QTP Descriptive Programming Unplugged

by Anshoo Arora and Tarun Lalwani

QTP Descriptive Programming Unplugged

Publisher: KnowledgeInbox
Author: Anshoo Arora & Tarun Lalwani
Editor: Vicki Watson

ISBN: 978-0-9836759-2-1

```
'Source code taken from "QTP Descriptive Programming Unplugged"
'By Anshoo Arora & Tarun Lalwani
'Download source from KnowledgeInbox.com/demos/QTPDPUnplugged_SourceCodes.zip
'Website: KnowledgeInbox.com/books/qtp-descriptive-programming-unplugged/
```

About the Authors

About Tarun Lalwani

 Tarun Lalwani is a Test Automation and Solutions Architect and the author of the two most widely-read books on QTP, 'QuickTest Professional Unplugged' and 'And I Thought I knew QTP!'. He has worked on various automated testing projects, utilizing technologies such as VBScript, VB6, VB.Net, C#.NET, Excel and Outlook Macros. Tarun is the founder of Test Automation Research and Labs (TARLABS); a company focused on Test Automation Products and Services. He is also the owner and lead author for KnowledgeInbox; a blog and publication house focused on Test Automation. Tarun was awarded with the 'Best Feedback Award' by HP for QTP 11 Beta testing and his book 'QuickTest Professional Unplugged' was named the Best Automation Book in the 2nd ATI Automation Honors awards. A regular contributor on AdvancedQTP and SQA forums, Tarun's work has been showcased on several websites, including www.relevantcodes.com and www.advancedqtp.com.

In Dec 2011, HP invited Tarun to its R&D center in Israel for a 4 day conference. The conference was aimed on taking his feedback on various aspects of QTP & BPT. This was the first time ever HP had invited any user from outside of Israel for feedback. The invitation highlights HP's interest in getting the user community involved in enhancing their tools.

Tarun can be contacted at www.linkedin.com/in/tarunlalwani or www.knowledgeinbox.com/contact-us.

About Anshoo Arora

Anshoo Arora is an author, Test Architect and software developer, best known for his Test Automation website, www.relevantcodes.com. He is continuously researching to find better ways of working with QTP, simplifying automation maintenance and creating extensible test suites/frameworks. Apart from QTP, he also works with Quality Center, LoadRunner, .NET programming, Selenium WebDriver, TestComplete and Web Technologies. Anshoo is a regular contributor at AdvancedQTP and SQAForums and is also the Technical Editor and Reviewer of QuickTest's first conceptual book, 'And I thought I knew QTP!'.

Write to him at anshoo@relevantcodes.com or visit his website Relevant Codes at http://www.relevantcodes.com.

Dedication

Our vision for this book is to share our knowledge and experience with the QTP community. It is a privilege for us to write this book and we hope that it will reach QTP Engineers across the globe. But not everyone in this world has the same advantages, let alone the blessing of education. Millions of children around the world today live life without hope of meeting their most basic needs, without any education, and without the promise of a brighter future.

Education empowers. Education inspires. Education can help to lead the way out of poverty, and provide the tools to guide the less fortunate towards a better life.

By purchasing this book, you will help a child break free from the cycle of poverty and gift them a future full of hope. For each copy sold, we will donate ₹10 to organizations working towards the worthy cause of child education. Help us to learn and foster learning.

Acknowledgements

From Tarun Lalwani

I actually started writing this book before my second book 'And I thought I knew QTP', but the idea of writing a technical novel overtook and I finished what was initially supposed to be my third book. Finally getting back to this book with another year of experience, however, meant even more polished content. This book has involved a lot of research and experimentation with different approaches and has therefore proved even more time–consuming. This, however, means more polished content and greater attention to detail.

I would like to thank Anshoo for accepting my request to co-author this book. He is one of the great finds for the QTP world, and in particular for me as we both seek the same goal, i.e. to share our knowledge with the Automation community.

I would also like to thanks my family members who have always been there to support me during the writing process and even after publication.

From Anshoo Arora

I would like to thank all my clients and colleagues for trusting in me and for giving me the opportunity to work with them.

A huge credit goes to Tarun, who has always strived for a better QTP community by constantly helping thousands of people over this course. Writing this book with him has been an incredible experience and a lot of fun.

I am grateful to everyone who visited and provided their feedback at Relevant Codes; it was their comments and encouragement which drove me to create the content that exists today.

And finally to my family: this is for you. Today, I wouldn't be doing anything without your support; nothing would have been possible.

About the Editor

Vicki Watson is a writer, editor and book designer whose publications have ranged from business books, teacher resource guides and parental handbooks to children's workbooks and poetry. After a career as a teacher and deputy headteacher, she decided to focus on her love of language and design and set up Callisto Green, a vibrant and dynamic writing and design venture and small publishing imprint. When she's not scribbling in her notebook, her many interests include playing the clarinet, rock-climbing, stargazing and playing chess.

Vicki can be contacted by emailing vicki@callistogreen.com or through her website at http://www.callistogreen.com.

Foreword
by Meir Bar-Tal

When Tarun Lalwani and Anshoo Arora asked me to assist in the review of this book, I felt both honored and obliged. Tarun and Anshoo are true pioneers in the field of Test Automation; whose contribution to the worldwide community is immeasurable. So, though the time schedule was tight, I undertook the challenge to make my humble contribution to this impressive project.

All through my reading I felt that QTP Descriptive Programming Unplugged is one of these books which make you think: "I wish I had this reference available in my last project". With this third book in Tarun Lalwani's QTP Unplugged series, now co-authored by our distinguished colleague Anshoo Arora, the Object Identification power of HP QuickTest Professional is handed to the Automation Developer like a cookbook.

The book, which could have been easily split into two volumes, leads the reader from the core concepts of Object Identification, through the challenges faced by the Automation Engineer, to the practical solutions which are the fruit of a sound and thorough research. All these are accompanied by well suited real-life, easy to grasp and well annotated examples.

The book is an extensive in-depth compilation with an emphasis on testing Web applications. It covers both GUI and SOA automation, and it tackles many misconceptions and pitfalls beginners face in their first steps. The numerous well documented code samples it provides ensure that understanding does not remain only at the theoretical, conceptual level.

To me, QTP Descriptive Programming Unplugged marks a very important event in the annals of automation knowledge. I am sure that the readers of this book will acquire skills that are rarely taught in QTP courses, and it will serve them as a reference and practical guide.

I wish to thank Tarun and Anshoo for giving me the opportunity to have a privileged glimpse into their colossal work and wish you the reader an enjoyable and fruitful journey.

Automation Architect, AdvancedQTP

* Meir Bar-Tal is an Automation Architect with over 12 years of technical, educational and leadership experience in Software Design, Development and Testing. Meir has helped companies establish solid foundations for their testing activities with a wide variety of software applications and systems and across different technologies and platforms. Meir is a well-known expert in Data-Driven, Keyword Driven and Hybrid methodologies and has published a number of influential articles on the applications of Design Patterns to Test Automation. For the last five years, he has been pushing forward an ambitious program towards the development of an Object Oriented automation framework named Sunscrit, a huge project which is still underway. Meir is the owner of www.AdvancedQTP.com of which he was a co-founder in 2007 and served as its Editor in Chief, Author and Forums Administrator ever since. Meir lives in Israel and cooperates closely with HP R&D and other colleagues to improve the user experience and productivity with HP Software tools..

Foreword

by Colin W. Fries

I've been in the test automation space since 2005, but was first introduced to HP's QuickTest Professional software in 2008, when I started a job with an HP client. Until then, I had performed a little bit of test automation using a home-grown service testing tool. However, I was keen to develop a working QTP skillset as quickly as possible. Interestingly enough, one of the things also driving this interest was that I was thrust into a situation where I was the automation expert, even though everyone above and around me knew that I knew about as much about the topic as they did. Nonetheless, I was expected to produce a working set of automated test cases as to reduce the manual testing burden of the QA team.

At first, I found that I wasn't very useful around this tool, so I did what everyone else in my position would have done – I asked for (and received) vendor training. I spent a week in Parsippany, New Jersey with a HP Business partner, learning the basic and advanced features of the tool. And when I came back to the office, I definitely had a few new tricks up my sleeve. But despite taking the basic and advanced courses, there were still a lot of questions and problems with our test suite that needed to be ironed out.

Prior to attending training, I'd spent a lot of time lurking on SQAForums.com and searching for answers to help fight the daily brushfires that were occurring. This is where I first encountered one of the authors of this book, Tarun Lalwani. At that point in time, Tarun was already a seasoned expert in the test automation space and was particularly adept at straightening out noobs such as myself. Over the years, he has answered hundreds of questions from the masses (I include myself here) and has given priceless advice and insight on everything from resolving syntax errors to developing automation frameworks. Because of Tarun's advice, the issues affecting us were resolved and we were able to create a working automated testing framework.

At about this time, I also became involved with Vivit, HP Software's independent user group. As it turned out, my local chapter focused on quality assurance software that HP had, at that point, recently acquired from Mercury. So I joined the chapter and eventually became one of its leaders. It was through this avenue that I came to know the other author of this book, Anshoo Arora. By this time, Anshoo was working for an HP Business partner and we began collaborating on bringing them in to present at a chapter meeting. I then met Anshoo in person at HP Discover, 2010, was impressed with his skill and ability, and instantly knew that the audience would be in for a treat when he gave his presentation and that his employer was lucky to have such a swell guy like him working for them. When he mentioned that he was collaborating with Tarun for the next installment of the QTP Unplugged series, I could hardly contain my excitement. After all, nothing excites a techie more than a new deep dive into his or her favorite tool, right?

So fast forward another, year, and again, I was attending the HP Discover conference when I received word from Anshoo that Tarun was going to be at the conference. Anshoo offered to facilitate an introduction, and of course, I jumped at the opportunity. It was a pleasure to meet him, and he struck me as a true authority in this field.

So what does this have to do with the book you're about to read and reference for the foreseeable future? When I met with Anshoo and Tarun, I realized that both of these men are passionate about their trade, and that their passion for test automation doesn't stop at the end of the business day. In talking to them, it quickly became apparent that they wanted to share what they've learned about this tool and its inner workings with their peers. After several years and a diversion or two, they've accomplished their goal by publishing this book. It is my belief that this book should be found in every automation shop utilizing HP's Functional Testing software. This book (and its predecessors, 'QuickTest Professional Unplugged' and 'And I Thought I knew QTP!') is a great resource for those who have experience writing or maintaining test automation frameworks in that it allows them to respond to the challenges of test automation against modern software applications. After reading this book, I hope you will come to the same conclusion. So enjoy; I'm sure that you'll find this to be very useful both now and in the future.

Quality Assurance Engineer III, Gateway EDI

Vivit Board of Directors, Secretary

* Colin W. Fries has been worked in the test automation space nearly his entire career and has spent the majority of his time in the healthcare industry. Colin has happily utilized QTP (and later, UFT) for the last five years and has extensive experience in writing, maintaining, and expanding upon Data-Driven, Keyword Driven and Hybrid frameworks. Colin is affiliated with the St. Louis chapter of QAI (Quality Assurance Institute), IIST (International Institute for Software Testing), and Vivit (the Independent HP Software Users' Group). For the past several years, Colin has been both a chapter leader and a member of the Board of Directors for Vivit. In this capacity, he has strived to provide education, community, and advocacy for its members. In his spare time, Colin enjoys running, cycling, researching test automation, and spending time with his wife and children

Foreword

by Christopher J. Scharer

Before writing the foreword to this book, I read it in its entirety, and although its content becomes increasingly more technical, each chapter builds on the previous one and includes several real-life examples. This book is very well written and made me become more interested the further I read. This book is focused toward conceptual knowledge of QuickTest Pro (QTP) with a deep dive into Descriptive Programming (DP). It is a must-have for anyone who is testing using QTP and complements Tarun's previous books, 'QuickTest Professional Unplugged' and 'And I thought I knew QTP!'. With so many companies moving to an Agile development/testing approach and application developers working side-by-side with automation engineers, it is becoming more common and even more important for an automation engineer to understand how to use DP.

With all the recent game changers in the IT industry, such as Cloud computing, Big Data, Mobile Testing and Web Services, I would definitely recommend reading this book and I really look forward to the next book that Tarun and Anshoo are working on currently, which I believe is going to focus on testing methodologies and frameworks. I also hope to be able to coordinate with them both to include a section on using Code Templates

Director (Vice President), Iowa, Nebraska & TQA-SIG Chapter Leader
Vivit Worldwide (http://www.vivit-worldwide.org)

* Christopher J. Scharer is an IT leader with over 15 years of technical experience in both the Software Development and Software Testing Lifecycles and Application Lifecycle Management (ALM). Christopher has been involved at every stage with experience in Data-Driven, Keyword Driven and Hybrid methodologies, and has helped companies achieve testing success in a wide variety of business applications (Banking, Finance, Health, Insurance, Mortgage, etc...). Christopher started the Vivit Worldwide LinkedIn group and has helped to organize the Nebraska Vivit Chapter, as well as several Vivit Midwest Regional Events. Most recently, Christopher was elected to the position of Vice President of Vivit Worldwide and works closely with HP executives to help provide quality to HP software users..

Contents

Preface

Test Automation plays a crucial role in Software Development Lifecycle. With businesses around the world pushing their IT teams to release software faster and sooner, Test Automation has become an essential part of the testing lifecycle. Test Automation helps perform redundant and repeatable tests against the application using an Automation tool.

QuickTest Professional (QTP), otherwise known as Functional Testing (FT) is one such tool being used in the Test Automation domain.

QTP offers support for functional automation of various platforms:

- Web
- VB
- Windows
- ActiveX
- JAVA
- .NET
- WPF
- Siebel
- SAP
- Peoplesoft
- Oracle
- PowerBuilder
- Stringray
- Terminal Emulators
- VisualAge Smalltalk

QTP supports these technologies using an extremely well laid-out Object Identification mechanism architecture, providing users with a set of predefined object types and properties for the given technology and its corresponding objects. Identification against test objects is performed by storing a set of known properties directly related to the type of object. For example, to identify a text box in a web page, QTP defines the object type as WebEdit and some of the common properties to identify such an object are html tag, type, id and name.

The QTP identification mechanism works perfectly as long as the application under test exposes test objects in such a way that its add-ins identify the interface presented by the underlying technology. If the relevant add-in is not associated with the test or if the ways test objects are exposed do not meet the criteria for Object Identification, QTP fails to identify objects correctly. At times, unsupported objects are defined using a generic WinObject. In such cases, certain workarounds must be implemented to enable QTP to accurately identify objects.

Even a small object identification issue can become a major problem. It is therefore of the utmost importance to understand how to work around the features of the tool and to consider the options available to overcome the issue.

The primary focus of this book is Object Identification with QTP. This book places great emphasis upon how to tackle the challenges one faces when implementing a real-life project. To illustrate, consider a page which presents a textbox generated at run-time and which has a dynamic NAME property; the property's value changes during each run-session. This can pose a great challenge in identification as there may be no unique property with which to identify the object, or the available properties may not be sufficient for a robust description. Hence it is important to be able to understand the implementation and also to come up with a robust description. This book will walk you through such real-life scenarios and implementation issues while providing several resolution techniques.

The book also covers Descriptive Programming and Object Repository concepts in depth and walks the reader through some of the really innovative ways in which these can be used for Object Identification and Test Implementation.

This book is written by two seasoned experts from the QTP community, Tarun Lalwani, who has published several other books (including the renowned '*QuickTest Professional Unplugged*') on QTP and is the founder of the website KnowledgeInbox, and Anshoo Arora, the founder of Relevant Codes, a website with focus on Test Automation. Both authors have worked for different international clients and have extensive real-time experience in Test Automation.

Who this Book is For

We recommend this book for those who use HP QTP (FT) or Business Process Testing (BPT). The book assumes that the reader has basic knowledge of both QTP and VBScript.

Important Note for the Readers

Some of the images have been clipped in the book. This is intentional, to ensure clarity and put focus on the concerned area of images.

Questions or Feedback Related to the Book

Feedback or questions related to this book can be sent through any of the below listed mode

Email: feedback@knowledgeinbox.com
Website: www.KnowledgeInbox.com/contact-us/
Facebook: www.facebook.com/qtpdpunpluggedbook/

Source Code in the Book

The source codes used in the book can be downloaded from: www.KnowledgeInbox.com/demos/QTPDPUnplugged_SourceCodes.zip

Ordering this Book

India: You can place an order online at www.KnowledgeInbox.com/store/

Other countries: Please check online at www.KnowledgeInbox.com/books/

For bulk orders, contact us at orders@KnowledgeInbox.com

Introduction to Objects

Believe it or not, our lives are surrounded by objects. From small to large, we encounter a huge variety of objects of various types on a daily basis. The neurons in our brain use information from our different senses, such as vision, smell, hearing and touch, to help us identify an object. In fact, the human brain works pretty seamlessly in performing this task. But for a normal computer program to match that power is not easy.

In order to automate applications, one of the most crucial elements is Object Identification. This is one of the tough challenges that Automation Engineers face around the world with various automation tools; any application can pose a challenge different in nature to any other application.

In object-driven automation, events against objects can only be executed if the software is able to correctly identify those objects. If the software fails in Object Identification, the application becomes impossible to automate. Object Identification is therefore a core concept in Test Automation. Moreover, the way an object is identified mostly depends on the technology that is used to implement the object. Consider the Window's Run window as shown in the image below:

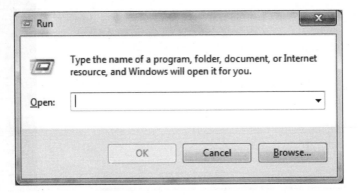

Figure 1.1 – Windows Run command window

Our aim is to click the Cancel button. When we spy the Cancel button using QTP's Object Spy, it identifies a hierarchy of objects with the Run window as the root object and the Cancel button as the child of the Run window.

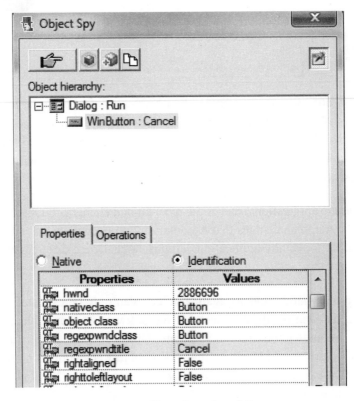

Figure 1.2 – Object Spy - Cancel Button

QTP is able to identify the Cancel button we wanted to click. Now we can add this object to the Object Repository and perform the click using the following code:

```
Dialog("Run").WinButton("Cancel").Click
```

This works because QTP internally knows how to recognize a native Windows object. QTP does this through the use of the corresponding add-ins. Every technology is represented as an individual add-in. When QTP is launched, it provides a list from which to select the relevant add-ins through the Add-in Manager.

Figure 1.3 – QTP Startup Add-in Manager

NOTE: For Windows native objects, no special add-in is required.

To demonstrate how the technology behind the GUI makes a difference, we have created a Java GUI for the same Run window we used earlier in this chapter:

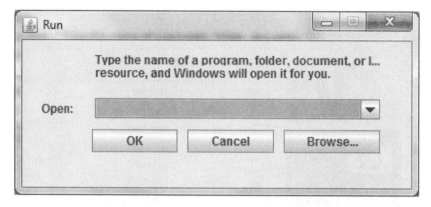

Figure 1.4 – Dummy Java based Run command window

Now if we Spy the same Cancel button again using QTP's Object Spy, we will notice one crucial difference as shown in Figure 1.5 – Object Spy - Java Run Command window.

QTP is only able to identify the top level window and nothing inside the window. This makes clicking on the Cancel button difficult as we cannot identify it as a unique object. The reason this is because the Java add-in is not loaded during startup. There may be circumstances when QTP may fail regardless of the add-in selected. In such a case, we must implement workarounds such as finding the location of the Cancel button and using its coordinates to fire a mouse-click event. Now let us load the Java add-in during QTP startup as shown in Figure 1.6 – Loading Java Add-in at startup

When we use the Object Spy again on the Run window made in Java, we will be able to identify the objects inside the Run window as shown in Figure 1.7 – Object Spy for Java Run window after loading Java Add-in

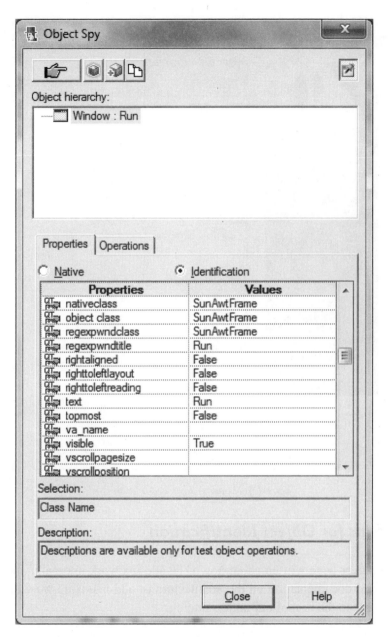

Figure 1.5 – Object Spy - Java Run Command window

Figure 1.6 – Loading Java Add-in at startup

QTP Add-ins for Object Identification

Very little has ever been written about how QTP add-ins work internally and HP has not openly provided documentation on the architecture of add-ins. Here we will throw some light on the topic to the best of our understanding.

No two add-ins are the same in QTP; each add-in operates in a different manner. For example, the SAP add-in uses the SAP GUI Scripting API provided by SAP internally, so any bug in the SAP GUI Scripting API gets propagated to QTP.

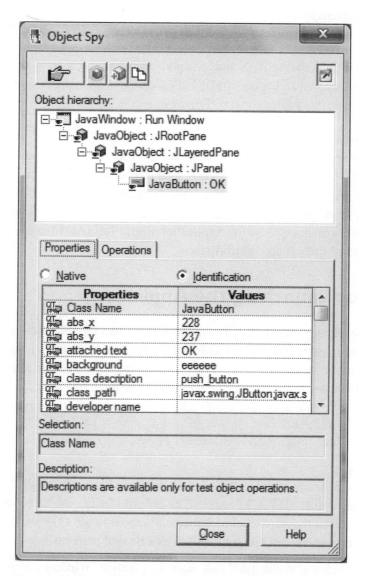

Figure 1.7 – Object Spy for Java Run window after loading Java Add-in

One such example is the max length, where the SAP GUI scripting engine returns the max length of a control as the length of text present in the control. This causes QTP to fail when performing a set operation if the text being set is bigger than the text already present. The SAP OSS note 1460861 - "Scripting: MaxLength property returns wrong value" describes the issue.

Similarly, the Siebel add-in uses the SIEBEL Automation API for interacting with the

Siebel High Interactivity client.

Other add-ins, such as ActiveX, Web, .NET and VB place hooks into the required processes. Let's launch QTP with the ActiveX and Web add-ins selected. Using Sysinternals Process Explorer, we can see that IE has certain DLL files loaded in its memory, and that these files are related to QuickTest Professional (QTP), as shown in Figure 1.8.

Acx_trap.dll, Acx_srv.dll, AcxSettings.dll and AcxOutputChannel.dll are some of the DLLs that QTP loads into the IE process to work on the ActiveX objects loaded by IE. Loading these DLLs into the process actually alters the state of the system being tested and means that we are testing our application with the help of external DLLs loaded into IE which may not be present when an actual user would be using the same application. These DLLs can, in rare instances, cause the Application Under Test (AUT) to crash or have some undesired behavior such as poor performance.

Timing for Launching the Application

You may have already heard that it is necessary to launch QTP before starting your application. The reason behind that requirement is that when QTP is launched, it places certain hooks in the system, each of which is targeted for a specific application. If the application is launched before QTP, then these hooks will not be present in the application and QTP will not be able to communicate with the application in the way intended.

However, this is not true for all applications or add-ins. Consider a few of the known exceptions:

- ⊙ The SIEBEL add-in uses SIEBEL Automation API, so if a SIEBEL application is launched before QTP, QTP will still be able to identify the Siebel objects. This is because even though Siebel runs inside a web Browser, QTP will not identify the Browser properly but rather identify it as a normal native window.

- ⊙ Any Windows application that uses just native Windows objects (Window, Dialog, WinEdit etc.) can be launched before QTP itself. QTP uses native system APIs (Let FindWindow, FindWindowEx etc.) to identify these objects and is therefore not dependent on the prior launching of QTP. Java applications also can be identified even if the application is launched before QTP. QTP uses three Windows environment variables (_JAVA_OPTIONS, IBM_JAVA_OPTIONS and JAVA_TOOL_OPTIONS) to inject its JVM hook and the application is hooked irrespective of whether QTP is launched or not.

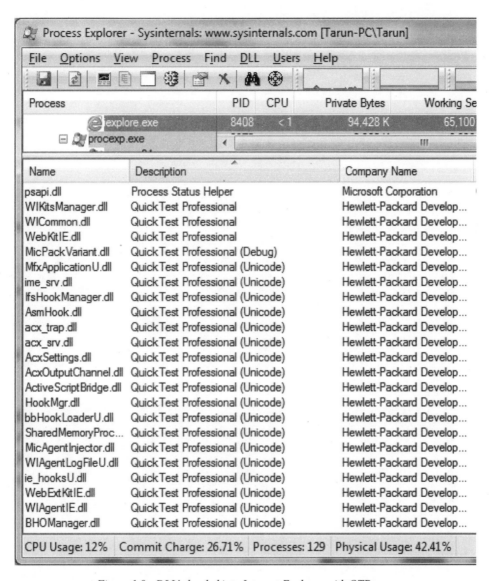

Figure 1.8 - DLL's loaded into Internet Explorer with QTP open

⊙ The SAP add-in uses SAP Scripting GUI and therefore a SAP GUI application will still be identified correctly even if launched before QTP.

2

Object Repository

Object Identification is the key concept to understanding the rest of this book. Everything we will read in this book is concerned with Object Identification using techniques such as Object Repository (OR) and Descriptive Programming (DP). But before we dive into the details of OR and DP, it's important to understand the concept of identification and how exactly it works.

When we record a script in QTP, it monitors all events that happen in the system. Based on QTP's configuration and the add-ins loaded in its memory, some of these events are captured in the test script. Not all events get recorded, e.g. mouse movements are not captured in context sensitive and low-level recording. When QTP records an event, the following process occurs:

1. Adding of objects to OR (with a logical name), which is necessary for replay

2. Adding of identification properties to objects in the OR so QTP can identify the object during replay.

3. Generating a code statement(s) in QTP which consists of Object, Action and Data. For example, in the below statement

```
Window("Win").WinEdit("Edit").Set "Tarun"
```

'Window("Win").WinEdit("Edit")' is the object, 'Set' is the action (or event) and '"Tarun"' is the data.

Our interest is in understanding the second step. QTP uses three sets of properties:

- ⊙ Mandatory Properties
- ⊙ Assistive Properties
- ⊙ Ordinal Identifiers

Mandatory Properties – These are set of properties that are always learned by QTP for a specified object. Even if QTP only needs a subset of these properties to identify the object, it would nevertheless learn all mandatory properties.

Assistive Properties – These are set of properties which are used only when QTP is unable to identify the object by Mandatory Properties alone. QTP adds these properties one by one to the Identification Properties and checks whether it can find a unique match. Once a unique match is found, QTP stops adding any of the remaining Assistive Properties.

Ordinal Identifiers – These are used only when QTP finds that the combination of Assistive and Mandatory Properties is leading to multiple object matches or no object match. In this instance, QTP has to decide which object it needs to identify. QTP provides three types of Ordinal Identifier to zero in on the desired object:

- ⊙ Index - Indicates the order in which the object appears in the application code relative to other objects.

- ⊙ Location - Indicates the order in which the object appears on the screen. Values are assigned from top to bottom, and then left to right.

- ⊙ CreationTime - Indicates the order in which the Browser was opened relative to other open Browsers. This is only available for the Browser object.

NOTE: Ordinal Identifiers can only be assigned for objects present in Object Repository. GetTOProperty method needs to be used to fetch the same. GetROProperty should not be used to read Ordinal Identifier values. There is no direct way to get the Ordinal Identifier value for objects derived using either the ChildObjects method or Descriptive Programming. We will learn more about ChildObjects and Descriptive Programming later in this book.

During the script replay, QTP follows the algorithm as shown in Figure 2.1 for Object Identification.

In order to identify the object, QTP first considers all the Identification properties. If it is able to find a unique match, then it stops. If there are zero or multiple matches found for the object, then QTP uses SMART Identification. If multiple matches are found and SMART Identification is not able to find a unique match, then QTP uses Ordinal Identifier to resolve the ambiguity. However, in the event of no matching instances being found, QTP raises an error.

NOTE: We recommend that SMART Identification should always be kept off. Later in the chapter we will discuss about its potential issues

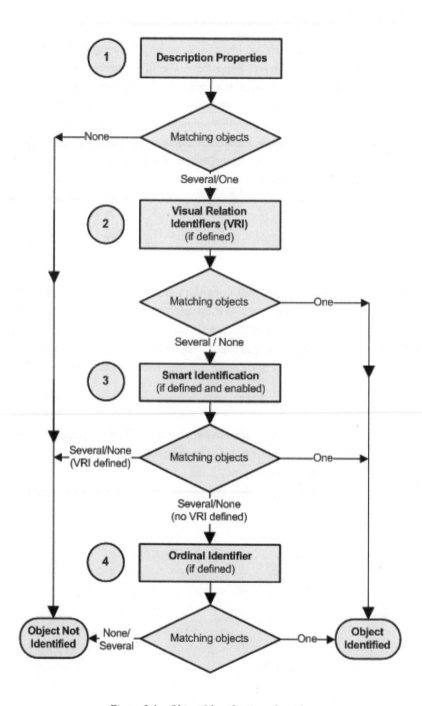

Figure 2.1 – Object Identification algorithm

Object Identification Settings

We saw earlier how QTP identifies an object during recording by using Mandatory, Assistive and Ordinal identifier properties. By default, QTP configures this setting to a system default but it can be customized. To customize these settings, go to Tools->Object Identification, where the Object Identification dialog is as shown in Figure 2.2. Select the environment for which you need to modify these settings and then select the Test Object from the tree. We can Add or Remove Assistive or Mandatory Properties and also enable or disable SMART Identification for the selected object.

These settings are machine-specific and not script-specific. Once the settings are changed, we can export them to a VBS file with QTP AOM code by clicking the Generate Script button.

Running the generated file on a machine will update all the Object Identification settings. To update settings on a remote machine which has QTP installed, we can edit the generated VBS and change the line.

```
Set App = CreateObject("QuickTest.Application")
'to:
Set App = CreateObject("QuickTest.Application","<RemoteMachineIPorName>")
```

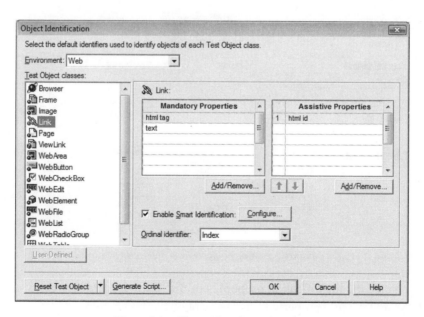

Figure 2.2 – Object Identification settings

Local Object Repository (LOR)

Every Action in a QTP script has an associated Local Object Repository. The LOR is stored with a BDB file extension and can be found in the respective Action's folder. Objects in a LOR can only be used in the Action they belong to. While recording, if the object does not exist in the associated Shared Object Repository (SOR) or LOR then QTP adds it to the LOR by default. It is not possible to force QTP to add objects to the SOR directly.

LOR can be viewed by using Resources->Object Repository from the menu or by pressing the CTRL + R key combination. By default, the LOR shows all objects present in LOR as well as objects present in SOR. Objects from SOR are read-only. We can filter purely local objects by using the Filter from the LOR window.

A LOR object always takes precedence over the same object from SOR. Consider the following case where a SOR associated with the test has five objects. We can copy the top level, 'KnowledgeInbox' Browser object, by right-clicking and using the 'Copy to Local' option. This creates a copy of the same object in the LOR.

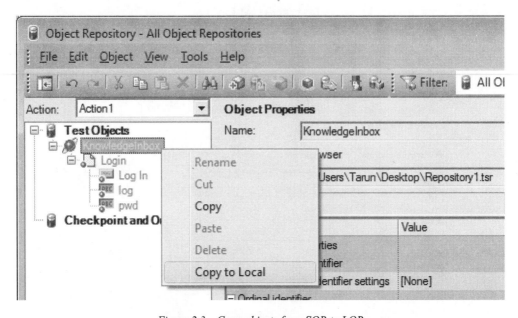

Figure 2.3 – Copy objects from SOR to LOR

Now let's change the identification properties of the 'KnowledgeInbox' Browser object in the LOR and add the title property to its Description as shown below:

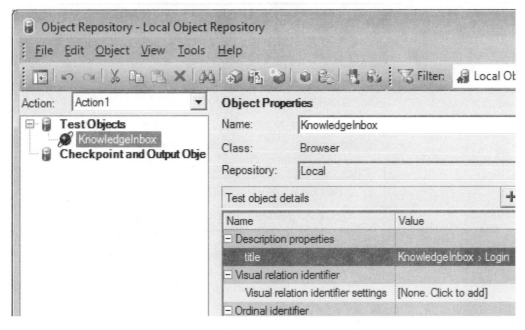

Figure 2.4 – Changing title property in LOR

After changing the title property for the Browser object, we use the following statement in our code:

```
Browser("KnowledgeInbox").Page("Login").WebButton("Log In").Click
```

The "KnowledgeInbox" Browser properties will be taken from the LOR and the remaining properties will be taken from the SOR. This alteration in the Object Identification Properties can make it hard to debug Object Identification-related errors. In such instances, when we highlight the object through the SOR it will be highlighted, but during the test run, the Object Identification may fail. This is because the object in the LOR will be altering the properties that we used in the SOR.

LOR window has two options for exporting the Object Repository:

⦿ Export Local Objects – This exports all the objects in the LOR to a TSR file.

⦿ Export and Replace Local Objects – This exports all the objects in LOR to a TSR file and removes them from the LOR.

NOTE: Exporting LOR to an existing TSR file will overwrite the file. That is, no merge operation will be performed during export.

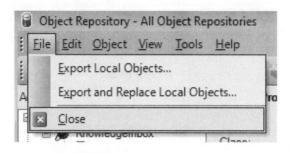

Figure 2.5 – Export options for LOR

Shared Object Repository (SOR)

The Shared Object Repository is a repository file (external to the test) which can be shared between various test scripts. Despite its name, the Shared Object Repository cannot be shared across users. Only one user can modify the SOR at a time. Other users can view the SOR in read-only mode.

NOTE: It is recommended that Version Control software be used to manage test automation assets to avoid accidental changes to the Object Repository.

A SOR is associated with a test at Action level. Actions and the SOR have a many-to-many relationship, i.e. an Action can have multiple SORs associated and an SOR can be associated with multiple Actions.

NOTE: SORs or LORs have no meaning until an Action is loaded. Assume we place 'Browser ("KnowledgeInbox"). Sync' statement into one of our associated libraries. Now when we run the test, QTP will throw an error as the object having no association with a library file. The statement will work correctly if the same is moved into a function and that function then is called inside an Action. Alternatively, we could move the statement into an Action.

SORs have TSR as the file extension. To create a new SOR, go to Resources->Object Repository Manager (ORM) and click the New icon.

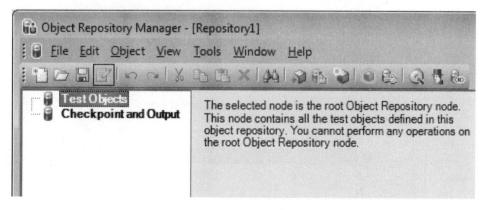

Figure 2.6 – Blank Shared Object Repository

 NOTE: It is not possible to record and have the objects created in the SOR directly. Objects can only be added to the SOR manually or through the Navigate and Learn feature discussed later in the chapter

Adding Objects to the SOR

Objects can be added in different ways to the SOR.

Adding an Object using Add Object Button

Objects can be added to a SOR by clicking the button and by selecting the object with the Hand pointer 🖱 . After clicking on the object, QTP shows the "Object Selection - Add to Repository" dialog shown in Figure 2.7. From this dialog, the whole hierarchy of the object is shown and we can select the object we wish to add.

> **NOTE:** QTP doesn't add all the objects from the listed hierarchy. It only adds those objects in the hierarchy which are necesarry for QTP to be able to re-identify the object properly.

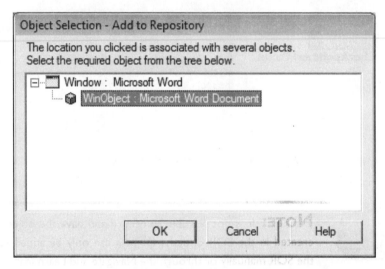

Figure 2.7 – Object selection dialog

Defining the Object Manually

We can add objects by defining them manually as well. To do this, click on the 🔲 Define

New Test Object button to view the 'Define New Test Object' dialog box. In this dialog, we need to select the Class (the Test Object type), the Name (logical name) and the Description property values.

QTP displays the list of Mandatory Properties by default in this dialog. To add additional properties for identification, click the ＋ button.

NOTE: This method is useful when either the application is not available to us for any reason or in cases where QTP displays the object hierarchy but doesn't add the objects to the OR. In such cases, we can note down the property values and add it using this method.

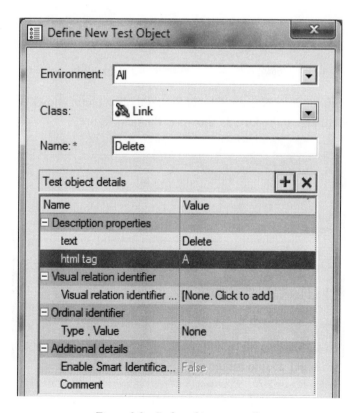

Figure 2.8 – Define object manually

Adding Objects through Object Spy

We can also add objects using the Object Spy tool. Click on the ▦ Object Spy button to launch Object Spy, select the object that needs to be added to the OR and then click on the ▦ button to add the object as shown in the next figure:

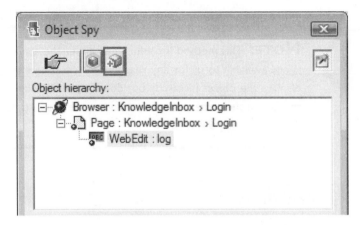

Figure 2.9 – Adding object through Object Spy

When we spy again on objects using Object Spy, the object icon shows whether or not the object is already present in the OR, as shown in the next figure:

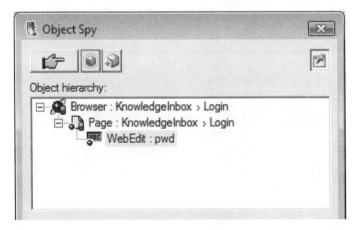

Figure 2.10 – Existing OR Objects shown with OR icon

NOTE: Adding objects directly from Object Spy is only available in QTP 11 or higher.

 NOTE: If Object Spy is launched from QTP's Test/Action view, objects will get added to the LOR of the active Action. If the Object Spy is launched through the Object Repository Manager, the objects will be added to the current, active SOR.

Navigate and Learn

This feature of Object Repository Manager (ORM) allows the user to navigate within an application and learn all its child objects. To activate Learn mode, go to Object->Navigate and select the Learn... menu or alternatively, press the F6 key. This will show the small 'Navigate and Learn' window at the top of the screen:

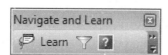

Figure 2.11 – Navigate and Learn objects

To learn objects from a screen, select the main window and click on the Learn button. QTP learns all the objects based on the current filter set. To change the filters click on the Filter icon, which will bring up the 'Define Object Filter' dialog as shown in Figure 2.12.

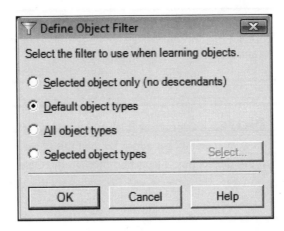

Figure 2.12 – Adding child objects with filters

The following options are available from the 'Define Object Filter' dialog:

- ⦿ 'Selected object only' (no descendants) will learn only the topmost object or the activated window.

- ⦿ 'Default object types' will capture only a predefined set of objects.

- ⦿ 'All object types' will capture all the objects from the application. It is not recommended to use this option as it can create many unwanted objects in the OR.

- ⦿ 'Selected object types' allows you to customize the filter. Pressing the Select button after choosing a radio button launches the 'Select Object Types' dialog box as shown in the next figure.

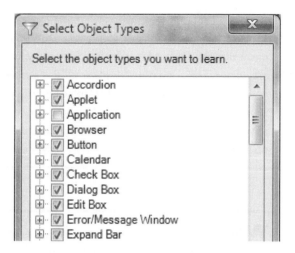

Figure 2.13 – Filter objects based on type

In this dialog we can filter the objects we want to select.

NOTE: Navigate and Learn can makes things easier by adding all the objects at once but it can add many unwanted objects in the SOR. This is not a good approach in case the screen has a lot of controls and our scripts only cover few of them. In such a case it is better to add objects manually.

Other Object-Related Features of OR

Highlighting the object in Application can be done by selecting the object in OR and clicking the ⬛ Highlight button. If QTP is unable to identify the object, it will raise one of the two possible errors shown in Figure 2.14 and Figure 2.15. The first error is due to the fact that properties used for identification are unable to identify an object. The second error is due to multiple matches from the current description. In this case we should use an Ordinal Identifier to make the match unique.

NOTE: If QTP is unable to identify an object, it doesn't mean that the Object Identification Properties of that object are wrong. There is a possibility that QTP is unable to identify one of the parent objects or that one of the parent object is identifying an undesired object. The entire parent hierarchy should therefore be checked to ensure that the rest of the objects in the hierarchy are being correctly identified.

 WARNING: If QTP highlights the object correctly and the SMART Identification is enabled for the object, then there is a possibility that QTP might have used SMART Identification for identification and in such cases your script can still error out. To make sure that object is being highlighted correctly, always set the SMART Identification for the object as False and then try to identify the object.

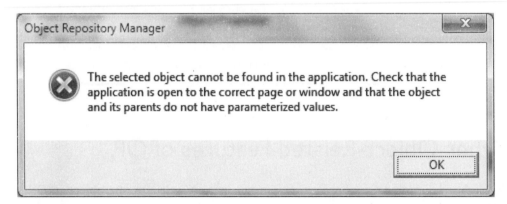

Figure 2.14 – Object not found in application error

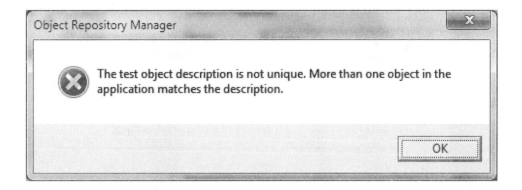

Figure 2.15 – Multiple object match error

Locating the Object in OR

We can also find out whether a given object in the application is already present in the OR or not. To locate an existing object, click on the ![icon] Locate in Repository button and then click on the object using the ![hand] Hand pointer. If the object already exists in the OR, QTP will locate and activate the same in the object tree or raise an error as shown in Figure 2.16.

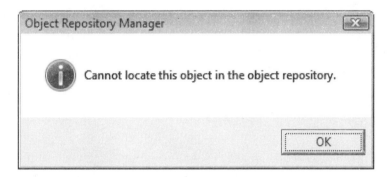

Figure 2.16 – Object not found in OR using Locate option

Updating an Object from the Application

In case an object has been changed after being added to the OR, we can update the properties again by clicking on the ![icon] Update from Application button.

WARNING: We can update an object of the same object type though it might not be the same object we had earlier, E.g. an existing textbox for a username can be updated with properties from a password textbox. This would create an object with the logical name of 'username' but would have the identification properties of a password textbox.

Object Repository Parameters (ORP)

Object Repository Parameters can be used to add parameters used for configuring property values. To launch the ORP dialog box, go to Tools->Manage Repository Parameters.

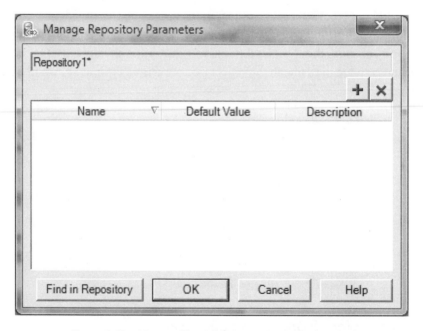

Figure 2.17 – Manage Object Repository Parameters dialog

Clicking on the $+$ button launches the 'Add Repository Parameter' dialog, where we can add the name of parameter and its default value.

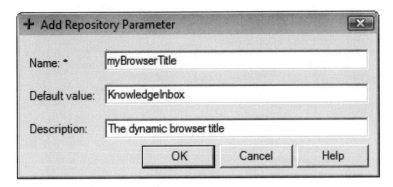

Figure 2.18 – Adding Repository parameter

Once the parameter is added, we use it to map to the property values. To map parameter values click on the <♦> button or press CTRL + F11.

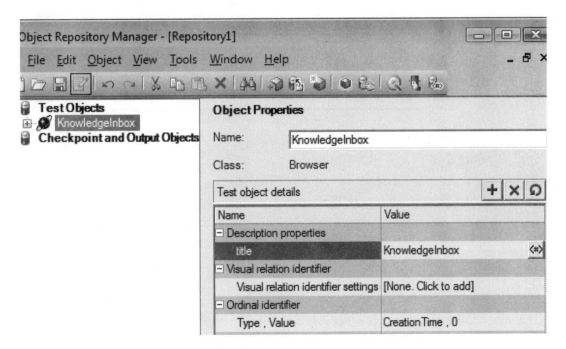

Figure 2.19 – Configure value for title property

In the Repository Parameter dialog (next figure), assign the parameter "myBrowserTitle" to KnowledgeInbox.

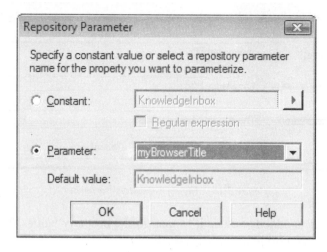

Figure 2.20 – Mapping Repository Parameter to title property

 NOTE: In a SOR, we can't directly map parameters to DataTable or Environment Variable as we do in LOR, which is why the need of an Object Repository Parameter arises.

When a SOR with Object Repository Parameter is associated with the test, the Object Repository is available for mapping. If there is no default value associated with a Repository Parameter, it would be shown in the Missing Resources tab as 'Unmapped Repository Parameters'.

Parameters can be mapped for a specific action or entire test (as shown in Figure 2.21), to a DataTable parameter, to an Environment variable or to a Random Number. We can also do this mapping at Run-time using the Repository Utility Object:

```
'Prints KnowledgeInbox (the default value)
Print Browser("KnowledgeInbox").GetTOProperty("title")
Repository("myBrowserTitle") = "Test"
'Prints Test (the updated value)
Print Browser("KnowledgeInbox").GetTOProperty("title")
```

NOTE: Updates made to the Object Repositorty Parameter using the Repository Object will persist for the duration of the Test i.e. if the value is changed in one Action, then all other actions will always see the updated value.

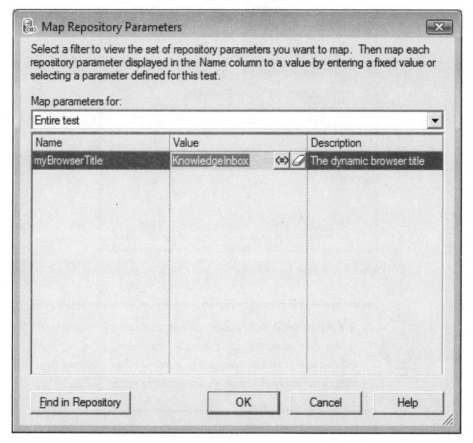

Figure 2.21 – Mapping Repository Parameter in the Test

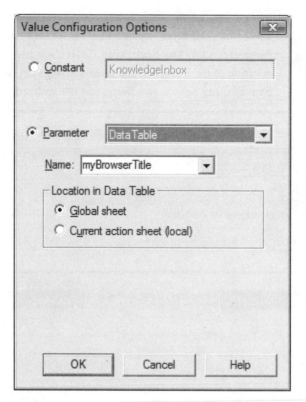

Figure 2.22 – Mapping title property to a DataTable parameter

WARNING: A limitation of using Repository Parameters is the fact that we can't specify the value as a regular expression. How HP managed to miss this is unclear but this feature is not available with parameterize values in OR.

Importing and Exporting OR from XML

The SOR can be exported as XML in a QTP-defined format. It is documented in QTP help file under the topic, 'HP QuickTest Professional Advanced References > HP QuickTest Professional Object Repository Schema'. To export the SOR, go to File->Export to XML.

The exported SOR can be imported using the File->Import from XML option.

NOTE: Exporting and re-importing the OR can at times reduce the size of the SOR and is a good way to compact it.

NOTE: Exporting SOR to XML includes CheckPoint information only in QTP 11. This feature is not available in previous versions.

NOTE: Importing the XML always creates a new SOR and doesn't merge the object with the existing SOR.

Update from Local Object Repository

We can merge objects from an existing Test to the current SOR. To do this, go to Tools->Update from Local Repository in the menu and click on the 🔲 button to select the test. Once the test is selected the dialog shows all the Actions available.

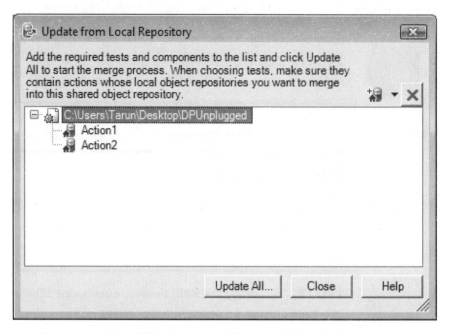

Figure 2.23 – Updating SOR objects from Test LOR

 NOTE: Multiple tests can be selected in the Update from Local Repository dialog box.

 NOTE: Only those Actions which have the SOR associated in the Tests can be added to the list. If a test has Action1 and Action2 but the current SOR is only associated with Action1, then the dialog would just show Action1 and not Action2.

 NOTE: Repositories for a test which are currently open in QTP cannot be merged without first closing the test.

Clicking on the 'Update All' button shows the Merge window and Merge results.

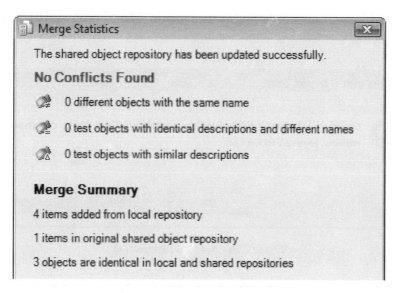

Figure 2.24 – Merge results

The Merge window will show the first merge action.

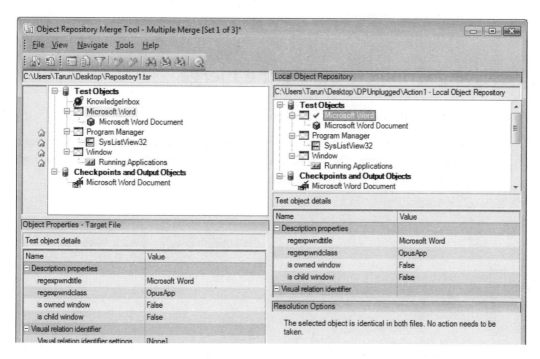

Figure 2.25 – Merge Actions

Click on the button to save the merge and move to the next conflict. The merge window will raise a confirmation dialog before saving.

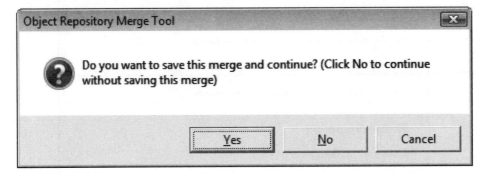

Figure 2.26 – Saving the merged OR

> **WARNING:** The merge process deletes all the objects from the LOR of selected scripts. Only those actions which were shown in the 'Update from Local Repository' dialog are impacted.

Resolving Conflicts during the Merge

There are two types of conflicts that can occur during a merge:

⊙ Description Conflict – In this case, two objects with the same hierarchy have different descriptions. The resolution would either be to take the description from the LOR or SOR or keep both objects.

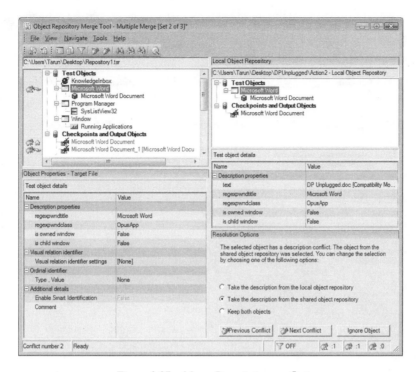

Figure 2.27 – Merge Description conflict

⊙ Duplicate Objects - In this case, a duplicate object exists. The resolution would be to either keep the LOR or SOR object or both the objects.

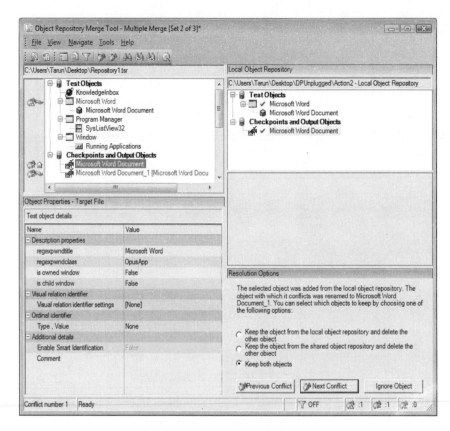

Figure 2.28 – Merge Duplicate object conflict

 NOTE: Choosing the 'Keep both objects' option will create two objects with different description. Some of the scripts which were using the Identifier values from the 2nd copy of the object, may not work any longer in such a case. If the number of scripts used by a Shared Object Repository is high, the merge process should be avoided, as the logical name changes during the merge process can break the scripts.

Object Repository Merge Tool

The Object Repository Merge Tool allows the merging of multiple Object Repositories. To launch the tool, in the ORM go to Tools->Object Repository Merge Tool and the 'New Merge' dialog will open as shown in Figure 2.29. Select the two Object Repositories to be merged and click OK. The merged repository is shown and if there are any conflicts, they can be resolved as we discussed earlier in the chapter.

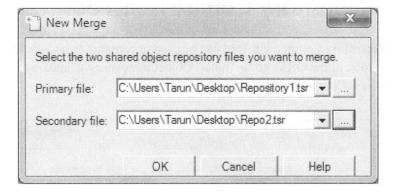

Figure 2.29 – Merge Object Repositories

 NOTE: One huge disadvantage of this merge process is that it cannot be saved onto the primary file but instead has to be saved to a new file. This means that if we want to merge ten Object Repositories, we will have to save the merged OR to a new OR every time and then use it as a primary OR for the next merge. This poor merge process design makes it impractical to use such an approach in real-life projects.

 NOTE: In case of an merge, the objects are not deleted from the secondary file. Unlike the case when "Update from Local Repository" option is used in LOR.

NOTE: Checkpoints can never be added directly into a SOR. They can only be imported through a direct or indirect merge from a Local Object Repository.

Object Repository Comparison Tool

The Object Repository Comparison Tool can be used to compare two Object Repositories. To launch the tool, in the ORM go to Tools->Object Repository Comparison Tool, which will open the New Comparison dialog:

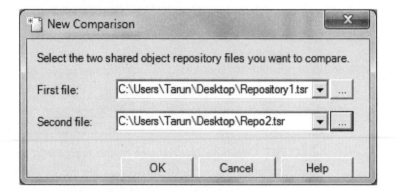

Figure 2.30 – Object Repository comparison tool

From here, you can see comparison stats:

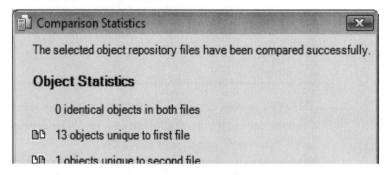

Figure 2.31 – Object Repository comparison stats

and comparison results:

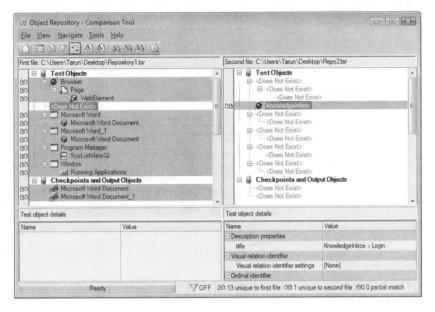

Figure 2.32 – Object Repository comparison results

Local OR vs Shared OR

LOR versus SOR has always been an important topic of discussion. LORs can be used when the Action has objects not required by other Actions; that is, all of its objects are unique in nature. They can be used when splitting of the AUT's workflow using reusable Actions is possible or for use-and-throw scripts where huge sets of data (data-driving) is to be created only once by driving input to the AUT.

SORs are better suited to when there are different reusable scripts which need to reuse the objects. But there are also a few challenges that we face when using SORs:

⊙ There is no history maintained for the changes made, making it difficult to track changes made by others.

⊙ There is no way to see which object is being used in which test case. This makes it difficult to carry out impact analysis of changes made to a particular object.

⊙ The SOR can be shared across scripts but cannot be shared across users for editing. This poses a huge limitation in large teams as only one person can edit the repository at a time.

⊙ While it is possible to create multiple Object Repositories and later merge them, the merge tool is poorly designed, which makes the merging of more than two ORs at the same time a difficult process.

SMART Identification

In one of our comments earlier, we spoke about SMART Identification. Let's first understand what SMART Identification is. SMART Identification (SI) is an algorithm that QTP uses when it is unable to identify an object or finds that the existing description results in multiple object matches. When we record an object in QTP, QTP learns all its properties and not just the identification properties stored in the OR. Consider the following webpage we created to demonstrate SI and its pitfalls:

http://knowledgeinbox.com/demologin.php

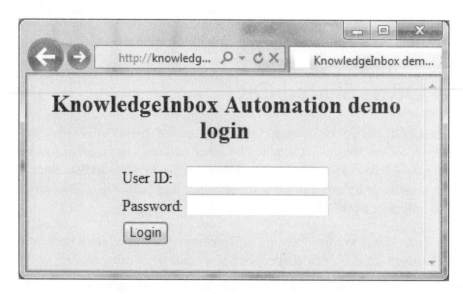

Figure 2.33 – KnowledgeInbox demo login page

The login only works with the username and password as 'tarun'. After a successful login, the following page is displayed:

Figure 2.34 – Successful login

After an unsuccessful login, the following error is displayed:

Figure 2.35 – Invalid login

To create Test for an unsuccessful login, we will add all the objects on these pages to a Shared Object Repository as shown below:

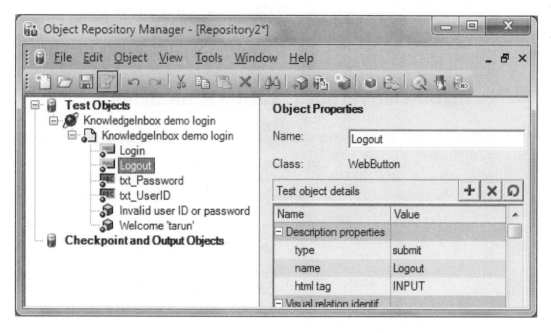

Figure 2.36 – Object Repository for KnowledgeInbox demo login page

If we export the above OR to XML and look at the Logout button, we will see

```
<qtpRep:ObjectRepository xmlns:qtpRep="http://www.mercury.com/qtp/
ObjectRepository">
  <qtpRep:Object Class="WebEdit" Name="txt_UserID">
    <qtpRep:Properties>
      <qtpRep:Property Name="micclass" Hidden="1" ReadOnly="1"
Type="STRING">
        <qtpRep:Value RegularExpression="0"><![CDATA[WebEdit]]></
qtpRep:Value>
      </qtpRep:Property>
      <qtpRep:Property Name="_xpath" Hidden="1" ReadOnly="1" Type="STRING">
        <qtpRep:Value RegularExpression="0"><![CDATA[//TR[normalize-
space()="User ID:"]/TD[2]/INPUT[1]]]></qtpRep:Value>
      </qtpRep:Property>
      <qtpRep:Property Name="visible" Hidden="1" ReadOnly="1" Type="BOOL">
        <qtpRep:Value RegularExpression="0"><![CDATA[-1]]></qtpRep:Value>
      </qtpRep:Property>
      <qtpRep:Property Name="type" Hidden="0" ReadOnly="0" Type="STRING">
```

```
        <qtpRep:Value RegularExpression="0"><![CDATA[text]]></qtpRep:Value>
      </qtpRep:Property>
      <qtpRep:Property Name="source_index" Hidden="1" ReadOnly="1"
Type="NUMBER">
        <qtpRep:Value RegularExpression="0"><![CDATA[15]]></qtpRep:Value>
      </qtpRep:Property>
      <qtpRep:Property Name="rows" Hidden="1" ReadOnly="1" Type="NUMBER">
        <qtpRep:Value RegularExpression="0"><![CDATA[0]]></qtpRep:Value>
      </qtpRep:Property>
      <qtpRep:Property Name="name" Hidden="0" ReadOnly="0" Type="STRING">
        <qtpRep:Value RegularExpression="0"><![CDATA[txt_UserID]]></
qtpRep:Value>
      </qtpRep:Property>
      <qtpRep:Property Name="max length" Hidden="1" ReadOnly="1"
Type="NUMBER">
        <qtpRep:Value RegularExpression="0"><![CDATA[2147483647]]></
qtpRep:Value>
      </qtpRep:Property>
      <qtpRep:Property Name="html tag" Hidden="0" ReadOnly="0"
Type="STRING">
        <qtpRep:Value RegularExpression="0"><![CDATA[INPUT]]></
qtpRep:Value>
      </qtpRep:Property>
      <qtpRep:Property Name="html id" Hidden="1" ReadOnly="1"
Type="STRING">
        <qtpRep:Value RegularExpression="0"><![CDATA[]]></qtpRep:Value>
      </qtpRep:Property>
      <qtpRep:Property Name="default value" Hidden="1" ReadOnly="1"
Type="STRING">
        <qtpRep:Value RegularExpression="0"><![CDATA[]]></qtpRep:Value>
      </qtpRep:Property>
      <qtpRep:Property Name="class" Hidden="1" ReadOnly="1" Type="STRING">
        <qtpRep:Value RegularExpression="0"><![CDATA[]]></qtpRep:Value>
      </qtpRep:Property>
    </qtpRep:Properties>
    <qtpRep:BasicIdentification>
      <qtpRep:PropertyRef>micclass</qtpRep:PropertyRef>
      <qtpRep:PropertyRef>_xpath</qtpRep:PropertyRef>
      <qtpRep:PropertyRef>type</qtpRep:PropertyRef>
```

```
        <qtpRep:PropertyRef>name</qtpRep:PropertyRef>
        <qtpRep:PropertyRef>html tag</qtpRep:PropertyRef>
    </qtpRep:BasicIdentification>
    <qtpRep:SmartIdentification Algorithm="Mercury.TolerantPriority"
Active="1">
        <qtpRep:BaseFilter>
          <qtpRep:PropertyRef>micclass</qtpRep:PropertyRef>
          <qtpRep:PropertyRef>type</qtpRep:PropertyRef>
          <qtpRep:PropertyRef>html tag</qtpRep:PropertyRef>
        </qtpRep:BaseFilter>
        <qtpRep:OptionalFilter>
          <qtpRep:PropertyRef>name</qtpRep:PropertyRef>
          <qtpRep:PropertyRef>html id</qtpRep:PropertyRef>
          <qtpRep:PropertyRef>max length</qtpRep:PropertyRef>
          <qtpRep:PropertyRef>default value</qtpRep:PropertyRef>
          <qtpRep:PropertyRef>class</qtpRep:PropertyRef>
          <qtpRep:PropertyRef>rows</qtpRep:PropertyRef>
          <qtpRep:PropertyRef>visible</qtpRep:PropertyRef>
        </qtpRep:OptionalFilter>
    </qtpRep:SmartIdentification>
    <qtpRep:LastUpdateTime>Saturday, June 30, 2012 14:58:38</
qtpRep:LastUpdateTime>
    <qtpRep:ChildObjects>
    </qtpRep:ChildObjects>
  </qtpRep:Object>
</qtpRep:ObjectRepository>
```

Let's look at one of the XML entries.

```
<qtpRep:Property Name="max length" Hidden="1" ReadOnly="1" Type="NUMBER">
<qtpRep:Value RegularExpression="0"><![CDATA[2147483647]]></qtpRep:Value>
```

The 'Hidden="1"' parameter tells us that the value is hidden and not used in Object Identification, but is stored for later use if SI needs to be performed. Now let us look at the SI properties:

```
<qtpRep:SmartIdentification Algorithm="Mercury.TolerantPriority" Active="1">
  <qtpRep:BaseFilter>
    <qtpRep:PropertyRef>micclass</qtpRep:PropertyRef>
```

```
  <qtpRep:PropertyRef>type</qtpRep:PropertyRef>
  <qtpRep:PropertyRef>html tag</qtpRep:PropertyRef>
</qtpRep:BaseFilter>
<qtpRep:OptionalFilter>S
  <qtpRep:PropertyRef>name</qtpRep:PropertyRef>
  <qtpRep:PropertyRef>html id</qtpRep:PropertyRef>
  <qtpRep:PropertyRef>max length</qtpRep:PropertyRef>
  <qtpRep:PropertyRef>default value</qtpRep:PropertyRef>
  <qtpRep:PropertyRef>class</qtpRep:PropertyRef>
  <qtpRep:PropertyRef>rows</qtpRep:PropertyRef>
  <qtpRep:PropertyRef>visible</qtpRep:PropertyRef>
</qtpRep:OptionalFilter>
</qtpRep:SmartIdentification>
```

The BaseFilter properties are always taken into account when looking for the object using SI, and QTP then uses one optional filter at a time until it finds a unique match. This means that if QTP is initially unable to identify the object, it will take micclass, type and html tag properties and try again to identify the object. If it is able to get a unique match, then that match will be used. If, however, there are no matches, an error will be raised. In the case of multiple matches, QTP will go through each property name in turn until it finds a unique match.

Now consider the following script to test our login functionality:

```
Browser("KnowledgeInbox").Page("demo login").WebEdit("txt_UserID").Set "Tarun"
Browser("KnowledgeInbox").Page("demo login").WebEdit("txt_Password").Set "Tarun"
Browser("KnowledgeInbox").Page("demo login").WebButton("Login").Click
Browser("KnowledgeInbox").Sync
If Browser("KnowledgeInbox").Page("demo login").WebButton("Logout").Exist Then
  Reporter.ReportEvent micPass, "Login", "Login was successful"
Else
  Reporter.ReportEvent micFail, "Login", "Login failed"
End If
```

The script will pass as expected, but now let us introduce an incorrect user id and password into the script:

```
Browser("KnowledgeInbox").Page("demo login").WebEdit("txt_UserID").Set "Lalwani"
Browser("KnowledgeInbox").Page("demo login").WebEdit("txt_Password").Set "Tarun"
Browser("KnowledgeInbox").Page("demo login").WebButton("Login").Click
```

```
Browser("KnowledgeInbox").Sync
If Browser("KnowledgeInbox").Page("demo login").WebButton("Logout").Exist Then
    Reporter.ReportEvent micPass, "Login", "Login was successful"
Else
    Reporter.ReportEvent micFail, "Login", "Login failed"
End If
```

If SMART Identification (SI) is enabled, we will notice that the script passes and test results will show that the script has used SI. The script passes because the SI algorithm incorrectly identifies the Login button as the Logout button

Using SMART Identification can therefore alter the way in which our test cases are supposed to behave and can sometimes create problems that go undetected because when a lot of tests are carried out, it is common place to analyze only the cases which have failed and not those which have passed.

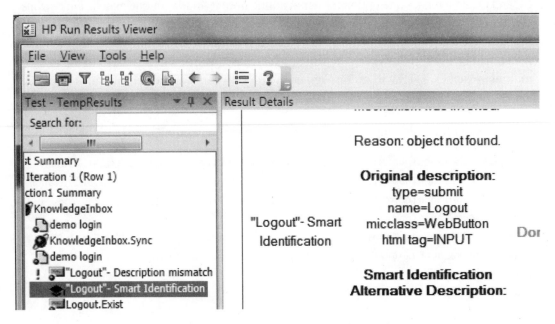

Figure 2.37 – Smart Identification use shown in Test result summary

NOTE: For a robust Automation solution, SMART Identification should be disabled as a rule of thumb.

Disabling SMART Identification

There are different ways to disable SMART Identification:

⊙ We can disable SMART Identification for a particular object in the Object Repository.

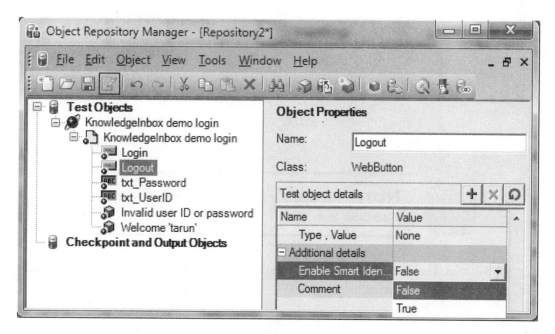

Figure 2.38 – Disabling SMART Identification for specific object in OR

◉ We can disable SMART Identification during replay using File->Settings.

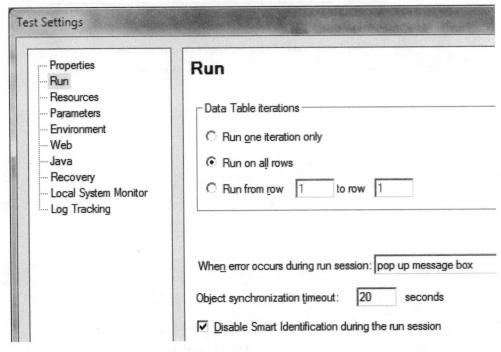

Figure 2.39 – Disable SMART Identification in Test Settings

 NOTE: This setting is applicable at test level and will not affect other tests.

◉ We can disable SMART Identification for a particular object type using Tools->Object Identification

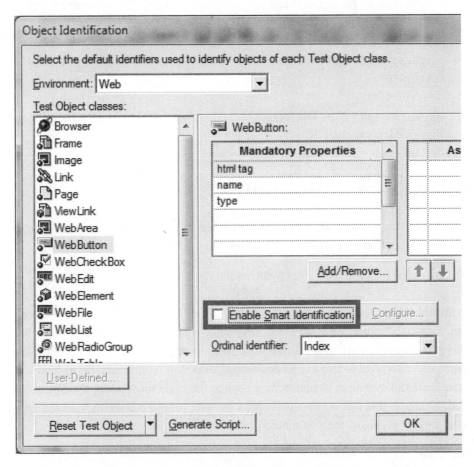

Figure 2.40 – Disable SMART Identification using Object Identification settings

This disables the SMART Identification for WebButton for all tests running on that system.

⦿ We can also disable SMART Identification using the following code in an associated library file:

```
Setting("DisableReplayUsingAlgorithm") = 1
'or using AOM code
Set QTPApp = CreateObject("QuickTest.Application")
QTPApp.Test.Settings.Run.DisableSmartIdentification = True
```

⦿ SMART Identification can be disabled for all objects in the OR by updating the exported XML. Export your OR to XML and then open it in a text editor. Replace

```
<qtpRep:SmartIdentification Algorithm="Mercury.TolerantPriority"
Active="1">
with
<qtpRep:SmartIdentification Algorithm="Mercury.TolerantPriority"
Active="0">
```

and then re-import the OR from XML. This will disable SMART Identification for all the objects in the OR.

Loading SOR at Run-time

Shared Object Repositories (SORs) can be loaded at run-time into an Action using the RepositoriesCollection object. The code snippet to load the OR is given below:

```
RepositoriesCollection.Add "C:\MySharedOR.tsr"
```

When the above code is executed inside Action1, it will load the Shared Object Repository only in Action1's scope. This will not have any impact on other actions and the SOR remains private to Action1 only. If the same SOR is required in another Action then that Action would also need to use the RepositoriesCollection.Add statement to load the SOR. This can create an overhead in maintenance when the code for loading the OR needs to be updated, although this can be easily avoided by wrapping the code to load the OR into a function present in one of the associated libraries.

```
'C:\SORLoad.vbs
Function LoadRepository()
  RepositoriesCollection.Add "C:\MySharedOR.tsr"
End Function
'Action1
Call LoadRepository()
```

In this approach, every Action initially calls the LoadRepository method, loads the required SOR into the Action. Executing the code twice when the SOR has already been associated to the current Action will make QTP raise an error.

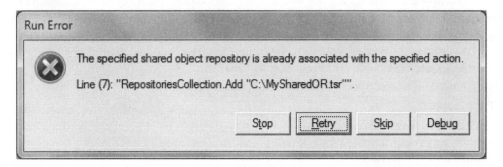

Figure 2.41 – Object Repository already exist error

To avoid such situations, we should always use the Find method to check whether the repository exists in the memory as shown in code below:

```
'-1 means the repository is not found in current action memory
If RepositoriesCollection.Find("c:\MySharedOR.tsr") = -1 Then
  RepositoriesCollection.Add "c:\MySharedOR.tsr"
End If
```

In case different Actions require different ORs, we can use the current Action name to decide which repository needs to be loaded. The code snippet below shows the updated LoadRepository method:

```
'C:\SORLoad.vbs
Function LoadRepository()
  RepositoriesCollection.Add "C:\MySharedOR.tsr"
    Select Case Environment("ActionName")
    Case "Login"
      RepositoriesCollection.Add "C:\MySharedOR_Login.tsr"
  End Select
End Function
```

Apart from hard-coding these repositories into the library file, we can also create a map of ActionName with corresponding SORs to be loaded from an external file.

Loading SOR at Design-time

Differing from Run-time, Design-time loading is for associating an Object Repository to a Test's Action and then saving the script. This association can be done by using the QTP Automation Object Model (AOM). This allows us to use the Action's ObjectRepositories method to associate a repository, rather than using the RepositoriesCollection object.

```
'Create a QuickTest Application for Automation
Set QTPApp = CreateObject("QuickTest.Application")
QTPApp.Launch
QTPApp.Visible = True
'Open an existing test
QTPApp.Open "C:\MyTest"
'Now, associate C:\MySharedOR.tsr to all actions present in the test
Dim i, oActions
Set oActions = QTPApp.Test.Actions
For i = 1 To oActions.Count
  If oActions.Item(i).ObjectRepositories.Find("C:\MySharedOR.tsr") = -1
Then
    oActions.Item(i).ObjectRepositories.Add "C:\MySharedOR.tsr"
  End If
Next
```

Descriptive Programming

Introduction

Descriptive Programming provides a way to perform interactions with runtime objects that are not in the Object Repository. Using this approach, QTP developers can create descriptions with the properties they see relevant to identify a test object instead of using an Object Repository, where QTP selects these descriptions based upon predefined rules.

Object Identification

To identify an object during playback, QTP stores values of one or more object identification properties in the Object Repository and uses them to identify the object uniquely at runtime. The next figure shows a simple Object Repository that contains descriptions for a webpage and three of its control objects:

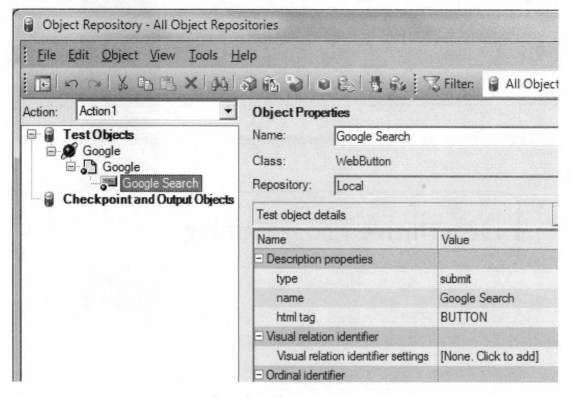

Figure 3.1 – Object Repository Window

The Google Search object in the OR has three recorded properties: type, name and html tag. Note that QTP recorded three properties (the mandatory properties defined for this test object), but that not all of them may be needed to recognize the object at Run-time.

Object Spy

These same properties can be viewed using QTP's Object Spy, an inbuilt tool that lists all relevant test object's identification and native properties. The Object Spy can be accessed using the ▣ icon in the QTP window. Using this tool, we can avoid adding objects to the repository in order to view its properties and associated values. The next figure shows a snapshot of the Object Spy showing properties of the Google Search button:

Figure 3.2 – Object Spy view for WebButton "Google Search"

Notice that the Object Spy displays the same properties for type, name and html tag as also listed in the snapshot of the Object Repository in Figure 3.1. However, there are a few additional properties associated with the Google Search button. At times, a combination of any of these can prove efficient in uniquely identifying a test object. Below is a list exposed by the Object Spy for an object:

- Identification property values
- Native property values
- Test object operations supported
- Native operations supported
- Test object hierarchy

More information can be found on the Object Spy tool in QTP Help from the following navigation: HP QuickTest Professional User Guide > Working with Test Objects > The Test Object Model > Object Spy Dialog Box.

Implicit and Explicit Properties

When we define an object description using Descriptive Programming (DP), there are certain properties that we don't need to provide explicitly. This is because QTP automatically assumes certain values based upon the test object type being referenced. For example, the 'Google Search' control in the previous figure is a WebButton and QTP assumes its HTML tag as INPUT and the TYPE tag as SUBMIT. The reason behind this is that a WebButton, or simply a button in the Web environment always has the HTML tag of INPUT and the TYPE tag of SUBMIT. This relationship, however, is not true for all types of objects. In a situation where we reference a generic WebElement, it is necessary to explicitly define every property of importance. Consider the following HTML source:

```html
<html>
  <head><title>Implicit Properties</title></head>
  <body>
    <div class="div1">
      <div class="div2">
        <p>Text</p>
      </div>
    </div>
  </body>
</html>
```

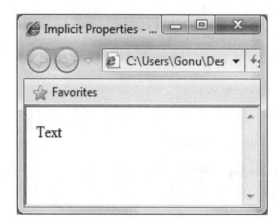

Figure 3.3 – Implicit Properties Demo

The object "Text" as shown in the previous figure has HTML TAG value of P. The micclass or Class Name is WebElement. The following code will fail when identifying the WebElement because the HTML tag value is not supplied.

```
Browser("name:=Implicit Properties").WebElement("innertext:=Text").
Highlight
```

However, when the HTML tag is explicitly provided, the code will run without errors.

```
Browser("name:=Implicit Properties").WebElement("innertext:=Text", "html
tag:=P").Highlight
```

The reason why the above fails is because the innerText value also matches the two parent DIV tags.

When to use Descriptive Programming

Below are some examples of when Descriptive Programming is considered a good alternative to Object Repository to define a test object:

- When objects in the application are dynamic. Consider the following two examples:
    - Clicking a link which changes according to the logged-in user of the application, x. "Logout <<UserName>>".
    - A multi-locale application which changes the currency symbol as locales change.
- When the Object Repository is getting very large. Performance may start to degrade as the size of the Object Repository increases.
- When you don't want to use an Object Repository at all. The following scenarios provide some rationales for why you might not use an Object Repository:
    - Consider an application which is not yet available for automation. Using the Object Repository approach, it is impossible to use QTP to record against the UI. However, it is possible to manually create the objects in the OR and update the identification properties when the application becomes available. It must be noted that creating objects manually using QTP UI is a cumbersome task. However, by creating a custom framework using DP, we can make the process of defining objects simpler. Of course, this approach assumes that we have reasonable understanding of application

workflow as well as descriptions of those page/screen objects against which testing is to be done.

o An application has similar objects on each of its screens. Imagine an application having the buttons Cancel, Back and Next on each screen. Recording interactions with these buttons on every page will add three objects per page to the Object Repository. So instead of adding these three identical objects repeatedly to the OR, we can just write three DP definitions and then use those definitions on any page.

◉ When it is required to perform an action on a web page at run-time without having the knowledge of each object's unique properties. Consider a scenario where we want to clear all the textboxes on a webpage. For this operation if we use the Object Repository, we would need to list all objects and perform the operation. However, in case of DP, we can use ChildObjects and perform set operation on all the text boxes on the webpage

Descriptive Programming Syntax

There are two ways to create Descriptive Programming statements:

◉ Using description objects.

◉ Using description strings.

Using Description Objects

A Description Object can be used to build object collections depending upon the properties used and their corresponding values. Each object in the AUT can be used to create a Description Object. This is a very powerful approach to creating object collections - each object in the collection will resemble each other by the properties specified by a Description Object.

Using this approach we create a description object and define the properties and values for identification. This is very similar to creating and initializing a dictionary object. Using this technique the Google Search button can be described as:

```
'Create a description object
Set btnGoogleSearch = Description.Create
```

```
'Add description identifiers
btnGoogleSearch("type").value = "submit"
btnGoogleSearch("type").RegularExpression = False
btnGoogleSearch("name").value = "Google Search"
btnGoogleSearch("html tag").value = "INPUT"
```

The Description Object is used to create a Properties Collection Object. This object can add a set of property-value pairs to match the description of an object that may exist in the AUT during a run session. In the previous example, the variable btnGoogleSearch is preceded by the Set statement and usage of the Set statement binds an object as a reference to another object. This means that btnGoogleSearch becomes an object reference to the Description Object represented by Description.Create.

Each description object's property supports both a value and RegularExpression assignment. By default the regular expression flag is True, indicating that its value assignment string is interpreted using VBScript's Regular Expression syntax. To click the Google Search button using this technique, the following code would be used:

```
'Click on the Button using description object btnGoogleSearch
Browser("Browser").Page("Page").WebButton(btnGoogleSearch).Click
```

 NOTE: Once we start using any Descriptive Programming syntax in a statement, the rest of the statement must continue to use DP syntax. In the above statement, Browser and Page objects are OR based whereas the WebButton object is Descriptive Programming based.

In the previous example, it took several lines of code to define the Google Search button using a description object. To simplify this, we can use a function to dynamically create this assignment for us:

```
'Function to convert a string or array to a description object
Sub CreateDescription(ByVal dpObjName, ByVal dpObjStringOrArray)
  'This will carry all the properties
  Dim propArray
```

```
        'This will carry the property name and it's corresponding value
    Dim valArray
    If VarType(dpObjStringOrArray) < vbArray Then
        'Convert the string into Array for creating the description
        propArray=Split(dpObjStringOrArray,",")
    Else
        'It's already an array
        propArray = dpObjStringOrArray
    End If
    'Create the description object
    ExecuteGlobal "Set " & dpObjName & "=Description.Create"
    Dim i
    For i = LBound(propArray) to UBound(propArray)
        'Split the property and value from property:=value
        valArray = Split(propArray(i), ":=")
        Execute dpObjName &"(""" & valArray(0) & """).Value=""" & valArray(1) &
""""
    Next
End Sub
```

The function CreateDescription can be used in the following ways:

```
'Usage with array
descArray = Array("html tag:=INPUT", "Name:=Submit")
CreateDescription "dpSubmit1", descArray

'Usage with string
descStr1 = "Name:=Submit"
CreateDescription "dpSubmit2", descStr1

'Usage with string concatenated by a comma
descStr2 = "Name:=Submit,html tag:=INPUT"
CreateDescription "dpSubmit3", descStr2
```

The description objects will be created with variable names as dpSubmit1, dpSubmit2 and dpSubmit3 respectively. Later we can directly use these variable as shown in code below:

```
Browser("Browser").Page("Page").WebButton(dpSubmit1).Click
```

The micclass Identifier

The micclass identifier describes the QTP test object class. For example the micclass:=WebButton is an implicit property of the WebButton object. When there is only a single button on a page we don't need to use any property description other than micclass:=WebButton. GetTOProperty("micclass") can be used to determine the test object class as shown in the next code statement.

```
'Displays Browser
MsgBox Browser("Browser").GetTOProperty("micclass")

'Displays Page
MsgBox Browser("Browser").Page("Page").GetTOProperty("micclass")
```

NOTE: 'Class Name' is not a property for the type of test object as QTP Object Spy shows it. In Object Spy, micclass is mapped to the class name.

Using Description Strings

In this method of Descriptive Programming we don't need to create a description object. Instead we can use a programmatic description string. An inline statement with programmatic description strings can be written in the following format:

```
ParentClass("property:=value").Child1("property:=value").
ChildN("property:=value").EventName
'or
Set Parent = ParentClass("property:=value").Child1("property:=value")
Parent.ChildN("property:=value").EventName
```

To recognize the Google Search button from the Object Repository, we use the following three description strings in the second line of code:

```
Browser("Google").Page("Google") _
  .WebButton("html tag:=INPUT","type:=submit","name:=Google Search")
```

Above, both Browser and Page objects have their properties stored in the Object Repository. The WebButton's properties and values are separated using the := delimiter.

> **NOTE:** A parent's properties can be stored in the Object Repository and its child properties can be written using programmatic descriptions. However, a parent's properties cannot be written using programming descriptions if its child is to be created using properties stored in the Object Repository.

The code statement as shown above can also be written using an object reference for the parent object:

```
'Get the page object reference
Set oPg = Browser("Google").Page("Google")

'Get the button object using string description
Set oButton = oPg.WebButton("html tag:=INPUT","type:=submit","name:=Google Search")
```

As we discussed earlier, it is not necessary to define all properties in order to identify the object. From the description created above, we can omit the HTML Tag and Type properties and still be able to uniquely identify the Google Search button:

```
'Get the button using a single property
Set oButton = oPg.WebButton("name:=Google Search")
```

Enumerating ChildObjects

QTP provides the ChildObjects method used to enumerate child objects of a given parent. The ChildObjects method lets us create a collection of objects that match a set of property-value pairs as specified by the supplied description object. Since object collections are to be formed within a prescribed parent, ChildObjects is always preceded by the parent. For example, to enumerate all the textboxes on a page we can use the following code:

```
'Create a description object
```

```
Set dpAllTxt = Description.Create

'Set the description for WebEdit only
dpAllTxt("micclass").value = "WebEdit"

'Get all the objects matching the description
Set allTextboxes = Browser("Google").Page("Google").ChildObjects(dpAllTxt)

'Loop through all of them
iCount = allTextboxes.Count   1
For i = 0 To iCount
  Set oTxt = allTextboxes.item(i)
  oTxt.Set "This is Text box #" & (i+1)
Next
```

ChildObjects enumerates all the child objects (regardless of the type) when we use an empty description object.

```
'Create a description object
Set dpAllChilds = Description.Create

'Get all the objects on the page as a blank description is used
Set allChilds = Browser("Google").Page("Google").ChildObjects(dpAllChilds)
iCount = allChilds.Count - 1

'Loop through all the objects on the page
For i = 0 To iCount
  MsgBox allChilds.item(i).GetTOProperty("micclass")
Next
```

 NOTE: Collection of objects derived from ChildObjects methods doesn't support For Each loop..

Custom CheckPoints

QTP offers several verification techniques using built-in CheckPoints that help us ensure our application is working as expected. CheckPoints help engineers verify if there has been a change in the application since the CheckPoint was created and with the help of reporting, they are a very useful tool in Test Automation with QTP. The following built-in CheckPoints are available in QTP:

- Standard CheckPoint
- Text CheckPoint
- TextArea CheckPoint
- Bitmap CheckPoint
- Database CheckPoint
- Accessibility CheckPoint
- XML CheckPoint

Even though built-in CheckPoints are very useful, there are a few limitations:

- They do not support programmatic descriptions.
- They only support one condition to pass or fail.
- They have limited reporting capacity.

To create multiple verification points for an object using built-in CheckPoints, it becomes necessary to create multiple individual CheckPoints. Because creating built-in CheckPoints requires navigating through an array of dialogs, it can become very time-consuming to create these checks. Moreover, if there is a change in the flow or UI, the same procedure would have to be repeated to update the CheckPoints or create new ones.

Apart from these limitations, there is another aspect to consider: flexibility. Engineers using built-in CheckPoints are bound by what QTP offers and there is very little flexibility present.

Custom CheckPoints are also utilized when the Engineer decides to implement automation using programmatic descriptions – where built-in CheckPoints are not feasible.

We will be using the HTML source below for developing custom CheckPoints:

```html
<html>
  <head>
    <title>Custom CheckPoints</title>
  </head>
  <body style="background:#ffffee;">
    <p>Please complete the form below to login:</p>
    <form>
      <table>
        <tr>
          <td width="100px">Username</td>
          <td><input name="username" value="Enter Username" /></td>
        </tr>
        <tr>
          <td width="100px">Password</td>
          <td><input name="password" value="Enter Password" /></td>
        </tr>
        <tr>
          <td width="100px"></td>
          <td><input type="button" name="login" value="Login" /></td>
        </tr>
      </table>
    </form>
  </body>
</html>
```

Check Test Object Existence

The most fundamental custom CheckPoint is to check whether or not the test object is available in the application UI. There are two ways to do this:

- ◉ Using .Exist
- ◉ Using .ChildObjects

Using .Exist

The Exist method provides a Boolean value indicating whether or not the object is available in the application UI:

```
If Browser("name:=Custom CheckPoints").WebEdit("name:=username").Exist(5)
Then
  Reporter.ReportEvent micPass, "Username", "Username textbox found"
Else
  Reporter.ReportEvent micFail, "Username", "Username textbox not found"
End If
```

The above can be extended as a built-in (RegisterUserFunc) method for any object that will simply check for its existence and report back:

```
Function ExistX(ByVal TObject, ByVal Timeout)
  ExistX = False
    If TObject.Exist(Timeout) Then
    Reporter.ReportEvent micPass, "ExistX", "Test object found"
    ExistX = True
  Else
    Reporter.ReportEvent micFail, "ExistX", "Test object not found"
  End If
End Function

'Usage:
Call Browser("name:=Custom CheckPoints").WebEdit("name:=username").
ExistX(5)
```

The above function can be used for either programmatic descriptions or Object Repository.

Using .ChildObjects

Another way of ensuring the object exists is by counting its instances through ChildObjects. The ChildObjects method provides an integer value indicating whether the count of the objects present in the application UI that match the test object. This technique can be quite useful when there are two or more instances of the object in the application UI. In this case, the Exist method will return False if an ordinal identifier is not used. This technique, however, retrieves the count which can then inform the engineer that there is in fact a need to use an ordinal identifier for the target object.

```
Dim oDesc
Set oDesc = Description.Create
oDesc("micclass").Value = "WebEdit"
```

```
oDesc("name").Value = "User"

If Browser("CheckPoints").Page("Page").ChildObjects(oDesc).Count > 0 Then
  Reporter.ReportEvent micPass, "Username", "The Username textbox was
found"
Else
  Reporter.ReportEvent micFail, "Username", "The Username textbox was not
found"
End If
```

Similarly, the above can also be created into a function that can return the number of test objects found in the application UI for the provided test object.

```
Function CountX(ByVal TObject)
  Dim TOProperties, i, Parent, oDesc

  Set TOProperties = TObject.GetTOProperties
   For i = 0 To TOProperties.Count - 1
    oDesc.Add TOProperties(i).Name, TOProperties(i).Value
  Next
   Set Parent = TObject.GetTOProperty("parent")
   CountX = Parent.ChildObjects(oDesc).Count
End Function

'Usage:
bExist = Browser("CheckPoints").Page("P").WebEdit("name:=User").CountX > 0
```

Converting an OR-based Script to a DP-based Script

Converting an OR-based script to a DP-based script requires careful selection of properties required by each DP statement to build a unique description for identification. Consider the OR-based statements below, recorded when interacting with the Windows calculator to multiply 2 by 5:

```
'Launch the calculator application
SystemUtil.Run "calc.exe"
```

```
'Activate the window
Window("Calculator").Activate

'Perform various operations
Window("Calculator").WinButton("2").Click
Window("Calculator").WinButton("*").Click
Window("Calculator").WinButton("5").Click
Window("Calculator").WinButton("=").Click

'Check the results
Window("Calculator").WinEdit("Edit").Check CheckPoint("Edit")
```

The OR for the above script is shown below:

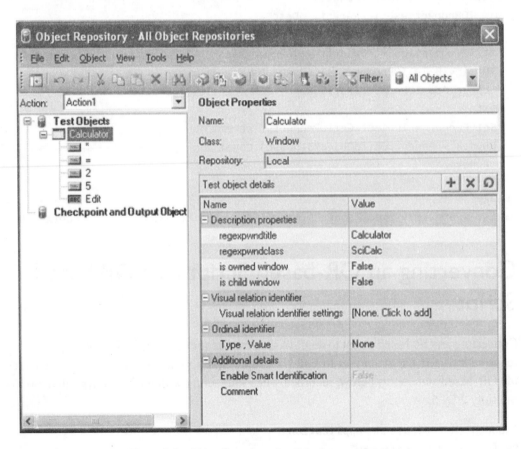

Figure 3.4 – Object Repository for Calculator application

Looking at the OR, we can see that the objects are recognized based on their text labels. The DP-based converted script will then use the following statements:

```
'Run the calculator application
SystemUtil.Run "calc.exe"

With Window("regexpwndtitle:=Calculator")
  'Activate the window
  .Activate
  'Perform various operations
  .WinButton("text:=2", "nativeclass:=Button").Click
  '* is regular expression and we should use a \ before that
  .WinButton("text:=\*","nativeclass:=Button").Click
  .WinButton("text:=5","nativeclass:=Button").Click
  .WinButton("text:==","nativeclass:=Button").Click
  'Check the results
  'We cannot create checkpoint object using DP but we can
  'run a already created checkpoint on a object identified using DP
  .WinEdit("nativeclass:=Edit").Check CheckPoint("Edit")
  .Close
End With
```

NOTE: We have used the regexpwndtitle:=Calculator property to recognize the calculator window. We could have also used regexpwndclass:=SciCalc which is unique to the calculator window. In case the window title keeps changing, a better option is to choose only the window's class or another property that remains static.

It is important to select the correct property (or properties) with which to identify an object in DP. Selecting properties like x, y, abs_x, etc. is never a good choice as these are subject to change with each run of the AUT and do not support use of regular expressions either. Properties like title and regexpwndtitle are in most cases reliable.

Using a VBScript DP Object Repository

Placing your DP object definitions in a VBScript library can logically emulate a QTP Object Repository. Consider the example below:

UserForm.vbs (function library)

```
'Declare DP string definitions
Const dpBrowser = "micclass:=Browser"
Const dpPage = "micclass:=Page"
Const dpFirstName = "name:=txtFirstName"
Const dpLastName = "name:=txtLastName"
Const dpSubmit = "name:=Submit"
```

There are three ways to include the above file in one or more scripts:

- ⊙ Associate the VBS file on the Test Settings Resource tab.

- ⊙ Use the ExecuteFile statement to load the file into one or more test Actions (no debugging capability available).

- ⊙ Use LoadFunctionLibrary to load the file with debugging capability.

Script

```
'Run the internet explorer application
SystemUtil.Run "iexplore.exe"
Browser(dpBrowser).Sync
'Enter data
Browser(dpBrowser).Page(dpPage).WebEdit(dpFirstName).Set "Tarun"
Browser(dpBrowser).Page(dpPage).WebEdit(dpLastName).Set "Lalwani"
'Click on the submit button
Browser(dpBrowser).Page(dpPage).WebButton(dpSubmit).Click
```

This technique can also be used to implement a multi-language testing script. Create different VBS files for each language, for example dpOR_EN.vbs, dpOR_FR.vbs or dpOR_DN.vbs.. Then use the following code to select the proper file, based on the language specified:

```
'Set the environment variable
'This should be loaded through a external file
```

```
Environment.Value("LanguageToTest")="FR"
'Check for which environment to execute in
Select Case Environment.Value("LanguageToTest")
  Case "EN"
    ExecuteFile "dpOR_EN.vbs"
  Case "FR"
    ExecuteFile "dpOR_FR.vbs"
  Case "DN"
    ExecuteFile "dpOR_DN.vbs"
End Select
'...
'The rest of the script goes here
'...
```

More information on this topic can be found in the Localization Techniques chapter.

Problems with Ordinal Identifiers

QTP only uses Ordinal Identifiers when there are multiple object matches for a given description.

```
'Check if a second browser exists
MsgBox Browser("micclass:=Browser","index:=1").Exist(0)
```

The above statement should indicate whether there is a second Browser instance open or not. However, in practice this is not the case because if there is a single Browser open, the above statement will still return true. Now consider the following statement:

```
'Check if a browser exists
MsgBox Browser("micclass:=Browser").Exist(0)
```

In situations where QTP is able to resolve the object based on the above description, it will return either True or False. But in situations where there are multiple open browsers, QTP must use an Ordinal Identifier (either Index or CreationTime) to uniquely identify each instance. Consider, for example, the following code:

```
'Check for existence of various browsers
bBrowser1 = Browser("CreationTime:=0").Exist(0) '1st opened browser
bBrowser2 = Browser("CreationTime:=1").Exist(0) '2nd opened browser
```

```
bBrowser3 = Browser("CreationTime:=2").Exist(0) '3rd opened browser
```

The return values from the previous code statements are show in the table below:

CreationTime Exist Values

Open Browser Count	Variable Value		
	bBrowser1	bBrowser2	bBrowser3
0	False	False	False
1	True	True	True
2	True	True	True

These results make it clear that in case of 0 or 1 open Browsers the CreationTime property was never used for identification. This creates a problem if we need to determine if 2 Browsers exist because the code below cannot be used to confirm this:

```
'Check if second browser exists
Browser("CreationTime:=1").Exist(0)
```

A workaround is to use the code as shown below to reliably test for a second opened browser. This code uses window handles (hWnd), which are always unique. By comparing the handles returned by both the CreationTime=0 and CreationTime=1 statements, we can know if the second Browser exists.

```
'Check if browser with creation time 0 exists
If Browser("CreationTime:=0").Exist(0) Then
   'There might be a possibility that only one browser exists
   'To make sure we can check the handle of 1st and 2nd browser
   hwnd1 = Browser("CreationTime:=0").GetROProperty("hwnd")
   hwnd2 = Browser("CreationTime:=1").GetROProperty("hwnd")
   'Check if the handles are equal
   If hwnd1 <> hwnd2 Then
     MsgBox "The 2nd Browser exists"
   Else
     MsgBox "The 2nd Browser does not exist"
   End If
Else
   Msgbox "No browser exists"
End If
```

Another technique is to use an invalid CreationTime of -1. The following statement will return False when there are 0 or more than 1 Browser open:

```
'Check for nonexistent browser
bNonBrowser = Browser("CreationTime:=-1").Exist(0)
```

Below is the complete code to reliably determine whether 0, 1 or multiple Browsers are open:

```
'Check if nonexistent browser exists. This trick helps us determine if the
'ordinal identifier was used during recognition of the object. If the
'return value is True then we are sure that the property was not used
bNonBrowser = Browser("CreationTime:=-1").Exist(0)
'Check for the 1st browser
bBrowser1 = Browser("CreationTime:=0").Exist(0)
'If bNonBrowser was true that means only 1 browser can exist
If bNonBrowser Then
  'Only 1 Browser
  Msgbox "Only 1 browser exists"
Else
  'If bNonBrowser is false: no browsers or multiple browsers exist
  If bBrowser1 then
    'If the first one exist then there are multiple browsers
    Msgbox "Multiple browser exists"
  Else
    'None exist
    Msgbox "No browser exists"
  End If
End If
```

Working with Multiple Browsers

QTP provides index and CreationTime Ordinal Identifiers for Web Browsers to differentiate between them at runtime. Consider the following script:

Script 1

```
'Launch internet explorer
```

```
SystemUtil.Run "iexplore.exe"
'Navigate to www.mywebsite.com
Browser("micclass:=Browser").Navigate "http://www.mywebsite.com"
```

The code snippet above creates a new Browser and opens the specified website in that Browser. Now let's modify the script to launch two Browsers instead:

Script 2

```
'Launch internet explorer
SystemUtil.Run "iexplore.exe"
'Launch a dummy internet explorer
SystemUtil.Run "iexplore.exe"
'Wait for the process to load
Wait 2
'Navigate to www.mywebsite.com. this time we cannot use micclass:=Browser
'as there are multiple browsers so we need to creation time
Browser("creationtime:=0").Navigate "http://www.google.com"
```

The Wait statement lets both Browsers launch properly. But the fourth statement specifies that the website will produce a 'multiple matches of object found' error because the Browser ("micclass:=Browser") statement is valid for both Browsers.

To differentiate between the two Browsers, we must use the Index or CreationTime property which is unique to each Browser:

```
'All of the following statements refer only to the 1st Browser:
Browser("micclass:=Browser","index:=0").Navigate "http://www.google.com"
Browser("micclass:=Browser","creationtime:=0").Navigate "http://www.google.
com"
Browser("index:=0").Navigate "http://www.google.com"
Browser("creationtime:=0").Navigate "http://www.google.com"
'All of the following statements refer only to the 2nd Browser:
Browser("micclass:=Browser","index:=1").Navigate "http://www.google.com"
Browser("micclass:=Browser","creationtime:=1").Navigate "http://www.google.
com"
Browser("index:=1").Navigate "http://www.google.com"
Browser("creationtime:=1").Navigate "http://www.google.com"
```

Browser Identification Issues

Use of the CreationTime or Index property to identify multiple Browsers may cause problems in the following situations:

- If before running the script there are one or more Browsers already open.

- If the script is not able to close Browsers it spawns subsequent iterations.

- When running the script from QC. In this particular situation, the QC browser might get counted as one of the script browsers, which could cause the script to fail.

Here are few ways to avoid these situations:

- Close all Internet Explorer processes before launching any Browser. This can be accomplished by using the following statement:

```
'Kill all internet explorer processes
SystemUtil.CloseProcessByName "iexplore.exe"
```

 NOTE: This may not work well when the script is running from QC as it might kill the QC browser as well.

- In the case of a script using an Object Repository Browser object with the CreationTime property defined, we can use SetTOProperty to update the CreationTime at Run-time (Note: SMART Identification should be disabled for this to work properly.). For example, the following line of code sets the Browser object to point to the third Browser:

```
'Change the creationtime use for Browser identification
Browser("Browser").SetTOProperty "creationtime", 2
```

The above methods do not, however, always provide reliable Browser references. Next we discuss some additional Browser identification techniques.

Browser Identification using OpenTitle

The Browser's OpenTitle property defines the Browser's initial title when it is first launched:

```
'description string for the browser
dpBrowser = "OpenTitle:=Google"
```

```
'Launch internet explorer and navigate to www.google.com
SystemUtil.Run "iexplore.exe", "www.google.com"
Browser(dpBrowser).Navigate "www.gmail.com"
```

We do, however, need to know the page title that corresponds to the opening URL, and running the above code twice causes an error due to the fact that there will then be two browsers with the same OpenTitle property. Unless these issues are avoided, this is therefore still not a foolproof method for Browser identification.

Browser Identification using a Unique OpenURL Property

The following method specifies a junk (but valid) URL that includes a unique integer:

```
'Generate a random URL every time
browserID = RandomNumber.Value(10000,99999)
'Get the open url string
dpBrowser = "OpenURL:=about:" & browserID
```

```
'Launch a new browser with opening url based on the random number
SystemUtil.Run "iexplore.exe", "about:" & browserID
Browser(dpBrowser).Navigate "www.google.com"
```

 NOTE: We used an "about:#####" format because if we had used a normal string, the Browser would have tried to search the website. The above code is independent of the number of Browsers already open and the only limitation it has is in the case of popup windows. If you know the URL/title of the popup then you can use OpenTitle/OpenURL.

Common Mistakes while using DP

This section will walk you through the common mistakes that are made in scripts while using Descriptive Programming. Knowing these mistakes beforehand and not making them during scripting saves a lot of time.

- ◉ **Adding spaces before ":="**: Using spaces for code clarity is not advised in the case of DP. Consider the code shown below:

```
'Will print True when the window exists and False when it does not
Print Window("text:=Run").Exist(0)
'A spaced after ":=" will work
Print Window("text:= Run").Exist(0)
'Will always return false because of additional space before :=
Print Window("text :=Run").Exist(0)
```

- ◉ **Overpopulated description**: An overpopulated description does not help in recognizing the object. We should use the minimum number of properties which are stable enough to recognize the object on every single run. Consider the following overpopulated description:

```
Set oDesc = Description.Create
oDesc("html tag").Value  = "TABLE"
oDesc("micclass").Value  = "WebTable"
oDesc("innertext").Value ="abcde"
oDesc("outertext").Value = "abcde"
oDesc("innerhtml").Value = "<tbody><tr><td>abcde</td></tr></tbody>"
oDesc("outerhtml").Value = "<table><tbody><tr><td>abcde</td></tr></tbody></table>"
oDesc("rows").Value = 1
oDesc("cols").Value = 1
```

Now consider the following advice when creating such a description:

- o Rows and columns are dynamic properties which might change if the table gets updated. These properties should therefore be avoided.

- o Only one of the properties from innertext, outertext, outerhtml and innerhtml should be used.

- o Outerhtml and innerhtml properties should be avoided as they contains various tags and are difficult to express.

- o When using Browser().Page().WebTable(oDesc) we can skip specifying the micclass and HTML tag properties because as soon as we enclose oDesc with the WebTable() test object, these two properties are mostly implied.

Considering the above points, we can reduce our description to simply:

```
Set oDesc = Description.Create
oDesc("outertext").Value = "abcde"
```

⊙ **Under-populated description**: Although we reduced the number of properties in the description object when we identified a table in the last section, when using the ChildObjects method, we should make sure of the following:

- o Maximum description properties should be used to reduce the final result set, although we should still follow the advice given in the previous section on overpopulated descriptions (except for the last one where we ignore micclass and HTML tag).

- o When using ChildObjects to find WebElements, "html tag" and "micclass" should always be provided to avoid errors.

- o Property names used in the description should be written in the same case as those provided in the QTP Help file because changing the case sometimes causes general run errors during script run. However, there is no documentation proving that description names are case-sensitive.

⊙ **Using 'Class Name' instead of 'micclass'**: The reason for HP preferring to show 'micclass' as 'Class Name' in the Object Spy is unknown, but it can mislead many DP users to creating a description with the non-existent property 'Class Name'.

```
'Below is the wrong way
Browser("Class Name:=Browser")

'Below is the right way
Browser("micclass:=Browser")

'Below is the wrong way
Set oDesc = Description.Create
oDesc("Class Name").Value = "Browser"
oDesc("title").Value = "My title"
```

```
'Below is the right way
Set oDesc = Description.Create
oDesc("micclass").Value = "Browser"
oDesc("title").Value = "My title"
```

⊙ **Case-sensitivity for non-regular expressions**: Properties become case-sensitive when the regular expression flag for a description is turned off.

```
Set pDesc = Description.Create
pDesc("text").Value = "Run"
pDesc("text").RegularExpression = True

'Both will work no matter what case the title has
Print Window("text:=RuN").Exist(0)
Print Window(pDesc).Exist(0)

'Turn the regular expression property off
pDesc("text").RegularExpression = False
'Will only work when the Title is "Run"
'Will not work for RUN, RuN or any other case
Window(pDesc).Exist(0)
```

⊙ **Not escaping the Regular Expression (r.e.) characters**: By default QTP treats all descriptive property values as Regular Expressions. Using the property values without escaping the r.e. will fail to identify the object. Imagine that we need to click a 'Logout Tarun' link using Descriptive Programming. The code to click on the link is given below:

```
sLinkText = "Logout Tarun"
Browser("creationtime:=0").Page("micclass:=Page").Link("text:=" &
sLinkText).Click
```

Now if the link changes to 'Logout (Tarun)', the below mentioned code won't work

```
sLinkText = "Logout (Tarun)"
Browser("creationtime:=0").Page("micclass:=Page").Link("text:=" &
sLinkText).Click
```

The reason it does not work is that '(' and ')' have special meaning in Regular expressions and are used to group a pattern. So the final equivalent of 'Logout (Tarun)' becomes 'Logout Tarun' because '(Tarun)' groups the pattern 'Tarun' and the '(", ")' itself has no meaning. To correct the issue we need to escape the characters which have special meaning in Regular Expressions. The code needs to be updated as shown below:

```
sLinkText = "Logout \(Tarun\)"
Browser("creationtime:=0").Page("micclass:=Page").Link("text:=" &
sLinkText).Click
```

If we are using object descriptions then we need to set the RegularExpression property to False:

```
Set oDesc = Description.Create
oDesc("text").Value = "Logout (Tarun)"
oDesc("text").RegularExpression = False
Browser("creationtime:=0").Page("micclass:=Page").Link(oDesc).Click
```

⊙ **Not all properties support the use of Regular Expression patterns**: QTP Help does not document which properties don't support patterns but this can be confirmed through the Object Repository UI. The checkbox for such properties is disabled in such cases. Properties like x, y, abs_x and abs_y do not support the use of patterns.

Writing DP Code using HTML Source Code

After opening the following HTML in Internet Explorer, you will immediately know how to locate the first and the last P elements because they have a unique class associated with them. However, the second and third elements can be quite challenging to identify uniquely using straightforward QTP methods, and understanding the HTML source then becomes a necessity. Moreover, if the second and third strings are dynamic, there will be very little possibility to identify them using the innerText.

```
<html>
  <head><title>Traversing Nodes</title></head>
  <body style="background:#ffffee;">
    <p class="para1">This is a paragraph.</p>
    <div class="divClassParent">
      <p>This is a paragraph.</p>
      <div class="divClassChild">
```

```
      <p>This is a paragraph.</p>
    </div>
  </div>
  <p class="para2">This is a paragraph.</p>
</body>
</html>
```

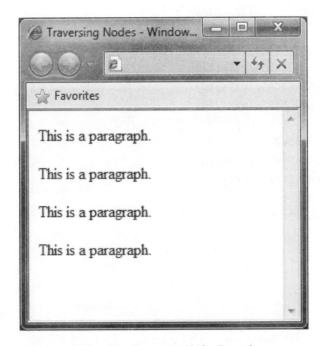

Figure 3.5 – Traversing Nodes Example

The follow code shows how to access all P tags using both standard QTP and HTML DOM styles:

```
'P Tag #1
Browser("name:=Traversing Nodes").WebElement("class:=para1").Highlight
'P Tag #2
Browser("name:=Traversing Nodes").WebElement("html tag:=DIV",
"class:=divClassParent").WebElement("html tag:=P", "index:=0").Highlight
'P Tag #3
Browser("name:=Traversing Nodes").WebElement("html tag:=DIV",
"class:=divClassChild").WebElement("html tag:=P").Highlight
'P Tag #4
Browser("name:=Traversing Nodes").WebElement("class:=para2").Highlight
```

Let's create another example using a HTML table with the same text element in each cell.

Consider the HTML source code below:

```
<html>
  <head><title>Traversing Nodes</title></head>
  <body style="background:#ffffee;">
    <table border="1" cellpadding="5">
      <tr class="row1">
        <td class="td1">Text</td>
        <td class="td2">Text</td>
        <td class="td4">Text</td>
        <td class="td5">Text</td>
      </tr>
      <tr class="row2">
        <td class="td1">Text</td>
        <td class="td2">Text</td>
        <td class="td4">Text</td>
        <td class="td5">Text</td>
      </tr>
    </table>
  </body>
</html>
```

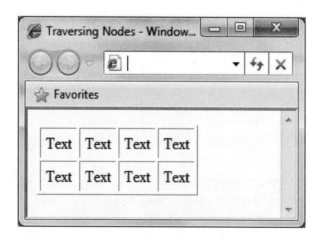

Figure 3.6 – Traversing Nodes Example

Notice the table cells in the snapshot above. They all have the same text. Is it really possible to find a way to uniquely identifying them? The answer is yes.

Even though the text element is the same, each element is housed in a separate cell with a unique class identifier for TR and TD. Therefore, even though the text element is exactly the same, it is possible to reference them uniquely using their row-column combination.

Using the same approach, the text elements can be recognized using the <TR> and <TD> elements.

Identifying elements in Row 1:

```
Set TR = Browser("name:=Traversing Nodes").WebElement("html tag:=TR",
"class:=row1")
'Row 1: Element 1
TR.WebElement("html tag:=TD", "class:=TD1").Highlight
'Row 1: Element 2
TR.WebElement("html tag:=TD", "class:=TD2").Highlight
'Row 1: Element 3
TR.WebElement("html tag:=TD", "class:=TD3").Highlight
'Row 1: Element 4
TR.WebElement("html tag:=TD", "class:=TD4").Highlight
```

Identifying elements in Row 2:

```
Set TR = Browser("name:=Traversing Nodes").WebElement("html tag:=TR",
"class:=row2")
'Row 2: Element 1
TR.WebElement("html tag:=TD", "class:=TD1").Highlight
'Row 2: Element 2
TR.WebElement("html tag:=TD", "class:=TD2").Highlight
'Row 2: Element 3
TR.WebElement("html tag:=TD", "class:=TD3").Highlight
'Row 2: Element 4
TR.WebElement("html tag:=TD", "class:=TD4").Highlight
```

So in this section, we have seen that it is possible to uniquely identify elements in an application using the right cues, even though the elements may have repeated occurrences within the same UI.

Test Object Override

Test Object Override means overriding a test object type through its identification properties. The concept will become clear when we look at an example. Descriptive Programming allows us to reference and work with various QTP test objects. Consider the following statement:

```
'Sync on the web page
Browser("micclass:=Browser").Page("micclass:=Page").Sync
```

From this statement we assume that there is only one Browser open and we provide only the default parameter, which is micclass:=Browser (as it is already an implicit property of the Browser object). Now one disadvantage of this code is that it becomes mandatory to include types such as Browser and Page. We can create generic statements using the concept of Test Object Override as shown in the following code:

```
'Sync on the web page
WinObject("micclass:=Browser").Navigate "www.test.com"
'Sync on the web page
WinObject("micclass:=Browser").WinObject("micclass:=Page").Sync
'Outside test object class does not make a difference as we
'are overriding the class inside
Page("micclass:=Browser").Browser("micclass:=Page").Sync
```

This technique provides a way to create generic frameworks which will work with any type of application by simply changing the description's micclass. This approach also helps when we want to assign or override a method using RegisterUserFunc for various object types. To override a Click method for all WebObjects, for instance, we would need to use RegisterUserFunc for all object types defined by the Web add-in. Using this technique means that we only need to use RegisterUserFunc with a single generic object class, and therefore this approach can be used to create technology-independent scripts where even the micclass or type of the object is used at Run-time.

Object References Unusable after Navigation

Reference to objects can be stored inside variables as shown in the code below:

```
'Store the object reference
```

```
Set oPg = Browser("Browser").Page("Page")
Set oSearch = oPg.WebEdit("name:=q")
Set oSearchBtn = oPg.WebButton("name:=Search")
'Use the object reference to the operation
oSearch.Set "Test"
'Go to the next page
oSearchBtn.Click
'Would throw an error that object cannot be identified.
'The Search button has the same description on new page also.
oSearch.Set "Test"
```

This statement would work perfectly assuming the page is not changed or refreshed. Any navigation to the next page would cause the set statement to fail with the error 'Unable to identify object'. The code given above would throw an error at the last statement.

The reason for this is because when we create a reference to the object and use it for the first time, QTP caches the object and maps it to a Run-time object. QTP does this caching to improve performance on the same object when used later. But when the application state has changed (page refreshed or changed) these object reference are no longer valid. Each QTP test object provides a hidden method named 'Init' to reinitialize the object cache. Using Init on the object makes sure that the object is re-identified. With QTP 11, a new method called RefreshObject has been introduced.

```
oSearch.RefreshObject
oSearch.Set "Test"
```

A Myth about DP

Before we proceed further in creating a deeper understanding of Descriptive Programming, it is important to highlight a myth about DP, that it can be used when QTP is unable to recognize the object using Object Repository. This statement is not true as DP does not add any extra functionality to QTP's object recognition.

If there is an object in the AUT that QTP is unable to identify even when proper add-ins are installed and loaded, there is no way within DP to identify the object. The only feature which DP provides is flexibility in terms of adding programming to the object recognition and avoiding a need for Object Repository. We will see how Object Casting discussed in the next section, can help us map objects to different object type (the same is achievable by manually defining the object in OR as well)

Object Casting

Object Casting is the technique of casting an object from one type to another and can be particularly useful when the object is a custom object and therefore not recognized as a specific test object. On Windows XP, the checkboxes inside the File Search window are recognized as WinObject by QTP. This happens because the nativeclass for the checkbox object is 'SA_Button', which is custom class. We can cast the object at Run-time as shown in the code below:

```
hWnd = Window("Search Results").WinObject("Search hidden files and").
GetROProperty("hwnd")
Window("Search Results").WinCheckBox("hwnd:=" & hWnd).Set "On"
```

In this code we first get some property for the object we want to cast, which should be uniquely able to identify the object. In the case of Windows, .NET or Java objects, the hwnd can do the job most of the time. Once we have the property, we use DP to change the test object type.

NOTE: This approach may or may not work on the custom object. The success of the approach depends on how the custom object behaves compared to the casted object internally. A custom object might have the same functionality when compared to a specific TestObject yet might be implemented in a totally different manner internally.

Performing an Action on Multiple Objects

There are situations where executing the same operation on all or multiple similar objects is required. A few examples of such scenarios are:

- Checking/unchecking all Checkbox controls.

⊙ Setting a blank value to all Textbox controls.

⊙ Selecting the first (or any other) value for every WebRadioGroup.

In general, such situations are handled using collections such as ChildObjects. The code below demonstrates this:

```
'Create a description for web checkbox
Dim oWebChkDesc
Set oWebChkDesc = Description.Create
oWebChkDesc("micclass").value = "WebCheckBox"
oWebChkDesc("html tag").Value = "INPUT"


'Get all objects matching this description
Dim allCheck, oCheckBox
Set allCheck = Browser("KnowledgeInbox").Page("KnowledgeInbox").
ChildObjects(oWebChkDesc)

Dim i
For i = 0 to allCheck.Count - 1
  Set oCheckBox = allCheck(i)
  oCheckBox.Set "ON"
Next
```

The above approach is sound, but with a major drawback. Because it is not generic, reusability becomes a concern if other object types are involved. An elegant solution would be to incorporate reusability by removing dependency from a single object type.

```
'Description: The function calls a method on a object by its name
'Params:
'  @Obj - The object on which the methods needs to be called
'  @MethodName - The name of the method to be called
'  @Params - Parameter to be passed to the Method. In case
'  of multiple parameters use Array
Function ExecActionMultipleObjects(Obj, MethodName, Params)
  'If the Params is not an Array we make it an Array
  'This makes it flexible to pass a single parameter without
  'creating an array for the same
  If VarType(Params) <> vbArray Then Params = Array(Params)
  Dim objDesc
```

```
 'Try to Extract the description from the object
 Set objDesc = Obj.GetTOProperties()
 'Generate the call statement parameters
 Dim i
 Dim paramCallText
 paramCallText = " "
 For i = 0 to UBound(Params)
   paramCallText =  paramCallText & "Params(" & i & "),"
 Next
 'Removed the trailing ","
 If Right(paramCallText,1) = "," Then
   paramCallText = Left(paramCallText, Len(paramCallText)-1)
 End If
  If objDesc.Count = 0 Then
   'The object is an derived object returned from ChildObjects
   'We Can't do anything special with this
   'Just try to execute the method on the Object passed to this function
   Execute "Obj." & MethodName & paramCallText
 Else
   Dim oParent
    'Get the Test Object's parent
   Set oParent = Obj.GetTOProperty("parent")
    'Get all children matching current object description
   Dim allChilds
   Set allChilds = oParent.ChildObjects(objDesc)
    If allChilds.Count = 0 Then
     'No matching objects were found. So let us just try to Set the value
     Execute "Obj." & MethodName & paramCallText
   Else
     'We now have multiple objects matching this description
     'Perform set operation for all children
     For i = 0 to allChilds.Count - 1
       Execute "allChilds(i)." & MethodName & paramCallText
     Next
   End If
 End If
End Function
```

The above function will extract the description from the object passed to it using

GetTOProperties. One issue to note is that when a collection is retrieved from ChildObjects, this method will not work. In such a case, the following extension method can be used:

```
Function SetAll(Obj, Text)
  CallMultiObjectMethod Obj, "Set", Text
End Function
RegisterUserFunc "WebCheckBox", "SetAll", "SetAll"
RegisterUserFunc "WebEdit", "SetAll", "SetAll"
```

The statement below shows how to use this function to set a value for all Checkboxes that are stored in the Object Repository:

```
Browser("B").Page("P").WebCheckBox("CheckBoxes").SetAll "ON"
```

When used with Descriptive Programming, both the following approaches will work:

Approach 1

```
Browser("B").Page("P").WebCheckBox("micclass:=WebCheckBox").SetAll "ON"
```

Approach 2

```
Dim oWebChkDesc
Set oWebChkDesc = Description.Create
oWebChkDesc("micclass").value = "WebCheckBox"
oWebChkDesc("html tag").Value = "INPUT"
Browser("B").Page("P").WebCheckBox(oWebChkDesc).SetAll "ON"
```

Using Descriptive Programming in Scripts

Consider the following descriptive script, which is used to log on to an application:

```
'Launch the browser
SystemUtil.Run "iexplore.exe"
Browser("creationtime:=0").Sync
Browser("creationtime:=0").Page("micclass:=Page").WebEdit("name:=Username").
Set "username"
Browser("creationtime:=0").Page("micclass:=Page").WebEdit("name:=Password").
Set "Password"
```

```
Browser("creationtime:=0").Page("micclass:=Page").WebButton("name:=Login").
Click
```

Although the script above is logically correct, the approach used for the same is not the best one when it comes to maintenance of the script. Since we have used hard coded values for the identification properties, a big test suite requiring identification property changes will mean updating a lot many scripts in the suite. Let's assume that we want to change the Name:=Password to Name:=Pwd, this change would pose 2 big issues, one we need replace it in every script it used, 2nd since we don't have a way to track the use of the object in any script we may end up digging into all scripts

We can use string based DP instead. In this case we will create variables containing string definitions of the description:

```
dpBrw = "creationtime:=0"
dpPg = "micclass:=Page"
dpFrame = "name:=Main"
dpTxtUserName = "name:=Username"
dpTxtPassword = "name:=Password"
dpBtnLogin = "name:=Login"
```

The above string definitions can be kept in a global library file and then loaded into the script. The script would be updated as below:

```
Browser(dpBrw).Sync
With Browser(dpBrw).Page(dpPg).Frame(dpFrame)
  .WebEdit(dpUserName).Set "username"
  .WebEdit(dpPassword).Set "Password"
  .WebButton(dpBtnLogin).Click
End With
```

In this way, all scripts refer to the created variables (dpBrw, dpPg, dpBtnLogin etc) for object definitions. Therefore, in case of maintenance updating variables in the library also updates all instances where these descriptions are used in scripts.

Problem with this approach is that when multiple properties are required to identify an object, we can't directly specify the identification properties in the string. Assume there are two login buttons on the screen and we need to click the first one. In this case, we would also need to specify the index. We can't update the dpBtnLogin string in the library file as follows:

```
dpBtnLogin = "name:=Login,index:=0"
```

Doing so will ask QTP to identify an object which has name as "Login,index:=0". This is a common mistake that is often made by novice users of DP. Instead of using a string based DP, we need to use object-based DP. We can update the library as follows:

```
Set dpBtnLogin = Description.Create
dpBtnLogin("name").value = "Login"
dpBtnLogin("index").value = 0
```

The above uses a hybrid of string-based and object-based DP. Using string-based DP means using less memory and shorter code, while using object-based DP means higher memory and lengthier code but less maintenance in scripts. This is because it allows adding multiple properties to the description and doesn't require any modification to the script.

This approach works well when the numbers of objects in the application is small. But when the number of objects increases, the library size also increases, making it difficult to maintain and lookup objects. Additionally, because all object definitions are in the same library, the library can't be updated by multiple users at the same time. To overcome this we will create a Keyword-based Object Repository.

Keyword-based Descriptive Programming Object Repository

This section describes how we can create a Keyword-driven Object Repository of programmatic descriptions. The following objects and properties are required for a custom object to implement this solution:

- Name or Keyword – Defines a unique name to identify each object. This is similar to defining a variable in your VBScript code therefore spaces and any special characters that are against VBScript rules are not permitted here.

- Type - Defines the Test Object class (micclass) of the target object (Page, Window, WebEdit etc.).

- Parent – Defines the keyword used for the parent object. Defining the keyword for the parent object helps us in the following ways:

  o   It becomes possible to fetch all objects associated with any given parent.

o   It helps to obtain complete details about an object by simply using its associated keyword without the need to provide any additional information in code. This helps ensure the code remains generic.

⊙   Identifier(s) – Defines the test object's properties used to identify the test object.

Let's see how our sample Object Repository would look like:

Name	Type	Parent	Identifier1	Identifier2
oBrw	Browser		creationtime:=0	
oPgLogin	Page	oBrw	micclass:=Page	
pgLogin_oTxt_UserName	WebEdit	oPgLogin	name:=Username	
pgLogin_oTxt_Password	WebEdit	oPgLogin	name:=password	
pgLogin_oBtn_Submit	WebButton	oPgLogin	name:=Submit	index:=0

Figure 3.7 – Sample Keyword-based Object Repository

 NOTE: In this example, we have used only 2 columns for Identifiers but you can add any number of columns to build unique descriptions. However, we recommend a maximum of 5 identifiers. Ideally speaking, the number of identifiers should be 2-3.

Next, we will explore a few different aspects of implementing this approach of building a custom Object Repository.

Implementing the Keyword based Object Repository

As we saw in the Figure 3.7, we must store some information about each object: Name, Type, Parent, Identifier1 and Identifier2. To facilitate this storage of information, we will create a new class called TestObject:

```
'Class to store object information
Class TestObject
   Dim Keyword
   Dim ObjectType
   Dim Parent
   Dim Identifier1
```

```
    Dim Identifier2
End Class
```

To maintain the object repository we will use a Dictionary object to store the information about each test object. Keys of the Dictionary will store the keywords whereas the items will store the target test objects as shown here:

```
'Create dictionary for storing objects in object repository
Dim ObjectRepository
Set ObjectRepository = CreateObject("Scripting.Dictionary")

Public Function AddObjectToOR(ByVal sKeyword, ByVal sObjectType, ByVal
sParent, ByVal sID1, ByVal sID2)
  Set oTestObject = New TestObject
  With oTestObject
    .Keyword = sKeyword
    .ObjectType = sObjectType
    .Parent = sParent
    .Identifier1 = sID1
    .Identifier2 = sID2
  End With

  'Create an object with sKeyword
  'Overwrite if the object already exists
  Set ObjectRepository(sKeyword) = oTestObject
End Function
```

In order to make our object repository case-insensitive, we simply add the next line of code after creating the Dictionary:

```
'Set text compare mode for keyword for object to be incase-sensitive
ObjectRepository.CompareMode = vbTextCompare
```

 NOTE: AddObjectToOR does not check whether the object already exists in the Object Repository. It creates and stores a new object if the object does not exist and overwrite the object definition in case the object already exists. This allows updating the OR at Run-time using a single function call. However, this behavior can be changed by modifying the function's code.

Instantiating a Test Object

Once we have loaded our custom Object Repository which was built using a Dictionary object, we can instantiate test objects at runtime by using the Execute statement. The user will have to provide the keyword for the object and the function will search for it by traversing keys of the Dictionary. The function will also check if the object has any parent specified. If there is a parent specified then its keyword will also be processed using the following function:

```
'ObjectRep function to get the object for a give keyword
Public Function ObjectRep(ByVal sKey)
  'Check if the Object exist or not
  If Not ObjectRepository.Exists(sKey) Then
    'Raise an error to notify the object does not exist
    Err.Raise vbObjectError + 1, "Object Repository", _
    "The specified object does not exist in the repository. Name - " & sKey
  Else
    'Get object information from the Repository
    Set oTestObject = ObjectRepository.Item(sKey)

    'In case of 1 ID generate strings as ObjectType("ID1") and in case
    'of 2 ID Generate ObjectType("ID1", "ID2")
    'We can improve the code here by using arrays and
    'the Join function to generate the identifier string
    If oTestObject.Identifier2 <>""Then
      sObjectDesc = oTestObject.ObjectType& "(""" & _
                    oTestObject.Identifier1 & """,""" & _
                    oTestObject.Identifier1 & """)"
  Else
      sObjectDesc = oTestObject.ObjectType& "(""" & _
                    oTestObject.Identifier1 & """)"
  End If

    'Check if this is the top level object
    If IsEmpty(oTestObject.Parent) Or oTestObject.Parent = "" Then
      'Get the top level objecy
      Execute "Set ObjectRep = " & sObjectDesc
  Else
      'Recursively call this function to get the parent object
```

```
        Set oParent = ObjectRep(oTestObject.Parent)
        'Generate the current object appending the parent
        Execute "Set ObjectRep = oParent." & sObjectDesc
    End if
  End If
End Function
```

 NOTE: To know more about Execute statement please refer to Appendix E – Eval & Execute

We have used two identifiers in the above function. To provide additional identifiers, we can use a single variable and store all identifiers as an Array, a Dictionary object or a user-defined Class object.

Using the Object Repository

Here is the sample code for using our Keyword based Object Repository:

```
'Add the objects to the Object Repository
AddObjectToOR "oBrw","Browser","", _
        "micclass:=Browser",""
AddObjectToOR "oPgLogin","Page","oBrw", _
        "miclass:=Page",""
AddObjectToOR "oPgLogin_oTxt_User","WebEdit", _
        "oPgLogin", "name:=user","index:=0"

'Get object reference of objects
Set MyBrowser = ObjectRep("oBrw")
Set MyPage = ObjectRep("oPgLogin")
Set MyButton = ObjectRep("oPgLogin_oTxt_User")

'Use the objects
Msgbox MyButton.Exist(0)
Msgbox ObjectRep("oBrw").Exist(0)
ObjectRep("oPgLogin_oTxt_User").Set "Tarun"
```

This approach helps reduce the length of code used as well. The DP equivalent of the last statement above would look like this:

```
'Set the value in the text box
Browser("micclass:=Browser").Page("micclass:=Page").WebEdit("name:=user","index:=0").Set "Tarun"
```

Storing the Object Repository

To store our Keyword based Object Repository let's now consider the following few options:

- ⦿ CSV Files – Comma-separate files can be used to store as the repository. This method is easy to implement in code but difficult to maintain in a team environment where simultaneous updates to data are required by multiple users. Though CSV files can be opened up in Excel programs but they still don't offer all the functionality of an Excel file (multiple tabs, file sharing etc).

- ⦿ Excel Files – Easiest to store and maintain. Multiple tabs (worksheets) can be used for different sections of the UI. Each worksheet can also store snapshots of the concerned applications' areas. We can also create shared Object Repositories used across multiple machines by allowing access through a shared network. Shared Excel sheets can be updated by multiple users at the same time giving it an edge over the QTP based SOR

- ⦿ Databases – Can be used to implement Shared Object Repositories through a database server. This option requires initial infrastructure setup but its advantages are same as we derive from using Excel files .

- ⦿ XML – Just like the previous 3 approaches, XMLs can also be used to store the Object Repository. Moreover, we can export the QTP's Object Repository into XML format. A downside of this storage option is that as the XML file gets large, it can become harder to use and maintain.

Below function shows how we can load the Object Repository in memory. The way array is generated in the function will depend on the format we use for the OR

```
Public Function LoadObjectRepository()
  Dim sKeyword(), sObjectType(), sParent()
  Dim sID1(), sID2()
  Dim oTestObject
```

```
'
'NOTE: this example assumes you have previously extracted all
'      of the user defined keyword, object type, parent, etc.
'      values into the above sKeyword(), sObjectType(), etc.
'      arrays. How these arrays are built depends on what technique
'      you used to store these OR definitions (which was described
'      in the previous section)

For i =  LBound(sKeyword) To UBound(sKeyword)
  AddObject2OR sKeyword(i), sObjectType(i), sParent(i), _
      sID1(i), sID2(i)
Next
End Function
```

Enhancing the Keyword-based Object Repository

We can enhance our custom Object Repository by implementing additional features.

Allowing Multiple Object Definitions

Our current implementation only allows the use of unique keywords for objects i.e. one object keyword can only have one definition. By overcoming this limitation, we can create multiple object definitions for any given test object, allowing removal of inconsistencies which may exist in different environments (QA, UAT, Production etc). To add this feature we will have to slightly modify the AddObject2OR and ObjectRep functions. Our earlier implementation stores the object definition as a test object class but now we will be storing it as an array of test object classes. Here is the updated function of adding objects:

```
'Flag to check if multiple definitions are allowed or not
Dim AllowMultipleDefinitions
AllowMultipleDefinitions = True

Public Function AddObjectToOR2(ByVal sKeyword, ByVal sObjectType, ByVal
sParent, ByVal sID1, ByVal sID2)
  Set oTestObject = New TestObject
  With oTestObject
```

```
        .Keyword = sKeyword
        .ObjectType = sObjectType
        .Parent = sParent
        .Identifier1 = sID1
        .Identifier2 = sID2
      End With


      objExist = ObjectRepository.Exists(sKeyword)


      Dim defArray
      If objExist And AllowMultipleDefinitions Then
        'If Object already exist and we allow multiple definitions
        'Get the current array of test objects
        defArray = ObjectRepository.Item(sKeyword)
        'Create room for one more test object definition
        ReDim Preserve defArray(UBound(defArray) + 1)
      Else
        'The object does not exist or we dont allow multiple
        'definitions. Overwrite the old one if one was there
        ReDimdefArray(0)
      End If

      Set defArray(UBound(defArray)) = oTestObject
      ObjectRepository.Item(sKeyword) = defArray
End Function
```

The ObjectRep function has become slightly more complex as we allow multiple definitions of an object. When we provide keyword for an object, it may happen that not only the object has multiple definitions but even one of its parents can have multiple definitions. It is highly recommended to limit using this feature for objects which have no child objects. For objects with multiple definitions, the ObjectRep function will automatically check which definition exists and then return the appropriate one. This happens in a recursive fashion where a parent object's existence will be checked first.

```
'Flag to check if multiple definitions need to be checked automatically
Dim AutoDetectOverride
AutoDetectOverride = True


Public Function ObjectRepEx(ByVal sKey)
```

```
      If Not ObjectRepository.Exists(sKey) Then
        'Raise an error to notify the object does not exist
        Err.RaisevbObjectError + 1, "Object Repository", _
        "The specified object does not exist in the repository. Name - "&sKey
      Else
        iDefCount = UBound(ObjectRepository.Item(sKey))

        If AutoDetectOverride Then
          If iDefCount = 0 Then
            'If there is only one definition then no need to check for exist
            Set ObjectRepEx = ObjectRepExByIndex (sKey, 0)
          Else
            For i = 0To iDefCount
              Set ObjectRepEx = ObjectRepExByIndex (sKey, i)
              If ObjectRepEx.Exist(0) Then
                'We found the definition of the object
                'which exist. Now return
                Exit Function
              End If
            Next
          End If
        End If

        'Object defined by sKey not found on screen. Return the 1st one
        Set ObjectRepEx = ObjectRepExByIndex (sKey, 0)
      End If
End Function

Public Function ObjectRepExByIndex(ByVal sKey, ByVal Index)
   'Check if the Object defined by sKey exists on the screen
   If Not ObjectRepository.Exists(sKey) Then
     'Raise an error to notify the object does not exist
     Err.RaisevbObjectError + 1, "Object Repository", _
       "The specified object does not exist in the repository. Name - "& sKey
   Else
     'Get object information from the Repository for the given index
     Set oTestObject = ObjectRepository.Item(sKey)(Index)

     'In case of 1 ID generate strings as
```

```
'ObjectType("ID1") and in case of 2 ID
'Generate ObjectType("ID1", "ID2")
'We can improve the code here by using arrays and
'the Join function to generate the identifier string

If oTestObject.Identifier2 <>"" Then
  sObjectDesc = oTestObject.ObjectType& "(""" & _
    oTestObject.Identifier1 &""",""" & _
    oTestObject.Identifier1 & """)"
Else
  sObjectDesc = oTestObject.ObjectType& "(""" & _
    oTestObject.Identifier1 & """)"
End If

'Check if this is the top level object
If IsEmpty(oTestObject.Parent) Or oTestObject.Parent = "" Then
  'Get the top level objecy
  Execute"SetObjectRepExByIndex = "&sObjectDesc
Else
  'Get the parent object recursively. We always want the
  'firsy object definition from parent.
  Set oParent = ObjectRepExByIndex(oTestObject.Parent, 0)

  'Generate the current object appending the parent
  Execute "Set ObjectRepExByIndex = oParent." &sObjectDesc
  End If
End If
End Function
```

In this enhancement, we have created two functions: ObjectRepEx and ObjectRepExByIndex. ObjectRepExByIndex can be used to get the object based on an index from multiple definitions. The object added first will have index as 0. ObjectRepEx function checks for each definition one by one and returns the first one that exists.

When calling the ObjectRepByIndex function for obtaining the parent object we always use 0 as the index. We can also use ObjectRepEx if we want permutations to be tested for parent objects as well, but this could lead to hard-to-debug bugs as we may not be sure which parent object definition was used at run-time.

Test Object Aliases

A test object alias is a name that references another test object already defined in our Object Repository. Consider the Object Repository example shown in Figure 3.8

In the table above, the oPgLogin is a test object alias for the oPg object. This allows us to more efficiently organize our OR because for every page object we can now create an alias of the oPg. The oBtn_Continue can also be considered as a template object which is used to define all the Continue buttons on different pages. This is advantageous when updating pages that contain this button, as we need only update the oBtn_Continue test object definition.

Name	Type	Parent	Identifier1	Identifier2
oBrw	Browser		micclass:=Browser	
oPg	Page	oBrw	micclass:=Page	
oPgLogin	oPg			
oBtn_Continue	WebButton	oPg	name:=Continue	
oPgLogin_oTxt_UserName	WebEdit	oPgLogin	name:=UserName	
oPgLogin_oBtn_Continue	oBtn_Continue			
Continue	oBtn_Continue			

Figure 3.8 – Object aliases in Keyword-based Object Repository

Now let's explore what needs to be done in the code to add this feature. First, we would like to check if the Type specified for an object is present as a Keyword for another object in the repository. Consider the following function:

```
'Function to resolve object aliases
Public Function ResolveAlias(ByVal sKey, ByVal Index)
  Set oTestObject = ObjectRepository.Item(sKey)(Index)
  sType = oTestObject.ObjectType
  If ObjectRepository.Exists(sType) Then
    'Object is a alias as the Type is already
    'present in the object repository
    Set oTestObject = ObjectRepository.Item(sType)(0)

    'Resolve any further aliases
    ResolveAlias = ResolveAlias(sType, 0)
  Else
```

```
    'No more aliases return the current object keyword
    ResolveAlias = sKey
  End if
End Function
```

We can now use this function within ObjectRepExByIndexandObjectRepEx functions:

```
'Function to get a specific object definiton from the OR
Public Function ObjectRepExByIndex(ByVal sKey, ByVal Index)
  'Check if the Object exist or not
  If Not ObjectRepository.Exists(sKey) Then
    'Raise an error to notify the object does not exist
      Err.Raise vbObjectError + 1, "Object Repository", _
        "The specified object does not exist in the repository. Name - "&sKey
  Else
    sKey = ResolveAlias(sKey, Index)
    'REST OF THE CODE GOES HERE
    '....
    '....
  End If
End Function
```

```
Public Function ObjectRepEx(ByVal sKey)
  If Not ObjectRepository.Exists(sKey) Then
    'Raise an error to notify the object does not exist
    Err.Raise vbObjectError + 1, "Object Repository", _
      "The specified object does not exist in the repository. Name - " & sKey
  Else
    sKey = ResolveAlias(sKey, 0)
    'REST OF THE CODE GOES HERE
    '....
  End If
End Function
```

Enumeration of Child Objects

Supporting enumeration of child objects can help extend the power of our custom DP Object Repository. Functions like RepChildObjects and RepChildObjectsByType can be created which return immediate children of any given object (parent). Consider a situation where we want to make sure that all concerned objects on a web page exist; for such a requirement we can add all critical objects to the OR. Then, we can use RepChildObjects method to retrieve these objects and check for their existence. This is not possible with the in-built QTP SOR.

```
Function RepChildObjectsByType(ByVal sKey, ByVal ObjectType)
  Dim oResult
  Set oResult = CreateObject("Scripting.Dictionary")
  oResult.CompareMode = vbTextCompare
  Set RepChildObjectsByType = oResult

  'Check if the Object defined by sKey exists on the screen
  If Not ObjectRepository.Exists(sKey) Then
    'Raise an error to notify the object does not exist
    Err.RaisevbObjectError + 1, "Object Repository", _
      "The specified object does not exist in the repository. Name - "&sKey
  Else
    'Get all keys from the ObjectRespository and see which ones have sKey
specified
    allKeys = ObjectRepository.Keys
    For each objectKey in allKeys
      If ObjectRepository.Item(objectKey)(0).Parent = sKey Then
        If ObjectType="" Or _
            LCase(ObjectType) = LCase(ObjectRepository.Item(objectKey)(0).
ObjectType) Then
          'We have found an object that has a parent  sKey
          'Return the object in the result dictionary
          Set oResult(objectKey) = ObjectRepEx(objectKey)
        End If
      End if
    Next
  End If
End Function

Function RepChildObjects(ByVal sKey)
  'Return all object types
  Set RepChildObjects = RepChildObjectsByType(sKey, "")
End Function
```

To test the same we can use the below sample code

```
'Add the objects to the Object Repository
AddObjectToOR2 "oBrw","Browser","", _
        "micclass:=Browser",""
AddObjectToOR2 "oPgLogin","Page","oBrw", _
        "miclass:=Page",""
AddObjectToOR2 "oPgLogin_oTxt_User","WebEdit", _
        "oPgLogin", "name:=user","index:=0"

AddObjectToOR2 "oPgLogin_oTxt_Password","WebEdit", _
        "oPgLogin", "name:=password",""
AddObjectToOR2 "oPgLogin_oBtn_Login","WebButton", _
        "oPgLogin", "name:=login",""

Set oFound = RepChildObjectsByType("oPgLogin", "WebEdit")
Print "Child Objects of oPgLogin object in OR with type WebEdit- " _
        & oFound.Count

Set oFound = RepChildObjects("oPgLogin")
Print "Child Objects of oPgLogin object in OR - " & oFound.Count
```

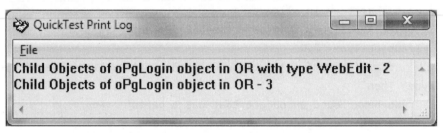

Figure 3.9 – Child Objects from the Keyword-based Object Repository

Using a Hybrid OR (DP plus a Regular OR)

We saw earlier in this chapter that using a custom DP Object Repository reduces the code size and provides extended functionality over the in-built QTP Object Repository. One key feature of this approach is that the custom repository can be easily mixed with the in-built Object Repository. Consider the hybrid OR as shown below:

Name	Type	Parent	Identifier1	Identifier2
oBrw	Browser		Browser	
oPg	Page	oBrw	Page	
oPgLogin	oPg			
oBtn_Continue	WebButton	oPg	Continue	
oPgLogin_oTxt_UserName	WebEdit	oPgLogin	Name:=UserName	
oPgLogin_oBtn_Continue	oBtn_Continue			
Continue	oBtn_Continue			

Figure 3.10 – Hybrid (DP + OR) Keyword-based Object Repository

Notice that the identifier for oBrw has been changed to Browser. When we use ObjectRep("oBrw"), the function will generate the object using Browser("Browser") which means the object Browser will be used from the QTP OR. Therefore, ObjectRep("oPgLogin_oTxt_UserName") will evaluate as:

```
Browser("Browser").Page("Page").WebEdit("name:=Username")
```

Similarly, ObjectRep("oBtn_Continue") will be evaluated as a statement where the description is taken from the built-in repository (Local or Shared):

```
Browser("Browser").Page("Page").WebEdit("Continue")
```

WARNING: Once we start using DP in a statement, the remaining hierarchy must also be DP. Starting a statement with DP prohibits us to continue code using objects from the OR. The hybrid OR approach also must comply with this.

Converting QTP SOR to Keyword-based DP OR

We just saw how to use a DP-based OR for new scripts, but what about existing scripts? We cannot update the whole code directly but we can at least export the existing SOR to our Excel based format using ObjectRepositoryUtil. ObjectRepositoryUtilAPI allow enumerating the objects present in a QTP SOR and by using the same, we will convert an Object Repository to an Excel Worksheet. More information on this API can be found in Chapter 13 – ObjectRepositoryUtil. The following code converts the Object Repository into an array where each element of that array is a collection of information about each object present in the SOR.

```
Dim Repository
Set Repository= CreateObject("Mercury.ObjectRepositoryUtil.1")
Repository.Load "C:\Temp\Test.tsr"
'Load the Object repository for conversion

'Set Repository = XMLUtil.CreateXMLFromFile("C:\Temp\TestOR.xml").
'This array will be be used to store all the object definitions
Dim outArray
ReDim outArray(0)

'Header rowof the excel sheet
outArray(0) = Array("Keyword", "Type", "Parent", "Identifier1",
"Identifier2", "Identifier3", "Identifier4", "Identifier5", "Identifier6")

'This function will recursively enumerate all the objects present in the OR
Call EnumarateObjectsIntoArray(Null,"", outArray)

'Save all the array details to a XLS
ExportArrayToXLS outArray,"C:\Temp\Test.xls"

Set Repository = Nothing

Function EnumarateObjectsIntoArray(Root, ByVal Parent, ByRef OutArray)
   Dim TOCollection, TestObject, PropertiesCollection, PropertyObj, Msg
   Dim sColumns

   'Get the childrens
   Set TOCollection = Repository.GetChildren(Root)

   For i = 0 To TOCollection.Count-1
     sColumns = Array ("","","","","","","","", "")

     'Get the Test Object
     Set TestObject = TOCollection.Item(i)

     'Get all TO properties for the test object
```

```
    Set PropertiesCollection = TestObject.GetTOProperties()

    'Get the object information
      sColumns(0) = Repository.GetLogicalName(TestObject) 'Name
      sColumns(1) = TestObject.GetTOProperty("micClass") 'Type
      sColumns(2) = Parent 'Parent

    'Populate the identification properties
    For n = 0To PropertiesCollection.Count-1
      Set PropertyObj = PropertiesCollection.Item(n)
      sColumns(3 + n) = PropertyObj.Name &":="& PropertyObj.Value
    Next

    'Increase the Array size by 1 and add the new object
    ReDim Preserve outArray(UBound(OutArray,1) + 1)
    outArray(UBound(OutArray,1)) = sColumns

    'Call the function recursively and pass the name of current object
    EnumarateObjectsIntoArray TestObject, sColumns(0), OutArray
  Next
End Function
```

We can now export this array to an Excel Worksheet using the following function:

```
'Function to export a 2-d array to excel file
Function ExportArrayToXLS(ByVal ValArray, ByVal FileName)
  'Declare constants
  ConstxlEdgeLeft = 7
  ConstxlEdgeTop = 8
  ConstxlEdgeBottom = 9
  ConstxlEdgeRight = 10
  ConstxlInsideVertical = 11
  ConstxlInsideHorizontal = 12
  ConstxlThin = 2
  ConstxlAutomatic = -4105
  ConstxlContinuous = 1

  Dim i, iCount
  Dim xlApp, xlWorkbook, xlWorksheet
```

```
'Create the excel application object
Set xlApp = CreateObject("Excel.Application")
xlApp.Visible = True

'Add a new workbook
Set xlWorkbook = xlApp.Workbooks.Add
Set xlWorksheet = xlWorkbook.Worksheets.Item(1)

'Change the name
xlWorksheet.Name = "ExportedOR"

sLastColumn = GetColumnName(UBound(ValArray(0)) + 1)
iCount = UBound(ValArray) + 1

'Update sheet row by row
For i = 1To iCount
  xlWorksheet.Range("A"&i&":"&sLastColumn&i) = ValArray(i-1)
Next

'Yellow color and bold font for header
xlWorksheet.Range("A1:"&sLastColumn&"1").Interior.ColorIndex = 6
xlWorksheet.Range("A1:"&sLastColumn&"1").Font.Bold = True

'Add borders to all cells
With xlWorksheet.Range("A1:"&sLastColumn& (iCount))
  For i = xlEdgeLeftToxlInsideHorizontal
    .Borders(i).LineStyle = xlContinuous
    .Borders(i).Weight = xlThin
  Next
End With

'Autofit all columns
xlWorksheet.Columns.Autofit

'Save sheet and close excel
'DisplayAlerts needs to be false to disable the overwrite file message
xlApp.DisplayAlerts = False
xlWorkbook.SaveAsFileName
```

```
    xlWorkbook.Close
    xlApp.Quit

    'Clean up
    Set xlWorksheet = Nothing
    Set xlWorkbook = Nothing
    Set xlApp = Nothing
End Function


Function GetColumnName(ByVal Index)
    GetColumnName = Chr(Asc("A") + (Index - 1) Mod 26)
    Index = (Index - 1) \ 26
    If Index <>0 Then GetColumnName = Chr(Asc("A") + (Index - 1) Mod 26) _
                            + GetColumnName
End Function
```

Visual Relation Identifiers

QTP 11 introduced a new type of Object Identification mechanism known as Visual Relation Identifiers (VRI). As the name suggests, this mechanism uses visual relationships between two or more objects to uniquely identify the target object. Before seeing how this identification works, we will first see a situation where this feature may be required. Consider the example below:

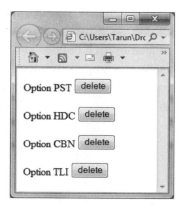

Figure 4.1 – VRI Demo Page

Now let's assume we want to click the Delete button next to Option CBN. Also assume that the above page along with the number of items displayed are dynamic. Below is the HTML source code of the webpage:

```html
<html>
  <body>
    <p>
      Option PST
      <input type="button" value="delete" onclick="deleteThis(23)" />
    </p>
    <p>
      Option HDC
      <input type="button" value="delete" onclick="deleteThis(24)" /></p>
    <p>
      Option CBN
      <input type="button" value="delete" onclick="deleteThis(25)" /></p>
    <p>
      Option TLI
      <input type="button" value="delete" onclick="deleteThis(26)" /></p>
  </body>
</html>
```

After looking at the HTML source, we can see that all the Delete buttons are very similar. The only unique aspect of each WebButton is the deleteThis function of onClick attribute. But, note that the argument for the deleteThis function (25 for Option CBN) is dynamic; this value may be fetched from a database or it may change during every page load/refresh. Also, we cannot use a pattern for the numeric value as other elements on the webpage may also call deleteThis with a different value. It is therefore not the best option to be used to identify the element in this case. We do, however, know that we can easily identify the name of the option – which is unique to each button. This is where visual relation to the label can be used to identify its neighboring WebButton. To start using VRI, let's first add the Option CBN to our Object Repository and use the concept of Visual Relations to identify the Delete button next to it.

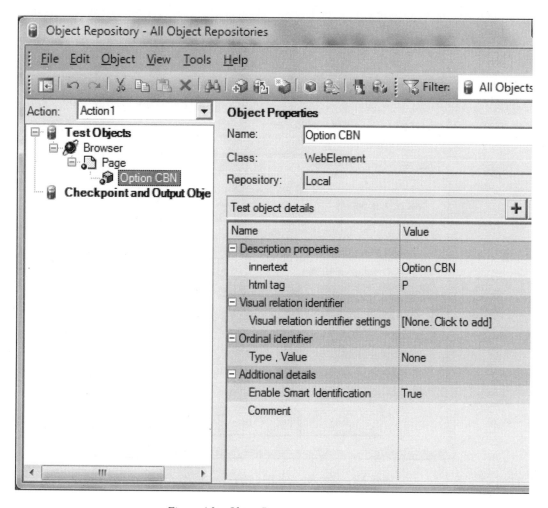

Figure 4.2 – Object Repository - Option CBN

Now let's manually add a WebButton object by clicking the 'Define New Test Object' ⬛ button and use 'Delete' for its name property.

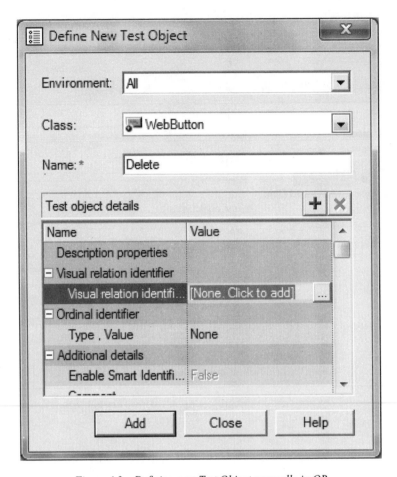

Figure 4.3 – Defining new Test Object manually in OR

Do not add the object yet. Instead, click on "Visual relation identifier settings" and in the new dialog click on the + button. A new dialog with the title "Select Test Object" will be displayed as shown here:

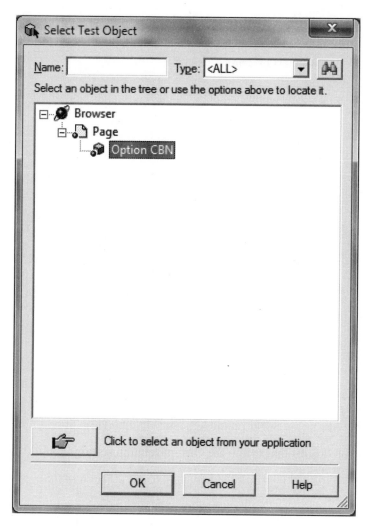

Figure 4.4 – VRI Select Test Object

Select the Option CBN WebElement and click the Preview button as shown below:

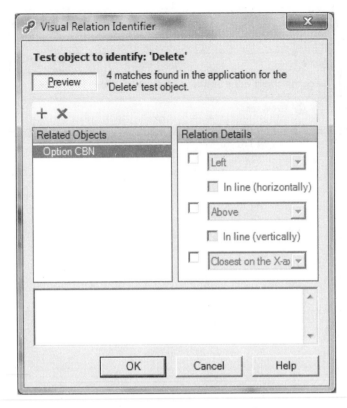

Figure 4.5 – VRI Preview Matching Objects

This will show the objects that match the current relation settings.

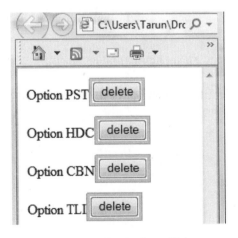

Figure 4.6 – VRI Matching Objects

Based on the option that works best, we can choose one of the three:

1. Checkbox 1 – Left or Right. This option enables the selection of the target object that lies visually to the left or right of the static object we plan to use.

2. Checkbox 2 – Above or Below. This option enables the selection of the target object that lies visually above or below the static object we plan to use.

3. Checkbox 3 – Closest to x-axis, Closest to y-axis, Closest to both axes or Contains. This option enables us to locate an element within the proximity of the static object we plan to use.

Selecting any of these options and clicking the preview button will show how many objects match the settings.

Let's select "Closest to X-Axis" and click the preview button. QTP will show that it matches four buttons.

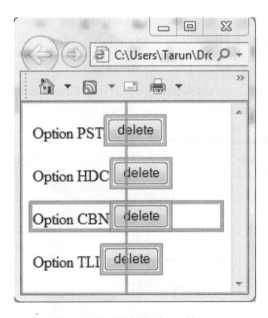

Figure 4.7 – VRI Matching Objects

For every preview option, QTP will display its markers to show the bright area (as shown in Figure 4.8) under which the object will be located, the area which is not considered is shown as dark (as shown in Figure 4.8). In our case, any of the options will work – "Closest to Y-axis", "Closest to both axis" and "Contains".

If we choose "Contains" and click the Preview button, we will notice that the white area is limited to the size of the "Option CBN" object.

Figure 4.8 – VRI Matching Objects

We have now successfully configured the VRI settings for our object and are now able to click the Delete WebButton adjacent to "Option CBN". But what if we would like to use this concept to select other options on this page?

To do so, it is possible to parameterize the "Option CBN" innerText and map it to an "option_innertext" Environment variable as shown below:

```
Environment("option_innertext") = "Option TLI"
Browser("Browser").Page("Page").WebButton("Delete").highlight
```

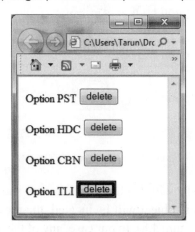

Figure 4.9 – VRI Highlight Object

Creating Visual Relation Identifiers using Code

It is also possible to create VRI identification using code.

```
Dim oRelObjectVRI

'Create a VRI Identifier
Set oRelObjectVRI = VisualRelations.Create

'Add a new relation object
Set oMainObject = oRelObjectVRI.Add

'Set the path to the relation object
oMainObject.RelatedObjectPath = "Browser("""B""").Page("""P""").
WebElement("""Option CBN""")"

'Set the relation
oMainObject.relativeposition = micRelContains
Set oMainObject = Nothing

'Set the VRI setting to the object
Browser("B").Page("P").WebButton("Delete").SetTOProperty "visual
relations", oRelObjectVRI
Browser("B").Page("P").WebButton("Delete").highlight
```

NOTE: The object assigned to RelatedObjectPath has to be an object present in the Object Repository.

The VRI object created can be assigned to an object existing in the Object Repository, but we can also create a description for the same using Descriptive Programming, as shown in the following code:

```
Dim oRelObjectVRI
'Create a VRI Identifier
Set oRelObjectVRI = VisualRelations.Create
```

```
'Add a new relation object
Set oMainObject = oRelObjectVRI.Add

'Set the path to the relation object
oMainObject.RelatedObjectPath = "Browser(""Browser"").Page(""Page"").
WebElement(""Option CBN"")"

'Set the relation
oMainObject.relativeposition = micRelContains
Set oMainObject = Nothing

'Set the VRI setting to the object
Dim oDesc
Set oDesc = Description.Create
oDesc("visual relations").value = oRelObjectVRI
Browser("Browser").Page("Page").WebButton(oDesc).Highlight
```

NOTE: As QTP imposes a restriction that the RelatedObjectPath must be an object present in the OR, VRI cannot be used just with pure DP.

5

ChildObjects

We looked at the ChildObjects method earlier in the Descriptive Programming chapter. This chapter discusses ChildObjects in detail and highlights the key concepts that users should be aware of.

Let's look again at how we use ChildObjects.

```
Dim oDesc
Set oDesc = Description.Create
oDesc("micclass").value = "WebEdit"
oDesc("name").value = "txt_.*"

'Find all the childObjects
Set allTextBox = Browser("B").Page("P").ChildObjects(oDesc)

Dim i
For i = 0 to allTextBox.Count - 1
```

```
  'Clear the textbox
  allTextBox(i).Set ""
Next
```

One thing we need to understand is that allTextBox is a collection of objects which is mapped to the runtime objects present at that moment in the application. If the state of the application changes, the collection will become invalid. The objects derived from ChildObjects are directly mapped to its runtime object and have no associated properties.

Consider an object collection of WebEdit objects that was created dynamically at runtime using the following HTML:

```
<html>
  <head>
  <title>TOPROPERTIES OF A RUNTIME COLLECTION OBJECT</title></head>
  <body>
    <input name="txt1" type="text" value="txt1" /><br/>
    <input name="txt2" type="text" value="txt2" /><br/>
    <input name="txt3" type="text" value="txt3" /><br/>
    <input name="txt4" type="text" value="txt4" /><br/>
    <input name="txt5" type="text" value="txt5" /><br/>
  </body>
</html>
```

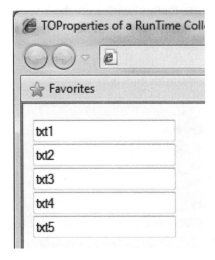

Figure 5.1 – Demo web page

The following code can be used to create the collection:

```
Dim desc, parent, colEdits
Set desc = Description.Create
desc("micclass").Value = "WebEdit"
Set parent = Browser("name:=TOProperties.*").Page("micclass:=Page")
Set colEdits = parent.ChildObjects(desc)
```

Visually speaking, we know that the colEdits collection must contain five objects of type (micclass) WebEdit. A loop can be used to retrieve properties of each object using GetROProperty. However, what will the code return if GetTOProperty were to be used instead? Below is a demonstration of values retrieved using GetROProperty vs GetTOProperty:

```
For ix = 0 To colEdits.Count - 1
  Print "Object_Index " & ix & "->" & colEdits(ix).GetROProperty("name")
Next
```

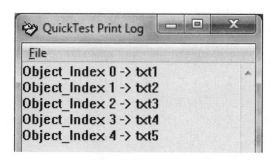

Figure 5.2 – Print results

Considering the output above, a user might expect the same values when using GetTOProperty. However, this is not the case. Consider the same loop using GetTOProperty:

```
For ix = 0 To colEdits.Count - 1
  Print "Object_Index " & ix & "->" & colEdits(ix).GetTOProperty("name")
Next
```

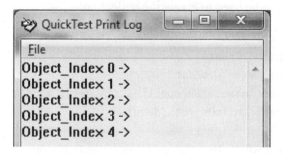

Figure 5.3 – Print results

Notice that the value of each property returned by the Print statement is Null.

The reason behind this behavior is quite simple. The property we have tried to retrieve is a property of a runtime object, not a design-time object. An object returned using the ChildObjects method (DispTOCollection) is always a runtime collection, thus any object present in the collection will only have runtime attributes. This holds true for all properties except micclass. The code below demonstrates that no other property for the target object will be retrieved except for the object's micclass:

```
For ix = 0 To colEdits.Count - 1
  Print "Object_Index " & ix & "->" & colEdits(ix).GetTOProperty("micclass")
  Print "Object_Index " & ix & "->" & colEdits(ix).GetTOProperty("html
tag")
  Print "Object_Index " & ix & "->" & colEdits(ix).GetTOProperty("value")
  Print "Object_Index " & ix & "->" & colEdits(ix).
GetTOProperty("outerhtml")
  Print "Object_Index " & ix & "->" & colEdits(ix).GetTOProperty("abs_x")
  Print "Object_Index " & ix & "->" & colEdits(ix).GetTOProperty("abs_y")
  Print "Object_Index " & ix & "->" & colEdits(ix).GetTOProperty("class")
  Print "Object_Index " & ix & "->" & colEdits(ix).GetTOProperty("disabled")
  Print "Object_Index " & ix & "->" & colEdits(ix).GetTOProperty("name")
  Print "Object_Index " & ix & "->" & colEdits(ix).GetTOProperty("readonly")
  Print "Object_Index " & ix & "->" & colEdits(ix).GetTOProperty("type")
  Print "Object_Index " & ix & "->" & colEdits(ix).GetTOProperty("x")
  Print "Object_Index " & ix & "->" & colEdits(ix).GetTOProperty("y")
  Print vbNewLine
Next
```

Below is the output from the Print statement for the first object in the collection:

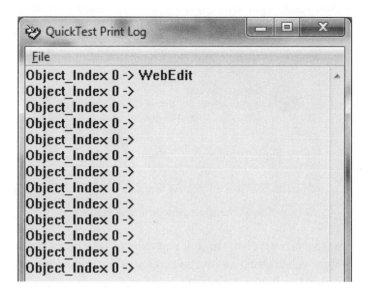

Figure 5.4 – Print results

In summary, for any runtime ChildObjects collection, GetTOProperty will only return the associated value for the micclass property. For all other properties, GetROProperty must be used.

If we needed to check for all links on a webpage, the code we would use would be as follows:

```
Dim oDesc
Set oDescLink = Description.Create
oDescLink("micclass").value = "Link"
oDescLink("html tag").value = "A"

'Find all the childObjects
Set allLinks = Browser("B").Page("P").ChildObjects(oDescLink)

Dim i
For i = 0 to allLinks.Count - 1
  'Clear the textbox
  allLinks(i).Click
  Browser("B").Back
  Browser("B").sync
Next
```

When we run the above code, QTP will throw a general run error while it is still in the loop.

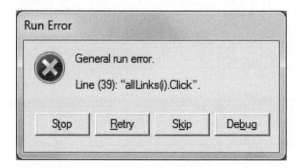

Figure 5.5 – General run error for ChildObjects loop

This happens because when we click the link and return to the previous page, the existing collection is no longer valid. Using an invalid runtime object reference causes the general run error. A workaround to the problem is to regenerate the collection every time inside the loop:

```
'Find all the childObjects
Set allLinks = Browser("B").Page("P").ChildObjects(oDescLink)

Dim i
For i = 0 to allLinks.Count - 1
  Set allLinks = Browser("B").Page("P").ChildObjects(oDescLink)

  'Clear the textbox
  allLinks(i).Click
  Browser("B").Back

  Browser("B").sync
Next
```

This approach will work but has a few constraints. When we click on a link and return to the previous page, the page remains the same in terms of the number of links and their position, but this approach may not always work. If we have a link on the main page which changes the language of the application by setting a cookie, clicking the link and using the back button will cause the main page to have changed completely. Now regenerating the collection inside the loop can create unexpected results.

Objects derived from the ChildObjects method differ from the usual ChildObjects in many ways. We will discuss the difference one by one.

Using Init or RefreshObject on Derived Objects

When we use Init or RefreshObject on an object derived from ChildObjects, it basically destroys the object. As we mentioned earlier, objects derived from the ChildObjects method have a direct-mapping to the runtime object. When we use RefreshObject on such an object, that mapping is destroyed. Since the derived objects don't have any description of their own, they cannot function. Consider the following example:

```
Set oDescSearch = Description.Create
oDescSearch("micclass").value = "WebEdit"
oDescSearch("name").value = "q"

Set oSearchText = Browser("B").Page("P").ChildObjects(oDescSearch).item(0)
oSearchText.RefreshObject
oSearchText.Set UCase(Text)
```

Running the above code raises the following error:

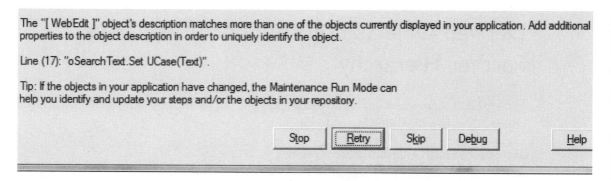

The "[WebEdit]" object's description matches more than one of the objects currently displayed in your application. Add additional properties to the object description in order to uniquely identify the object.

Line (17): "oSearchText.Set UCase(Text)".

Tip: If the objects in your application have changed, the Maintenance Run Mode can help you identify and update your steps and/or the objects in your repository.

| Stop | Retry | Skip | Debug | Help |

Figure 5.6 – Object Not found error for referenced object

For this reason, we should make sure that we never call RefreshObject on an object that is derived from ChildObjects.

Derived Objects don't Support RegisterUserFunc

Until QTP 11 there was a limitation that impeded using registered methods on derived objects. Consider the following code sample:

```
Function NewSetMethod(obj, Text)
  obj.Set UCase(Text)
End Function
RegisterUserFunc "WebEdit", "NewSet", "NewSetMethod"

Set oDescSearch = Description.Create
oDescSearch("micclass").value = "WebEdit"
oDescSearch("name").value = "q"

Set oSearchEdit = Browser("B").Page("P").ChildObjects(oDescSearch).item(0)
oSearchEdit.NewSet "tarun lalwani"
```

The above code will throw an error message saying the object doesn't support the property or method.

Derived Objects don't Support Objects in Further Hierarchy

Until QTP 11 there was a limitation that impeded using further object hierarchy on derived objects. Consider the following code sample:

```
Set oDescSearch = Description.Create
oDescSearch("micclass").value = "WebTable"

Set oSearchTable = Browser("B").Page("P").ChildObjects(oDescSearch).item(0)
oSearchTable.WebEdit("name:=q").Set "tarun lalwani"
```

The above code will similarly throw an error message saying that the object doesn't support the property or method.

NOTE: The workaround to fix this issue is to create a new description and use ChildObjects again on the derived objects.

ChildObject Returns Zero Objects for WebElements

Consider the HTML source below:

```
<div>
  <div>
    <span>test</span>
  </div>
</div>
```

And the following ChildObjects code:

```
Dim oDesc
Set oDesc = Description.Create

oDesc("html tag").value = "DIV"
Set allObjects = Browser("Browser").Page("Page").ChildObjects(oDesc)

'Expected Count is 2 but we will get 0
MsgBox allObjects.Count
```

The above code will return the count as 0 because we have not specified the WebElement tag. This is not true for all tags as TD and TR tags will work without specifying micclass. To fix the issue, just update the code as follows:

```
Dim oDesc
Set oDesc = description.Create
oDesc("html tag").value = "DIV"
oDesc("micclass").value = "WebElement"
Set allObjects = browser("Browser").Page("Page").ChildObjects(oDesc)
```

```
'Displays count 2 as expected
MsgBox allObjects.Count
```

 NOTE: Using a wrong case for micclass and generic Web type (WebElement) will produce an incorrect result. oDesc("micclass").value = "webElement" will also return 0 . The right case is "WebElement".

Detecting if an Object has been Derived using ChildObjects

There is no direct method available for one to detect if an object has been derived from using ChildObjects, but we can use our understanding of how the derived objects differ from normal objects. The method, however, is not foolproof.

```
Function IsDerivedObject(Obj)
  IsDerivedObject = False
  If Obj.GetTOProperties().Count = 0 Then
    'This is surely a derived object, otherwise we cannot have count as 0
    IsDerivedObject = True
  ElseIf Obj.GetTOProperties().Count = 1 Then
    'Now if we only have a micclass property then let's assume
    'that it is derived. Though that may not be true.
    'Like in case of Browser("micclass:=Browser")
    If Obj.GetTOProperties().Item(0).name = "micclass" then
      IsDerivedObject = True
    End if
  End if
End Function
```

HTML DOM

Introduction

The HTML DOM is a Document Object Model for representing HTML documents. DOM is a W3C standard which is platform and language independent and defines a standard set of objects in a tree structure of elements. It provides a standard approach to access and manipulate HTML documents. All elements, along with their text and attributes can be accessed and manipulated through the DOM tree.

The QTP Page object's .Object property provides access to the HTML DOM:

```
'Get the DOM document object
Set oDocument = Browser("Browser").Page("Page").Object
```

When to Use HTML DOM

Sometimes a QTP test object fails to provide a property that is required to solve a particular problem or implement a specific solution. A few reasons why HTML DOM may be the preferred solution are outlined below:

- QTP only provides access to radio buttons through the WebRadioGroup rather than providing access to individual elements

- QTP provides no way to access webpage style sheets to find out any CSS implemented for it

- Normal QTP operations are not equipped to accomplish tasks. Examples include:

  - o Dynamically traversing upwards in object hierarchy (unless all required parent objects are present in the OR)

  - o When operations are not supported by QTP, e.g. retrieving the session cookie

- Performance is of importance

- Interacting with an object's style and currentStyle objects

- The application fails to respond to normal QTP operations

Using HTML DOM has the performance argument. Imagine a webpage with 500 text boxes to be filled with the same data. A QTP script using Descriptive Programming would look like this:

```
'Loop through all 500 webedits
For i = 1 To 500
  Browser("Browser").Page("Page").WebEdit("name:=txt_Box" & i).Set "data" &
i
Next
```

The code above completes setting data to the textbox in just over 70 seconds.

Figure 6.1 – Time taken to set text using QTP

The same script using the HTML DOM would look like this:

```
'Loop through all web edits using DOM
For i = 1 to 500
  Browser("Browser").Page("Page").object.all("txt_Box" & i).Value = "data"
& i
Next
```

Using HTML DOM, it takes just under 24 seconds. This simple comparison shows the magnitude of performance difference between the two techniques.

Figure 6.2 – Time taken to set text using DOM

HTML DOM is substantially faster because there is no object recognition overhead required to find and interact with each WebEdit on the page. For the same reason, performance is also improved when extracting values from a large WebTable.

Despite the performance improvements the user must keep in mind that HTML DOM is different for all currently supported Browsers (IE vs Firefox vs Chrome) so workarounds must be used to handle cases for each. Also, because HTML DOM is so fast, it can at times have a negative impact on the functional behavior of the AUT.

Also, QTP may throw a general exception for no obvious reason when working with Web test objects. Using HTML DOM to interact with that object can provide a workaround in these situations.

When Not to Use HTML DOM

Some situations when HTML DOM should not be considered are shown below:

- When a QTP test object is working as expected.
- When there is no significant performance overhead.
- When your script is used by other automation developers with little knowledge of HTML DOM.

HTML DOM Objects

This section provides insight into the HTML DOM objects.

HTML Node

Every tag in the HTML source represents a node in the HTML DOM tree. When writing HTML for a webpage, once you start a tag, all the tags following it become its child nodes until the tag itself is closed. Each tag (node) can have a variety of attributes, some predefined and others user-defined.

Consider the following HTML node:

```
<INPUT type="textbox" value="Name" name="txt_Name" myval="Test">
```

In the above HTML markup, the predefined attributes of the INPUT node are: type, value and name. The attribute myval is user-defined.

The Document Object

The Document object represents the entire document. It is the topmost node in the DOM tree also called the root node. It has no sibling or parent nodes. All nodes on a webpage are child-nodes of the Document node.

HTML Element Object

The HTML Element can refer to any node in the HTML source. Every Element represents a set of properties and methods, some of which are used in QTP for object identification and performing actions. Don't get confused with the way QTP names properties as opposed to how they are named with HTML DOM. For example, the QTP property 'html tag' is the same as 'nodeName' or 'tagName' in HTML DOM.

HTML Elements Collection

The HTML Element Collection object is a collection of one or more elements. Consider the following HTML code:

```
<INPUT name="txt_Name" type="text">
<INPUT name="txt_Name" type="text">
```

JavaScript code to retrieve a collection of the above two input nodes is shown here:

```
'Get a DOM Element Collection by name
Set txt_Boxes = Browser("").Page("").Object.getElementsByName("txt_Name")

For i = 0 to txt_Boxes.Length - 1
  txt_Boxes.item(i).Value = "Tarun"
  'The default property is item so it can skipped
  txt_Boxes(i).Value = "Anshoo"
Next
```

The QTP equivalent code is shown as follows:

```
'Access to the browser COM
Set browserObj = Browser("").Object

'Access to the browser's document object
Set pageObj = Browser("").Page("").Object

Set txt_Boxes= browserObj.document.getElementsByName("txt_Name")
```

```
'or
Set txt_Boxes= pageObj.getElementsByName("txt_Name")

For i = 0 To txt_Boxes.Length - 1
  txt_Boxes.item(i).Value = "Tarun"
  'The default property is item so it can skipped
  txt_Boxes(i).Value = "Tarun"
Next
```

We will be using the Document object directly in our next few examples. The following code shows how to retrieve the Document object using several different techniques:

```
'Method 1
Set Document = Browser("").Page("").Object

'Method 2
Set Document = Browser("").Object.document

'Method 3
Set Document = Browser("").Page("").Frame("").Object.document

'Method 4
Set Document = Browser("").Page("").WebEdit("").Object.document
```

Link and Button (Click)

A link in a webpage is defined using the 'A' tag. Below is an example of two links which navigate to KnowledgeInbox.com and RelevantCodes.com respectively. The HTML also contains a button that displays an alert:

```
<a href="http://knowledgeinbox.com" id="tarun">KnowledgeInbox</a><br />
<a href="http://relevantcodes.com" id="anshoo">RelevantCodes</a><br />
<input type="button" name="btn" onclick="alert('HELLO!')" value="Clicky" />
```

A few ways to click on these three objects using HTML DOM are shown below:

```
document.Links("tarun").click
document.Links("anshoo").click
document.getElementById("tarun").click
```

```
document.getElementsByName("btn")(0).click
document.all("tarun").click
document.all("anshoo").click
document.getElementsByTagName("input")[0].click
```

The code above can be run against a Browser using the EmbedScript or RunScript methods of Browser and Page respectively. In order to use the code without having to utilize these two methods, it is possible to write QTP equivalent code using .Object.

```
With Browser("").Page("")
  .Object.getElementById("tarun").Click
  .Object.getElementById("anshoo").Click
  .Object.getElementsByTagName("input")(0).Click
End With
```

Textbox

A Textbox in a web page is defined using an INPUT tag where the attribute 'type' equals 'text'. The textbox below has the following attributes: type, myprop, name, id and value:

```
<input type="text" myprop="test" name="name" id="firstname" value="initial"
/>
```

In QTP, the Set method is used to enter a value into a textbox. The HTML DOM equivalent is the 'value' property.

```
'Setting value in 'firstname' textbox
Browser("").Page("").Object.getElementById("firstname").value = "Tarun"

'Setting value in 'name' textbox
Browser("").Page("").Object.getElementsByName("name")(0).value = "Anshoo"
```

The code below shows how to traverse a collection of INPUT nodes and enter a value.

```
Set collection = Browser("").Page("").Object.getElementsByTagName("input")
For Each element In collection
  If element.myprop = "test" Then
    element.value="Tarun"
    Exit For
  End If
```

Next

Combo Box or List box

Combo and list boxes have various options that a user can select. This object is defined in HTML using the SELECT tag. Sample HTML source code is as follows:

```
<SELECT size="1" name="demo_ComboBox">
  <option value="Actual Value 1">Displayed Value 1</option>
  <option value="Value 2" >Value 2</option>
  <option value="Value 3" >Value 4</option>
</SELECT>
```

The following shows various ways of selecting the value in the combo or list box:

```
'Get the combobox object by name
Set objCombo = Browser("").Page("").Object.getElementsByName("demo_
ComboBox").item(0)

'Would give 3 in our case
numOptions = objCombo.Options.length

' "Actual Value 1" in our case
firstOptionValue = objCombo.Options(0).value

' "Displayed Value 1" in our case
firstOptionText = objCombo.Options(0).text

'To select one of the options use the below code
objCombo.Options(0).Selected = true
objCombo.value = "Actual Value 1"
```

Checkbox

A checkbox is also an input node. It is shown as a checkbox due to its type attribute, which equals "checkbox". The HTML below creates a checkbox with a name attribute:

```
<input type="checkbox" name="demo_CheckBox">
```

The code below shows one possible HTML DOM usage for setting the `checked` property to True:

```
'Get the check box object by name
Set objChkBox = Browser("").Page("").getElementsByName("demo_CheckBox").
item(0)

'Check the checkbox
objChkBox.Checked = True
```

Radio Group

Similar to a list box or combo box, radio buttons also offer a list of choices. A radio group can only have one selected item. In order to group radio buttons into a radio group, each button node is given the same Name attribute. Sample HTML source code would be:

```
<input type="radio" name="Sex" value="male" checked="checked" />
<input type="radio" name="Sex" value="female" />

'Bind to the radio button by name
Set objRadio = Browser("").Page("").getElementsByName("Sex").item(1)

'Will select female
objRadio.checked = True

Set objRadio = Browser("").Page("").getElementsByName("Sex").item(0)
'Will select male
objRadio.checked = True

'Will select female even if we point to the male object node
objRadio.value = "female"
```

HTML Table

A table is defined in HTML with the Table tag. QTP shows it as a WebTable (Web is prefixed because of the technology used). Below is a table with two rows (`tr tag`) each containing two cells (`td tag`):

```
<table id="myTable" border="1">
```

```
<tr>
  <td>Row1 cell1</td>
  <td>Row1 cell2</td>
</tr>
<tr>
  <td>Row2 cell1</td>
  <td>Row2 cell2</td>
</tr>
</table>
```

Table object provides two collections: 'Cells' provides access to all cells present in the table. 'Rows' provides access to all rows present in the table. Because each row can contain one or more cells, they can also be used to access cells in a specific row.

```
'To access the 1st row and 1st column cell, use the following code
Set objTable = Browser("").Page("").getElementById("myTable")
sOuterText = objTable.rows(0).cells(0).outerText
sOuterText = objTable.cells(0).outerText

'To access the 2nd row and 1st column cell, use the following code
sOuterText = objTable.rows(1).cells(0).outerText
```

```
'will give total # of rows in the table
iRowCount = objTable.rows.length

'will give total # of cells in the table
iCellCount = objTable.cells.length

'will give total # of cells in the 1st row of the table
iFirstRowCellCount = objTable.rows(0).cells.length
```

We have now discussed most of the common DOM elements. Let's now look at other possible uses of DOM with QTP.

Binding to an Element using HTML DOM

This section shows various ways in which DOM can be used to connect to HTML nodes. Consider the following input node:

```
<INPUT name="txt_Name" id="firstname" type="text" value="Tarun">
```

There are several ways to bind to this element, as shown below:

```
Set txt_Elem = Document.getElementsById("firstname")

'Checking if the element is present or not
If txt_Elem is Nothing then Msgbox "Element Is not present"

'Bind to the element using getElementsByTagName and the tag attribute
With Browser("").Page("")
  Set txt_Elem = .getElementsByTagName("INPUT").item(0)
  Set txt_Elem = .getElementsByTagName("INPUT").item("txt_Name")
  Set txt_Elem = .getElementsByTagName("INPUT").item("firstname")

  'Bind to the element using getElementsByName
  Set txt_Elem = .getElementsByName("txt_Name").item(0)
End With
```

The last four statements will throw an exception if there is no element found with either the Input tag or using the Name attribute. To avoid this runtime error, we can check the length of the collection returned by either the getElementsByTagName or the getElementsByName methods, as follows:

```
'Check the length of collection returned by getElementsByName
Set Document = Browser("").Page("").Object
If Document.getElementsByName("txt_Name").length <> 0 then
  Set txt_Elem = Document.getElementsByName("txt_Name").item(0)
Else
  MsgBox "Element is not present"
End if
```

In the examples above, we saw how to access a DOM node in the Document to perform DOM operations. However, at times it can become necessary to access the QTP test object representation of the DOM node. For example, it would not be possible for us to use the `Set` method to enter a value in the textbox because `Set` is a QTP method. This brings us to the next section, which shows how to access the QTP test object from any DOM node.

Converting a DOM Object to a QTP Test Object

The HTML DOM sourceIndex property represents the index of a node in the DOM tree and can be used to get its corresponding QTP test object. In other words, we can use the runtime DOM value of sourceIndex to convert the DOM object into a QTP test object. The following code shows various techniques for getting the DOM sourceIndex:

```
'Getting the sourceIndex using QTP code + DOM
srcIndex = Browser("").Page("").WebEdit("").Object.sourceIndex

'Using QTP code only
srcIndex = Browser("").Page("").WebEdit("").GetROProperty("attribute/
sourceIndex")

'Using QTP code only
srcIndex = Browser("").Page("").WebEdit("").GetROProperty("source_Index")

'Using DOM only
Set oText = document.getElementsByName("txt_name")(0)
srcIndex = oText.sourceIndex
```

Once we have the sourceIndex and know what type of object we are working with, we can then use the following code:

```
' Set a value using source_Index as the only property
Browser("").Page("").WebEdit("source_Index:=" & srcIndex).Set "Test"
Browser("").Page("").WebEdit("sourceIndex:=" & srcIndex).Set "Test"
```

NOTE: There is difference between the naming convention of DOM and QTP. The DOM uses sourceIndex while QTP uses source_Index. However, we can access objects using either.

Traversing HTML Tree Nodes

HTML DOM is very useful when traversing nodes. This section demonstrates traversing nodes from parent to child, child to parent and between children to retrieve the immediate node using DOM.

To understand this approach, consider the HTML source below:

```
<html>
  <head><title>Traversing Nodes</title></head>
  <body>
    <p class="para1">This is a paragraph.</p>
    <div class="divClassParent">
      <p>This is a paragraph.</p>
      <div class="divClassChild">
        <p>This is a child paragraph.</p>
      </div>
    </div>
    <p class="para2">This is a paragraph.</p>
  </body>
</html>
```

If we want to get the immediate parent of the DIV element above with CLASS divClassChild, it is not possible to retrieve the correct value with standard QTP methods. Here is the QTP code that will retrieve the parent object of the DIV element, but instead of retrieving the DIV with CLASS divClassParent, it will return Page:

```
MsgBox Browser("name:=Traversing Nodes").Page("micclass:=Page") _
  .WebElement("html tag:=DIV", "class:=divClassChild") _
  .GetTOProperty( "parent" ).GetROProperty("micclass")
```

Figure 6.3 – micclass of the parent object

As we dig further into the HTML Source and apply DOM methods we can, however, retrieve the correct node:

```
MsgBox Browser("name:=Traversing Nodes").Page("micclass:=Page") _
  .WebElement("html tag:=DIV", "class:=divClassChild") _
  .Object.parentNode.nodeName
```

Figure 6.4 – HTML Tag for the parent node

Let's again consider the same HTML source and the same element DIV with CLASS divClassChild. If we traverse one node before the DIV tag, we will find the tag P. We can use the previousSibling property associated with the DIV element to access the P node, as follows:

```
MsgBox Browser("name:=Traversing Nodes").Page("micclass:=Page") _
  .WebElement("html tag:=DIV", "class:=divClassChild") _
  .Object.previousSibling.nodeName
```

Figure 6.5 – HTML Tag for the previous sibling

Using the same technique, but changing the nodeName property to innerText, we can retrieve the text associated with the P element:

```
MsgBox Browser("name:=Traversing Nodes").Page("micclass:=Page"). _
 WebElement("html tag:=DIV", "class:=divClassChild"). _
 Object.previousSibling.innerText
```

Figure 6.6 - Text for the previous sibling node

Checking Appearance using Style Sheets

QTP test objects do not support any method for accessing the style sheets of an HTML element. However, this can be made possible by using the currentStyle and style objects.

Checking Object Visibility

Certain pages hide HTML elements using CSS which can either come from a style sheet or from <style> tags in a Document. Even though these objects may be hidden from the human eye, using the QTP Exist method on these elements always returns True. Consider the following style sheet fragment:

```
<style>
  .visi1 { visibility:"visible" }
  .visi2 { visibility:"hidden" }
  .disp1 { display:"block" }
  .disp2 { display:"none" }
</style>
```

and the following HTML source code:

```
<div class="disp2" id="checkHidden">
  <p>DHTML using DISPLAY</p>
</div>
```

The DIV node above has CLASS attribute which equals disp2. The attribute disp2 has a CSS attribute display which equals NONE. This attribute will hide the element from the human eye, but it will still 'exist' in the document. There are different ways to check whether the object is hidden using CSS.

Technique 1

This is a two-tiered approach. Firstly, check the attributes of the target element and secondly, match those attributes against the document style:

```
'Get the page object
Set oPg = Browser("micclass:=Browser").Page("micclass:=Page")

'We need to know that the class of the potentially hidden object is disp2
If oPg.WebElement("html id:=checkHidden").GetROProperty("class") = "disp2"
Then
  Msgbox "The object is hidden using style disp2"
Else
  Msgbox "The object is visible"
End if
```

NOTE: It is also possible for `script` tags to execute JavaScript against a node to hide the element.

NOTE: This approach can be a little tricky because it is possible for the node's id attribute to hide the element along with the class. Because of this, we may have to write the code for each attribute. This dependency to check for multiple properties can make this a high-maintenance approach. A more flexible way of handling this is shown next in Technique 2.

Technique 2

This technique is similar to the first and checks the element's class attribute using DOM instead.

```
'Get the page object
```

```
Set oPg = Browser("micClass:=Browser").Page("micClass:=Page")

'Get the object's DOM class
If oPg.WebElement("html id:=checkHidden").object.className = "disp2" Then
  Msgbox "The object is hidden using style disp2"
Else
  Msgbox "The object is visible"
End if
```

Technique 3

This technique directly checks for CSS properties using DOM, a much more efficient approach in cases where styles are changing frequently.

```
'Get the page object
Set oPg = Browser("micclass:=Browser").Page("micclass:=Page")

'Check the display property of the currentStyle
If oPg.WebElement("html id:=HideMe2").object.currentStyle.display = "none"
Then
  Msgbox "The object is hidden using style display none"
Else
  Msgbox "The object is visible"
End if
```

 NOTE: The currentStyle object can be used to validate many attributes such as font name and font size. Using currentStyle, we can also make an automated test case to validate the CSS selectors for elements in the AUT. Below are a few examples:

```
currentStyle.backgroundColor
currentStyle.fontFamily
currentStyle.fontSize
currentStyle.textAlign
```

For details, refer to msdn.microsoft.com for currentStyle.

Selecting a Radio Button by Text

Radio buttons are generally identified using their value property and not by the text appearing within them. Consider the following HTML source code:

```
<INPUT type=radio name=addressType value="hm"> Home Address
<INPUT type=radio name=addressType value="ofc"> Office Address
```

So, the QTP code to select a radio button for this radio group would be:

```
'Select the radio button option
Browser("").Page("").WebRadioGroup("addressType").Select "hm"
Browser("").Page("").WebRadioGroup("addressType").Select "ofc"
```

There are instances when choosing items by value may not be feasible or when selecting by the associated text makes more sense. In order to select by text, we can use the getAdjacentText method of. Even though getAdjacentText works in this situation, it may not always be the case for a different HTML source. Consider the following code:

```
<TABLE>
  <TR>
    <TD>
      <INPUT type=radio name=addressType value="hm">
    </TD>
    <TD>
      Home Address
    </TD>
  </TR>
  <TR>
    <TD>
      <INPUT type=radio name=addressType value="ofc">
    </TD>
    <TD>
      Office Address
    </TD>
  </TR>
</TABLE>
```

In the above HTML, the Home Address text is not adjacent to the radio button but is inside a TD element. In this situation, if we can find a common path between all radio buttons, we can come up with a solution to select the target elements by text (instead of the underlying value). In this case, each radio button resides in a TD node, making TD the parent. Knowing this, we can create a function to get the target object from the given path:

```
'Path is to be separated by colon
'The keyword that can be used for navigation are:
'parent - for a parent node. To reach a parent with specific tag use pipe:
parent|TD
'next/right - to navigate to a next node
'previous/left - to navigate to a previous node
'child/children - navigate to the specified child node
Public Function GetDOMObjectByPath(ByVal DOMObject, ByVal Path)
  'Split the path based on ; as the delimiter
  Path = Split(LCase(Path), ";")
  Set GetDOMObjectByPath = DOMObject
  'Loop through all the navigation keywords
  For i = LBound(Path) To UBound(Path)
    If Path(i) <> "" Then

      'Check if any tag was specified using a |
      If InStr(Path(i), "|") Then
        'If yes then get the tag
        sTag = UCase(Split(Path(i), "|")(1))

        'Get the navigation keyword
        Path(i) = Split(Path(i), "|")(0)
      Else
        'No Tag specified
        sTag = ""
      End If

      'Check the navigation keyword
      Select Case Path(i)
        Case "parent"
          'Loop until we get the first parent node
          'or the one with tag specified (in case any)
          Do
            Set GetDOMObjectByPath = GetDOMObjectByPath.parentNode
```

```
          Loop Until (sTag = "") Or _
              (GetDOMObjectByPath Is Nothing) Or _
              (GetDOMObjectByPath.tagName = sTag)
        Case "next", "right"
          'Loop until we get the next node
          'or the one with tag specified (in case any)
          Do
            Set GetDOMObjectByPath = GetDOMObjectByPath.nextSibling
          Loop Until (sTag = "") Or _
              (GetDOMObjectByPath Is Nothing) Or _
              (GetDOMObjectByPath.tagName = sTag)
        Case "previous", "left"
          'Loop until we get the previous node
          'or the one with tag specified (in case any)
          Do
            Set GetDOMObjectByPath = GetDOMObjectByPath.previousSibling
          Loop Until (sTag = "") Or _
              (GetDOMObjectByPath Is Nothing) Or _
              (GetDOMObjectByPath.tagName = sTag)
        Case "child", "children"
          'Check if the current node has a children or not
          If GetDOMObjectByPath.childnodes.Length = 0 Then
            Set GetDOMObjectByPath = Nothing
            Exit Function
          Else
            If sTag <> "" Then
              'If there was tag specified then get the first child with
              'the given tag
              If GetDOMObjectByPath.getElementsByTagName(sTag).Length <> 0
Then
                Set GetDOMObjectByPath = GetDOMObjectByPath.
getElementsByTagName(sTag).Item(0)
              Else
                'No such tag present
                Set GetDOMObjectByPath = Nothing
                Exit Function
              End If
            Else
              'No tag specified return the first child node
```

```
            Set GetDOMObjectByPath = GetDOMObjectByPath.childNodes.Item(0)
            End If
         End If
      End Select
   End If
 Next
End Function
```

We can now use this function in QTP in the following manner:

```
'Get the DOM document
Set Document = Browser().Page().Object
Set firstRadio = Document.getElementsByName("addressType")(0)

'1st method to get the reference TD tag
Set oRefObject = GetDOMObjectByPath(firstRadio, "parent;next")
'2nd method to get the reference TD tag
Set oRefObject = GetDOMObjectByPath(firstRadio, "parent|TD;next|TD")
```

Once we have the reference object, we need to fetch the text associated with the object. This can require us to use outerText, innerText or textContent on the reference object or require us to read the text from the left or the right of the object. The getAdjacentText can be used to read text near to the object and takes a string parameter with four possible values: afterEnd, afterBegin, beforeBegin and beforeEnd. To select the radio button we can use the following function:

```
'objWbRGP - the Radio button object
'Text - Text to be searched
'Index - In case of multiple matches
'Path - Path to be used to get the reference object
'TextLocation - Location of the text from the reference object
Public Function SelectRadioByTextIndex(objWbRGP, Text, Index, Path,
TextLocation)
  'RegEx object to test regular expressions
  Dim RegEx: Set RegEx = New RegExp

  'Match the pattern with the whole string
  RegEx.Global = True
  'Pattern to be matched
```

```
RegEx.Pattern = Text
'Ignore the case
RegEx.IgnoreCase = True

'Get the name of the radio button from the RO property
radioName = objWbRGP.GetROProperty("name")

'Get all the DOM  radio buttons with the name
Set allRadios = objWbRGP.object.document.getElementsByName(radioName)

'Current count of matched
Dim iMatches: iMatches = -1

'Loop through all of the the radio buttons
For Each oRadio In allRadios
   'Get reference object from the radio button using the specified path
   Set oReferenceObject = GetDOMObjectByPath(oRadio, Path)

   'Check the text location
   If IsNull(TextLocation) Or IsEmpty(TextLocation) Or TextLocation=""
Then
       TextLocation="after"
   Else
      TextLocation=LCase(TextLocation)
   End If
   'Get the text of the reference node text
   nodeText = oReferenceObject.outerText

   'Check the text location and get the text
   Select Case TextLocation
     Case "after" ,"next", "right", "afterend"
       RefText = oReferenceObject.getAdjacentText("afterEnd")
     Case "before", "left", "beforebegin"
       RefText = oReferenceObject.getAdjacentText("beforeBegin")
     Case "beforeend"
       RefText = oReferenceObject.getAdjacentText("beforeEnd")
     Case "afterbegin"
       RefText = oReferenceObject.getAdjacentText("afterBegin")
   End Select
```

```
      'Check if it matches the node text or the adjacent text
      If RegEx.Test(nodeText) Or RegEx.Test(RefText) Then
        'Increase the matches index
        iMatches = iMatches + 1

        'Check if the match index is equal to the current match index
        If iMatches = Index Then
          'Check the radio button
          oRadio.checked = 1

          'Return its value
          SelectRadioByTextIndex = oRadio.Value
          Exit Function
        End If
      End If
    Next

    'Return -1 for no macthes found
    SelectRadioByTextIndex = -1
End Function

'Register the method
RegisterUserFunc "WebRadioGroup","SelectRadioByTextIndex",
"SelectRadioByTextIndex"
```

7

Visual Relation Identifiers using HTML DOM

A limitation of Visual Relational Identifiers is that it cannot be used with programmatic descriptions. Not all automation frameworks use the Object Repository, so making use of Visual Relation Identifiers (VRI) for Object Identification (in a Web environment) is not possible out-of-the-box. There is, however, a workaround using HTML DOM as demonstrated in this section.

We use the following DOM properties to traverse nodes:

DOM Property	Description
childNodes	Retrieves a collection of HTML elements and TextNode objects that are immediate descendants of the target.
firstChild	Retrieves the reference to the first child in the childNodes collection.
lastChild	Retrieves the reference to the last child in the childNodes collection.
nextSibling	Retrieves the reference to the following-node of the target, which is also the next child of the same parent as the target.
parentNode	Retrieves the reference to the parent object of the target.

DOM Property	Description
previousSibling	Retrieves the reference to the preceding-node of the target, which is also the preceding child of the same parent as the target.

In the next example, we will see how to work with target controls using their neighbors, but without the use of Visual Relational Identifiers.

Example 1: A simple registration form

Let's use the HTML source below with the properties in the table above to demonstrate the same functionality of Visual Relational Identifiers without using the Object Repository.

```html
<html>
  <head>
    <title>VRI using HTML DOM</title>
  </head>
  <body style="background:#ffffee;font-family:Calibri;">
    <h2>Registration Form</h2>
    <table>
      <tr>
        <td>Email:</td>
        <td><input type="text" /></td>
      </tr>
      <tr>
        <td>Username:</td>
        <td><input type="text" /></td>
      </tr>
      <tr>
        <td>Password:</td>
        <td><input type="text" /></td>
      </tr>
      <tr>
        <td>Confirm:</td>
        <td><input type="text" /></td>
      </tr>
      <tr>
        <td></td>
        <td><input type="button" value="Register" /></td>
      </tr>
```

```
      </table>
    </body>
</html>
```

The resulting form is as follows:

Figure 7.1 – Demo web page

Looking at the image visually, you will notice that each textbox corresponds to some text label to its left. Using this approach, each text node can be used to identify the WebEdit node.

Notice the snapshot from Object Spy (next figure) for the properties of the WebEdit controls of the registration form:

Properties	Values
Class Name	WebEdit
abs_x	552
abs_y	224
class	
default value	
disabled	0
height	22
html id	
html tag	INPUT
innerhtml	
innertext	
kind	singleline
max length	2147483647
name	WebEdit
outerhtml	<INPUT>
outertext	
readonly	0
rows	0
type	text
value	
visible	True
width	147

Figure 7.2 – Text box Identification properties

None of the controls have any unique properties that can aid in simplified identification. This case is a good candidate for Visual Relational Identifiers (VRI) because the target object does not have the properties required for unique identification, but its neighbor can be used to bridge that gap. However, as mentioned at the beginning of this chapter, VRI only works with Object Repository. If Descriptive Programming is used, other options such as HTML DOM, XPath and CSS selectors are available.

In a real-time scenario there may be several such controls and no unique properties by which to define them. To complete the form, let's now examine the HTML source we're working with:

```
<tr>
  <td>Email:</td>
  <td><input type="text" /></td>
</tr>
```

All other controls are laid out in the similar fashion: a TD text node is a sibling of another TD that has a child node INPUT. Both TD nodes have the same parent: TR. This relationship is shown below:

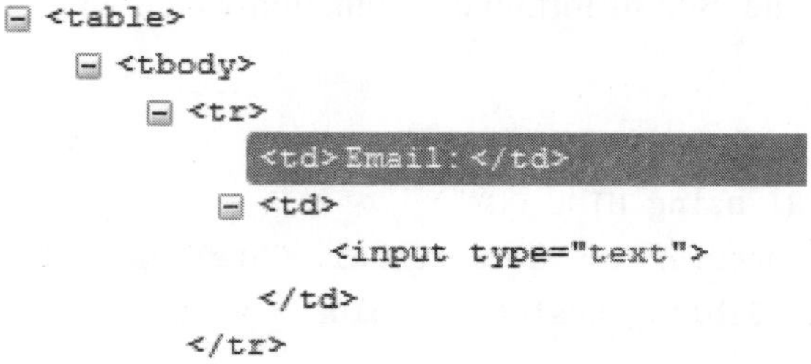

```
⊟ <table>
    ⊟ <tbody>
        ⊟ <tr>
                <td> Email: </td>
            ⊟ <td>
                    <input type="text">
                </td>
            </tr>
```

Figure 7.3 – Firebug DOM Tree

Knowing the relationship defined in the figure above, DOM properties can be utilized to fill the form and complete the registration process. Since we are using the Email: node as the anchor, we will be using the following 2 properties to reach to the INPUT node:

◉ nextSibling: Move from text TD node (<td>Email:</td>) to its sibling TD node (<td><input type="text"></td>).

◉ firstChild: Move from TD node (#2) to its child INPUT node.

The code below shows the usage of these two properties to complete the form:

```
With Browser("name:=VRI using HTML DOM")
  'Email:
  .WebElement("innertext:=Email:", "html tag:=TD").Object _
    .nextSibling.firstChild.value = "anshoo.arora@email.com"

  'Username:
  .WebElement("innertext:=Username:", "html tag:=TD").Object _
    .nextSibling.firstChild.value = "anshoo"

  'Password:
  .WebElement("innertext:=Password:", "html tag:=TD").Object _
    .nextSibling.firstChild.value = "pass0000"

  'Confirm:
  .WebElement("innertext:=Confirm:", "html tag:=TD").Object _
    .nextSibling.firstChild.value = "pass0000"

  .WebElement("value:=Register").Click()
```

```
End With
```

The logic above can be used to formulate a function which will supply data to the input fields:

```
Sub SetFormValue(textLabel, value)
  With Browser("VRI using HTML DOM")
    .WebElement("innertext:=" & textLabel, "html tag:=TD")_
      .Object.nextSibling.firstChild.value = value
  End With
End Sub


SetFormValue "Email:", "anshoo.arora@email.com"
SetFormValue "Username:", "anshoo"
SetFormValue "Password:", "pass0000"
SetFormValue "Confirm:", "pass0000"
```

Example 2: Login form

We have completed the registration process successfully. Now, we must login to the application to test whether the registration was successful. The HTML for the login page is shown below:

```
<html>
  <head>
    <title>VRI using HTML DOM</title>
  </head>
  <body style="background:#ffffee;font-family:Calibri;">
    <h2>Login Form</h2>
    <form>
      <table>
        <tr>
          <td>Username:</td>
          <td><input type="text" /></td>
        </tr>
        <tr>
          <td><span>Password:</span></td>
          <td><div><input type="password" /><div></td>
        </tr>
```

```
    <tr>
      <td>Login:</td>
      <td>
        <div>
          <span><input type="submit" value="Login" /></span>
        </div>
      </td>
    </tr>
   </table>
  </form>
 </body>
</html>
```

Figure 7.4 – Demo Login Form

To complete the login form from the sample HTML source, the UserName, Password and Login labels can be used to interact with their neighboring objects.

Notice from the HTML source that each reference node (Username, Password and Login) appears before the target node. There are, however, differences in the way we approach each. Let's start with the Username field.

```
<tr>
  <td>Username:</td>
  <td>
    <input type="text" />
  </td>
</tr>
```

When we look at the form visually, the textbox appears right next to the Username text. To bind to the textbox then, we must first move to the following-node (TD) then drill down to the textbox (INPUT) node:

```
'Bind to the Username text
Set UsernameTD = Browser("name:=VRI using DOM") _
  .WebElement("innertext:=Username:", "html tag:=TD").Object

'Bind to the following-node TD
'nextSibling is used to move from TD of Username to the next TD node
Set SiblingTD = UsernameTD.nextSibling

'Connect to the textbox
'firstChild points to the first child node of TD, which is INPUT
Set Textbox = SiblingTD.firstChild
Textbox.Value = "Tarun"
```

Similar to firstChild, childNodes(0) can also be used:

```
'Bind to the textbox
'childNodes(0) points to the first child node of TD, which is INPUT
Set Textbox = SiblingTD.childNodes(0)
Textbox.Value = "Tarun"
```

Let's now see how to set a value in the Password textbox. This is a little trickier. In the previous example, we jumped the reference node twice using nextSibling and firstChild/childNodes(0). The HTML source for the Password row is shown below:

```
<tr>
  <td><span>Password:</span></td> <!-- TD #1 -->
  <td><div><input type="password" /><div></td> <!-- TD #2 -->
</tr>
```

To set a value in the Password textbox, we will jump the reference node four times:

1. parentNode: move up from <SPAN>Password</SPAN> to <TD>.

2. nextSibling: move horizontally from TD #1 to TD #2.

3. firstChild: using the TD #2 node as an anchor, select the DIV node.

4. firstChild: using the DIV node as an anchor, select the INPUT node from the DIV node.

```
'Bind to the Password text
Set PasswordSPAN = Browser("name:=VRI using DOM") _
  .WebElement("innertext:=Password:", "html tag:=SPAN").Object

'Move up to the parent node (parent TD node)
Set TD_1 = PasswordSPAN.parentNode

'Move to the next sibling node (sibling TD node)
Set TD_2 = TD_1.nextSibling

'Drill down to the DIV node (child DIV)
Set DIV = TD_2.firstChild

'Drill down to the textbox node
Set Textbox = DIV.firstChild
Textbox.Value = "password"
```

Finally, let's see how we can click the Login button. Below is the HTML:

```
<tr>
  <td>Login:</td>
  <td><div><span><input type="submit" value="Login" /></span></div></td>
</tr>
```

To click the Login button, we can directly use the VALUE property or use the element relationships as described earlier in this section. Both techniques are shown below:

```
'Using the 'value' property
Browser("name:=VRI using DOM").WebButton("value:=Login").Click
```

If the same is to be done using DOM relationships, we must again move four nodes to get to the target node:

1. nextSibling: move from <TD>Login:</TD> to the next TD node.

2. firstChild: using the TD node as an anchor, select the DIV node.

3. firstChild: using the DIV node as an anchor, select the SPAN node.

4. firstChild: using the SPAN node as an anchor, select the INPUT node.

The implementation is shown here:

```
'Create connection with Login: text
Set LoginTD = Browser("name:=VRI using DOM") _
  .WebElement("innertext:=Login:", "html tag:=TD").Object

'Move to the next sibling node
Set TD_2 = LoginTD.nextSibling

'Move to the first child element in the TD childNodes collection
Set DIV = TD_2.firstChild

'Move to the first child element in the DIV childNodes collection
Set SPAN = DIV.firstChild

'Move to the first child element in the SPAN childNodes collection:
LoginButton
Set Button = SPAN.firstChild
Button.Click
```

WebTables

A huge amount of testing today is done on Web/HTML. A TABLE tag in HTML can be used to present data or perform layouts on the webpage. This chapter will focus on some of the key tasks that need to be performed when dealing with WebTables. But before we start with these tasks, we want to discuss WebTable identification.

WebTable Identification in QTP

When we add a WebTable object to the Object Repository (OR), it identifies the object using the Index Ordinal Identifier as shown in the image below:

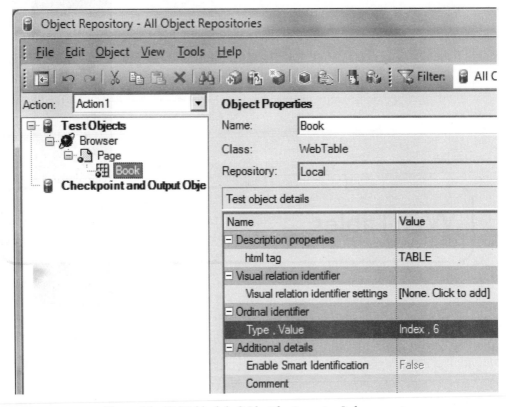

Figure 8.1 – WebTable default Identification using Index property

The Index property is one of the most unreliable ways of identifying the table and should only be used as a last resort. The following table shows some of the possible Identifiers best suited to WebTables:

Identification Property	Description
html id	If the table has an id tag defined, it is best to use this property: `<TABLE id="dmainTableTest">` In most cases this property will be unique to identify the desired table.

Identification Property	Description
innerText	If we know that the table we want to identify will always have some constant text (generally the headings) in it, we can use that text to identify it. Assume that our table always has a series of Edit and Delete links. We can identify the table using the following innerText: `innerText:=.*Edit.*Delete.*` Note: If a web page has multiple tables or nested tables, this approach may not give unique results.
columns	QTP 10 introduced the Columns property containing the names of all the columns in the table delimited by a semicolon. If there are no columns specified, then QTP will take the cells in the first row of the table as columns. To identify a table with two columns, Book and Order, we can use: `columns:=Book;Order`
CSS	CSS attributes can be used to identify the table and will be discussed in more detail in Chapter 12.
XPath	We can also identify a table using XPath and will discuss this further in Chapter 11, Object Identification using XPath.
Using an object inside the table	If we can identify an object present in the table, we can also use it for identification of Table as well. There are two ways to achieve this. One way is to use XPath. Consider the figure below: | Book	Order
QuickTest Professional Unplugged Author: Tarun Lalwani	☐
And I thought I knew QTP Author: Tarun Lalwani	☐
Descriptive Programming Unplugged Author: Tarun Lalwani & Anshoo Arora	☐	

Identification Property	Description

	If only this table on the webpage has checkboxes, we can just identify any of the checkboxes and try and reach to its parent table. This is a very simple method when working with XPath. We can use the following XPath to identify the table:
	
	`xpath:=(//INPUT[@type='checkbox'])[1]/ancestor::TABLE`
	
	But if we are not using XPath then we need to make use of HTML DOM:
	
	<pre>'Get the QTP WebTable from a specified object
	Public Function GetWebTableFromElement(ByVal pObject)
	  Dim oTable, oParent
	  'Get the parent table, a DOM object
	  'Note: the function GetParentOfElement is shown later in
	  'the chapter
	  Set oTable = GetParentOfElement (pObject.Object, "TABLE")
	  'Get QTP test object parent of supplied object
	  Set oParent = pObject.GetTOProperty("parent")
	  If oTable is Nothing Then
	    Set GetWebTableFromElement = Nothing
	  Else
	    'Return the table using the source index
	    Set GetWebTableFromElement = oParent.WebTable("source_
	Index:=" & oTable.sourceIndex)
	  End If
	End Function
	RegisterUserFunc "WebCheckBox", "ParentTable",
	"GetWebTableFromElement"</pre>
	We can use the above approach as shown below:
	
	<pre>Dim oTable
	'Use any of the checkbox to get the table
	Set oTable = Browser("B").Page("P").WebCheckBox("index:=0").
	ParentTable
	MsgBox oTable.GetCellData(2,1)</pre>

Finding a Row with Specified Text

Consider this WebTable:

Book	Edition	Order
QuickTest Professional Unplugged Author: Tarun Lalwani	1st Edition	☐
QuickTest Professional Unplugged Author: Tarun Lalwani	2nd Edition	☐
And I thought I knew QTP Author: Tarun Lalwani	1st Edition	☐
Descriptive Programming Unplugged Author: Tarun Lalwani & Anshoo Arora	1st Edition	☐

Figure 8.2 – Demo web page

If we need to check the checkbox for 'Descriptive Programming Unplugged' (last row), we would need to find the cell containing the text. WebTable object provides a method called GetRowWithCellText to search for specified text as shown below:

```
iRow = Browser("B").Page("P").WebTable("Book").GetRowWithCellText("Descriptive
Programming Unplugged")
```

In this case, we know that the book title will only appear in the first column so we can also specify the column number:

```
iRow = Browser("B").Page("P").WebTable("Book").GetRowWithCellText("Descriptive
Programming Unplugged", 1)
```

Also, in this case, the first row is the heading row, so we know that the search should begin from the second row:

```
iRow = Browser("B").Page("P").WebTable("Book").GetRowWithCellText("Descriptive
Programming Unplugged", 1, 2)
```

If the row is not found, -1 value is returned:

```
iRow = Browser("Browser").Page("Page").WebTable("Book").
GetRowWithCellText("Tarun Lalwanis")
If iRow = -1 Then
  Msgbox "Text not found"
End If
```

Performing Operations on Objects Inside the Table

In our previous example, we searched for 'Descriptive Programming Unplugged'. Now let's see how we can check the checkbox which corresponds to this book.

```
iRow = Browser("Browser").Page("Page").WebTable("Book").
GetRowWithCellText("Descriptive Programming Unplugged")

'Get the checkbox in specified row and 2nd column (Order)
Set oCheckBox = Browser("Browser").Page("Page").WebTable("Book").ChildItem(iRow,
2, "WebCheckBox", 0)
oCheckBox.Set "ON"
```

In this case, it is assumed that the checkbox will be present in the specified cell, but if that is not so, we should first check the cell for the existence of the checkbox. There are two ways to accomplish this, as shown below:

Method 1 - Check for returned object

```
'Get the checkbox in specified row and 2nd column (Order)
Set oCheckBox = Browser("Browser").Page("Page").WebTable("Book").ChildItem(iRow,
2, "WebCheckBox", 0)
If oCheckBox is nothing Then
  Msgbox "The checkbox doesn't exist"
End If
```

Method 2 - Check the object count

```
iCount = Browser("Browser").Page("Page").WebTable("Book").ChildItemCount(iRow,
2, "WebCheckBox")
If iCount = 0 Then
  Msgbox "The checkbox doesn't exist"
End if
```

Finding a Row Containing Specific Text

We saw earlier how the GetRowWithCellText method provides us with a way to search for specific text present in the cell. But there is no method which allows us to search a row with text in multiple columns of the table. Consider the following table:

Book	Edition	Order
QuickTest Professional Unplugged Author: Tarun Lalwani	1st Edition	☐
QuickTest Professional Unplugged Author: Tarun Lalwani	2nd Edition	☐
And I thought I knew QTP Author: Tarun Lalwani	1st Edition	☐
Descriptive Programming Unplugged Author: Tarun Lalwani & Anshoo Arora	1st Edition	☐

Figure 8.3 – Demo web page

If we want to search for the second edition of 'QuickTest Professional Unplugged', we have to use a loop with GetRowCellText and find the row as shown below:

```
Dim bExit, bFound, iRow, iStartRow
bExit = False
bFound = False
iStartRow = 1
Do
  iRow = Browser("Browser").Page("Page").WebTable("Book").
GetRowWithCellText("QuickTest Professional Unplugged",1, iStartRow)
  If iRow = -1 Then
    bFound = False
    bExit = True
  Else
    'Next time we will search for one row further
```

```
    iStartRow = iRow + 1
    If Trim(Browser("Browser").Page("Page").WebTable("Book").GetCellData(iRow,
2)) = "2nd Edition" Then
        'We have found of the row
        bExit = True
        bFound = True
    End If
  End If
Loop while bExit = False
If bFound Then
  Msgbox "Found the row at - " & iRow
Else
  Msgbox "Row could not be found"
End If
```

The code will become even more complex if we add more and more columns to our search criteria, so to overcome this we will write a new function:

```
Function GetRowWithText(Obj, ByVal Text, StartFromRow, RegExpression)
  bReg = LCase(RegExpression) = "true"
  Set oDOM = Obj.Object
  If bReg Then
    Set oReg = new RegExp
    oReg.Pattern = Text
    oReg.Global = True
    oReg.IgnoreCase = True
  Else
    Text = UCase(Trim(Text))
  End If
  Dim iColStart, iRowStart
  If IsNull(StartFromRow) Then
    iStartRow = 0
  Else
    iStartRow = StartFromRow - 1
  End if
  Dim i, j
  For i = iStartRow to oDOM.rows.length - 1
    Dim rowText
    'Get the text of the row
    rowText = Trim(UCase(oDOM.rows(i).innerText))
```

```
    If Not bReg Then
      If Text = cellText Then
        GetRowWithText = i + 1
        oDOM.rows(i).scrollIntoView
        Exit Function
      End If
    Else
      'Check if the rowText matched the pattern
      If (oReg.test(rowText)) Then
        GetRowWithText = i + 1
        oDOM.rows(i).scrollIntoView
        Exit Function
      End If
    End if
  Next
    'Nothing found lets exit
  GetRowWithText = -1
End Function
RegisterUserFunc "WebTable", "GetRowWithText", "GetRowWithText"
```

NOTE: The above function has been created using IE DOM. This may not work for other Browsers.

To use this function we can use the following:

```
MsgBox Browser("Browser").Page("Page").WebTable("Book").
GetRowWithText(".*QuickTest Professional Unplugged.*2nd.*", 2, True)
```

When we run the above code we will find that the function returns -1 even when the pattern is correct. This is because even though "." in Regular Expression matches any character, it doesn't match new line characters in the text. We therefore need to add an additional \s tag to our pattern as shown below:

```
MsgBox Browser("Browser").Page("Page").WebTable("Book").
GetRowWithText(".*QuickTest Professional Unplugged(.|\s)*2nd.*",2, True)
```

Now the function will return the correct value of 3.

Clicking Inside a WebTable

There are no in-built methods provided for the WebTable to click one of its cells but there are several ways described in this section to achieve the same.

METHOD 1

```
'Get the tables DOM object
Set oDOMTable = Browser("").Page("").WebTable("").object
'To click on (1, 1) we can use:
Row = 1
Col = 1
oDOMTable.rows(Row - 1).Cells(Col - 1).Click
```

METHOD 2

We can also bind to the corresponding WebElement object of the target cell and then click it.

```
'Get the DOM table object
Set oDOMTable = Browser("").Page("").WebTable("").object
Row = 1
Col = 1
'Get the source index of the table
sIndex  = oDOMTable.rows(Row - 1).Cells(Col - 1).sourceIndex
'Click on the WebElement using it's source index
Browser("").Page("").WebElement("source_Index:=" & sIndex).Click
```

METHOD 3

This method uses the Object Identification hierarchy. Each row is a child object of the Table and each cell is a child of its table Row. So to click cell (1, 1), we can use the following code:

```
'Get the WebTable test object
Set oWebTable = Browser("").Page("").WebTable("")
Row = 1
Col = 1


'Get the Row WebElement of the object
```

```
Set oRow = oWebTable.WebElement("html tag:=TR","index:=" & (Row-1))


'Get the Cell WebElement of the object from the row element
Set oCell = oRow.WebElement("html tag:=TD","index:=" & (Col -1))


'Click on the cell
oCell.Click
```

NOTE: This approach may not work correctly if the Table has nested Tables inside it.

METHOD 4

This method can be used when we want to click on an object which is located inside a table cell:

```
'Get the WebTable test object
Set oWebTable = Browser("").Page("").WebTable("")
Row = 1
Col = 1
'Get the number of WebEdits present in specified Row, Col
iEditCount = oWebTable.ChildItemCount(Row, Col, "Link")

If iEditCount = 0 Then
  MsgBox "No WebEdit present in 1, 1"
Else
  'Get the 1st WebEdit present in 1, 1
  Set oWebEdit = oWebTable.ChildItem(Row, Col, "Link", 0)

  'Set the value
  oWebEdit.Set "This is 1st WebEdit in 1, 1"
End if
```

Asynchronous Table Loading

Some pages use asynchronous calls for loading content. In such cases, content is delivered without having to refresh the page. In this situation, since the objects are already are present but the content is changing, using ".Exist", ".Sync" or "WaitProperty" on one of the objects can't be used to determine when data loading is complete.

In the next example we have an object reference to a WebTable being updated with data asynchronously. The trick here is to evaluate the RowCount of the WebTable after a specified interval—when the number of rows in the table gives the same value after a specified interval of delay, we can assume that updating of the table is complete. Consider the code below:

```
'Reference the table being asynchronously loaded
Set objTbl = Browser("..").Page("..").WebTable("..")
oldRowCount = 0
'Stop when the row count is stable for 2 iterations
While (oldRowCount <> objTbl.RowCount)
 'Get the new row count
 oldRowCount = objTbl.RowCount
 'Wait for 3 seconds and try again
 Wait 3
Wend
```

NOTE: The delay timing may need some tweaking based on the application being tested and response time of the same.

This code retrieves and evaluates the WebTable row count every three seconds. Data loading is presumably done when the row count is the same for two iterations.

Retrieving the Parent WebTable from an Element

The GetTableFromElement we created earlier returns the DOM table object, so let's create another function which will return a QTP WebTable Test object instead, by using information from the DOM table object we have. We will use the HTML source we used at the beginning of this chapter to demonstrate this technique:

```
<table>
```

```
  <tr>
    <table border="1">
      <tr>
        <td>Attribute</td>
        <td>Value</td>
        <td>Description</td>
      </tr>
    </table>
    <table border="1">
      <tr>
  <td>align</td>
        <td>left</td>
        <td>Alignment of the element</td>
      </tr>
    </table>
  </tr>
</table>


'Get the QTP WebTable from a specified object
Public Function GetWebTableFromElement(ByVal pObject)
  Dim oTable, oParent
  'Get the parent table, a DOM object
  'Remember to include the Function GetParentOfElement!
  Set oTable = GetParentOfElement (pObject.Object, "TABLE")
  'Get QTP test object parent of supplied object
  Set oParent = pObject.GetTOProperty("parent")
  If oTable is Nothing Then
    Set GetWebTableFromElement = Nothing
  Else
    'Return the table using the source index
    Set GetWebTableFromElement = oParent.WebTable("source_Index:=" & oTable.
sourceIndex)
  End If
End Function


'Function to get parent node on element
Function GetParentOfElement(ByVal pObject,ByVal pParentTagName)
  On error resume next
```

```
'In case a QTP Test object is passed, convert it
'to the DOM Object. This allows using the
'function on both DOM and QTP Test Objects
Set pObject = pObject.Object
Err.Clear
On Error Goto 0
'Search for object's parent node
Set oParent = pObject
'Seacrh for the node with specified Tag Name
Do
Set oParent = oParent.parentNode
'if oParent == Nothing then we didn't find any parent object
'with the specified tag
Loop While Not (oParent is Nothing) And oParent.tagName <> pParentTagName
'Return the object found, else return Nothing if a tag is not found
Set GetParentOfElement = oParent
End Function
```

The above function can be used in the following way to find the QTP table:

```
Set QTPTable = GetWebTableFromElement(Browser("name:=.*GetRowColumn.*")_
.WebElement("innertext:=Value"))
QTPTable.Highlight
```

Similarly, the function can be used as a RegisterUserFunc so its presence is seen in the test-object's IntelliSense:

```
RegisterUserFunc "<TargetWebObject>", "GetWebTableFromElement",
"GetWebTableFromElement"
```

Testing Complex HTML Tables

Previously in web-design, UI Designers used the TABLE tags to create a tabular look and feel. This TABLE tag implementation makes it easier for Automation Engineers to process data and perform actions on objects inside the table. Consider the following table:

Book	Order
QuickTest Professional Unplugged Author: Tarun Lalwani	☐
And I thought I knew QTP Author: Tarun Lalwani	☐
Descriptive Programming Unplugged Author: Tarun Lalwani & Anshoo Arora	☐

Figure 9.1 – Demo web page

The HTML implementation is as follows:

```
<html>
```

```
<head></head>
<body>
  <style type="text/css">
    .mainheader{background-color:SkyBlue;border:0px solid SkyBlue;}
    .maintile{border:1px solid #CCCCCC;background-color:white;width:  25%}
    .mainrow{border:2px solid #CCCCCC;border-style:solid;}
    .bookname{border-style:solid;border:1px solid #CCCCCC;background-
color: #F1F3F4;width:95%;}
    .bookcheck{border-style:solid;border:1px solid #CCCCCC;background-
color:DarkGray;width:2%;}
    .author {color:#666666;font-size:80%;}
  </style>
  <table class="maintile">
    <thead class="mainheader">
      <tr>
        <th>
          Book
        </th>
        <th>
          Order
        </th>
      </tr>
    </thead>
    <tbody>
      <tr class="mainrow">
        <td class="bookname">
          QuickTest Professional Unplugged<br>
          <span class="author">Author: Tarun Lalwani</span>
        </td>
        <td class="bookcheck">
          <input type="checkbox" value="AD01" id="chkBook_001">
        </td>
      </tr>
      <tr class="mainrow">
        <td class="bookname">
          And I thought I knew QTP<br>
          <span class="author">Author: Tarun Lalwani</span>
        </td>
        <td class="bookcheck">
```

```
          <input type="checkbox" value="AD02" id="chkBook_002">
        </td>
      </tr>
      <tr class="mainrow">
        <td class="bookname">
          Descriptive Programming Unplugged<br>
          <span class="author">Author: Tarun Lalwani & Anshoo Arora</
span>
        </td>
        <td class="bookcheck">
          <input type="checkbox" value="AD03" id="chkBook_003">
        </td>
      </tr>
    </tbody>
  </table>
 </body>
</html>
```

Now, let us assume that we have to verify all the book names that appear in the table. One approach would be to read the cell values to get the book names. We can create a dictionary out of the book names and use it to create our own verification points.

```
Dim i, iCount
Dim oWebTable
Set oWebTable = Browser("X").WebTable("Book")

'Create a dictionary of book names
Dim oDictBooks

Set oDictBooks = CreateObject("Scripting.Dictionary")
oDictBooks.CompareMode = vbTextCompare

'Start from 2, we need to ignore header row
For i = 2 to oWebTable.RowCount
  sBookName = oWebTable.GetCellData(i, 1)

  'We will get the full text in the cell
  'Full text: QuickTest Professional Unplugged Author: Tarun Lalwani
  'Using Split on this string will give us the book name
```

```
    sBookName = Split(sBookName, "Author:")(0)

    oDictBooks.Add sBookName, sBookName
Next

If oDictBooks.Exists("QuickTest Professional Unplugged") Then
  Reporter.ReportEvent micPass, "Book Found", _
    "Book Found - QuickTest Professional Unplugged"
Else
  Reporter.ReportEvent micFail, "Book Not Found", _
    "Book Not Found - QuickTest Professional Unplugged"
End if
```

The above method makes it quite easy for us to loop through the data on UI and complete the necessary validations. Now consider the DIV HTML implementation of same table without using the <table> tag. Even though the upcoming structure will look like a table, it is not. Instead, it is made to look like a table as a result of its CSS styling.

```
<html>
  <head></head>
  <body>
    <style type="text/css">
      .maintile
      {
        background-color: SkyBlue;
        width: 30%;
        border: 2px;
        height: 20px;
      }
      .mainheader
      {
        background-color: SkyBlue;
        width: 105%;
      }
      .mainrow
      {
        width: 100%;
        background-color: SkyBlue;
        height: 20px;
```

```
    }
    .bookname
    {
      width: 90%;
      height: 20px;
      float: left;
      background-color: #F1F3F4;
    }
    .bookcheck
    {
      width: 10%;
      height: 100%;
      float: right;
      background-color: DarkGrey;
    }
    .author
    {
      color: #666666;
      font-size: 80%;
    }
    .mainheaderbook
    {
      margin-left: 10%;
      width: 30%;
      float: left;
    }
    .mainheadercheck
    {
      width: 10%;
      float: right;
      margin-right: 5%;
    }
    .book
    {
      font: 100%;
    }
</style>
<div class="maintile">
  <div class="mainheader">
```

```
        <div class="mainheaderbook">
          Book</div>
        <div class="mainheadercheck">
          Order</div>
      </div>
      <div class="mainrow">
        <div class="bookname">
          <span class="book">QuickTest Professional Unplugged</span><br>
          <span class="author">Author: Tarun Lalwani</span>
        </div>
        <div class="bookcheck">
          <input type="checkbox" value="AD01" id="chkBook_001">
        </div>
      </div>
      <div class="mainrow">
        <div class="bookname">
          <span class="book">And I thought I knew QTP</span><br>
          <span class="author">Author: Tarun Lalwani</span>
        </div>
        <div class="bookcheck">
          <input type="checkbox" value="AD02" id="chkBook_002">
        </div>
      </div>
      <div class="mainrow">
        <div class="bookname">
          <span class="book">Descriptive Programming Unplugged</span><br>
          <span class="author">Author: Tarun Lalwani & Anshoo Arora</span>
        </div>
        <div class="bookcheck">
          <input type="checkbox" value="AD03" id="chkBook_003">
        </div>
      </div>
    </div>
  </body>
</html>
```

In the above source, there are no WebTable objects. When we spy on it, there will only be WebElements as shown in the following image comparison:

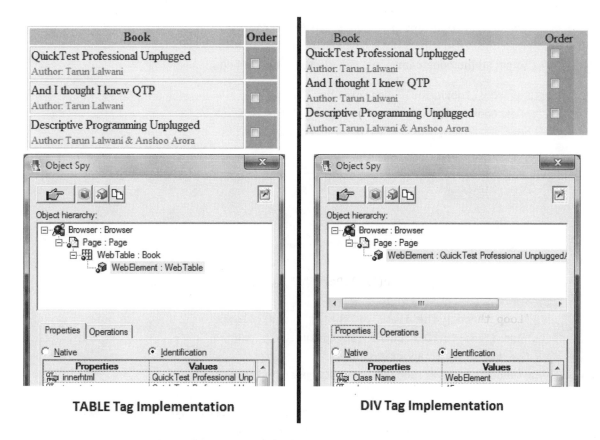

TABLE Tag Implementation   **DIV Tag Implementation**

Figure 9.2 – TABLE vs. DIV based Implementation

In the new implementation, we can see that the data appears to be in tabular format but that each cell is identified individually as a WebElement. Losing the WebTable object from the hierarchy makes it difficult for us to get all the book names and perform actions on the checkboxes next to them. In QTP 10 or lower, we don't have the option to use CSS Identifiers and therefore require an object description such as this one:

```
Set oDescBookNames = Description.Create
oDescBookNames("html tag").value = "DIV"
oDescBookNames("micclass").value = "WebElement"
oDescBookNames("class").value = "bookname"
```

With QTP 11, we can use the CSS Identifier directly:

```
Set oDescBookNames = Description.Create
```

```
oDescBookNames("micclass").value = "WebElement"
oDescBookNames("css").value = "DIV.bookname"
```

To get all the book names, we can use the following code:

```
Set oDescBookNames = Description.Create
oDescBookNames("micclass").value = "WebElement"
oDescBookNames("css").value = "DIV.bookname"

'Create a dictionary of book names
Dim oDictBooks

Set oDictBooks = CreateObject("Scripting.Dictionary")
oDictBooks.CompareMode = vbTextCompare

Set allBooks = Browser("X").Page("X").ChildObjects(oDescBookNames)

'Loop through the items of the allBooks collection
'Add items to oDictBooks (Scripting.Dictionary)
For i = 0 to allBooks.Count -1
  sBookName = allBooks(i).GetROProperty("outertext")

  'We will get the full text in the cell, so lets take what we need
  sBookName = Split (sBookName, "Author:")(0)

  oDictBooks.Add sBookName, sBookName

  Print sBookName
Next
```

The code above appears simple enough in order to pull up information from a DIV table too, but in order to keep the HTML short for this example, we didn't add too many columns. In a real-life application, there may be many more columns in this table. Different DIV layouts will need different solutions so the amount of coding effort required will also be higher.

If it was possible to operate such a layout as a table, that would be a great convenience to any Automation Engineer, but currently there are no existing solutions and hence we will showcase how to develop a mapped HTML table to do this. We will develop a class to create the map and implement some of the basic methods.

```
Class MappedHTMLTable

End Class
```

Before we dive into the rest of the implementation, we need a method that can let us easily and quickly create a description object.

```
Function Desc(ByVal Params)
  'Its a description. Just return it and exit
  If TypeName(Params) = "DispPropertyCollection" Then
    Set Desc = Params
    Exit Function
  Else
    Dim arrDesc, eachDesc, oDesc
    Set oDesc = Description.Create
    arrDesc = Split(Params, ";")

    'Process each property from the string. Format is as below
    'Property1=value1;Property2=value2
    For Each eachDesc In arrDesc
      eachDesc = Split(eachDesc, "=")
      If Trim(eachDesc(0)) <> "" Then
        oDesc(trim(eachDesc(0))).Value = trim(eachDesc(1))
      End If
    Next

    'If micclass was not given then set it as WebElement
    If isEmpty(oDesc("micclass").value) Then
      oDesc("micclass").value = "WebElement"
    End If

    Set Desc = oDesc
  End If
End Function
```

The function can be used in the following way to create descriptions quickly:

```
Set oDesc = Desc("css=DIV.bookname")
```

```
Set oDesc = Desc("html tag=INPUT;name=q")
Set oDesc = Desc("micclass=WebElement;html tag=DIV;class=bookname")
```

Now we will start adding small functionality to our mapped table. The table will have a main object inside which the rows and the columns reside. So we can update the MappedHTMLTable class as below:

```
Class MappedHTMLTable
  Private oMainObject
  Private oRows
  Private oRowsDesc

  'Function to the pass the main parent object
  Sub SetTableObject(ByVal pMainObject)
    Set oMainObject = pMainObject
  End Sub

  'Function to pass the description to reach each row
  Sub SetRowsDesc(ByVal oDesc)
    Set oRowsDesc = oDesc
  End Sub
End Class
```

We have now added two methods – one to set the main table object and the second to set the row descriptor. Let's now look more closely at our HTML DIV representation:

```
<div class="maintile">
  <div class="mainheader">
    <div class="mainheaderbook">
      Book</div>
    <div class="mainheadercheck">
      Order</div>
  </div>
  <div class="mainrow">
```

The DIV with Class 'maintile' is the one which represents the table for us and the DIV with 'class=mainrow' represents each row in the table. So we can use our class as follows:

```
Dim oMapTable
Set oMapTable = New MappedHTMLTable
```

```
Call oMapTable.SetTableObject(Browser("X").WebElement(Desc("css=DIV.
maintile")))
Call oMapTable.SetRowsDesc(Desc("css=DIV.mainrow"))
```

One key operation in our class is to get the count of rows, so there is one property for rows and one method for RowCount.

```
Public Property Get Rows
  If oRows is Nothing Then
    Set oRows = oMainObject.ChildObjects(oRowsDesc)
  End If

  Set Rows = oRows
End Property

Public Property Get RowCount
  RowCount = Rows.Count
End Property

Sub Class_Initialize()
  Set oRows = nothing
End Sub
```

We now need to be able to fetch a row and its text:

```
Function GetRow(rowIndex)
  If rowIndex < 1 or rowIndex > RowCount Then
    Set GetRow = Nothing
    Exit Function
  End if

  Set GetRow = Rows.Item(rowIndex - 1)
End Function

Function GetRowData(rowIndex)
  GetRowData = GetRow(rowIndex).GetROProperty("outertext")
End Function
```

Now we have support for row-level details but we are still missing logic for column-level details. To incorporate column support we will create a dictionary with column names and column object descriptions. Since each column in a DIV table can have different object identification properties, we cannot use a common object description as we used for rows. So in our mapped table, instead of referring to columns using indexes, we will be referring to them using names.

```
Function AddColumn(ColumnName, oDesc)
  Set oColumnsDict(Trim(ColumnName)) = oDesc
End Function

Function RemoveColumn(ColumnName)
  oColumnsDict.Remove Trim(ColumnName)
End Function

Function ColumnExists(ColumnName)
  ColumnExists = oColumnsDict.Exists(Trim(ColumnName))
End Function

Sub Class_Initialize()
  Set oRows = nothing
  Set oColumnsDict = CreateObject("Scripting.Dictionary")
  oColumnsDict.CompareMode = vbTextCompare
End Sub
```

Now we can add virtual columns to our map table as shown below:

```
oMapTable.AddColumn "Book", Desc("css=SPAN.book")
oMapTable.AddColumn "Author ", Desc("css=SPAN.author")
oMapTable.AddColumn "Order", Desc("css=DIV.bookcheck
input;micclass=WebCheckBox")
```

Now let's add two methods to get the column text and the column object:

```
Function GetColumn(rowIndex, columnName)
  Set GetColumn = GetRow(rowIndex).ChildObjects(oColumnsDict(columnName))
(0)
End Function

Function GetCellData(rowIndex, columnName)
  GetCellData = GetColumn(rowIndex, columnName).GetROproperty("outertext")
```

```
End Function
```

To utilize the above method, we need to use the following:

```
Msgbox oMapTable.GetCellData(1,"Book")
Msgbox oMapTable.GetCellData(1,"Author")
oMapTable.GetColumn(1,"Order").Set "ON"
```

Our final class code will be as below:

```
Class MappedHTMLTable
  Private oMainObject
  Private oRows
  Private oRowsDesc
  Private oColumnsDict

  Function AddColumn(ColumnName, oDesc)
    Set oColumnsDict(Trim(ColumnName)) = oDesc
  End Function

  Function RemoveColumn(ColumnName)
    oColumnsDict.Remove Trim(ColumnName)
  End Function

  Function ColumnExists(ColumnName)
    ColumnExists = oColumnsDict.Exists(Trim(ColumnName))
  End Function

  'Function to the pass the main parent object
  Sub SetTableObject(ByVal pMainObject)
    Set oMainObject = pMainObject
  End Sub

  'Function to pass the description to reach each row
  Sub SetRowsDesc(ByVal oDesc)
    Set oRowsDesc = oDesc
  End Sub

  Public Property Get Rows
```

```
      If oRows is Nothing Then
        Set oRows = oMainObject.ChildObjects(oRowsDesc)
      End If

      Set Rows = oRows
   End Property
   Public Property Get RowCount
      RowCount = Rows.Count
   End Property

   Sub Class_Initialize()
      Set oRows = Nothing
      Set oColumnsDict = CreateObject("Scripting.Dictionary")
      oColumnsDict.CompareMode = vbTextCompare
   End Sub

   Function GetRow(rowIndex)
      If rowIndex < 1 or rowIndex > RowCount Then
        Set GetRow = Nothing
        Exit Function
      End if

      Set GetRow = Rows.Item(rowIndex - 1)
   End Function

   Function GetRowData(rowIndex)
      GetRowData = GetRow(rowIndex).GetROProperty("outertext")
   End Function

   Function GetColumn(rowIndex, columnName)
      Set GetColumn = GetRow(rowIndex).ChildObjects(oColumnsDict(columnName))
(0)
   End Function

   Function GetCellData(rowIndex, columnName)
      GetCellData = GetColumn(rowIndex, columnName).GetROproperty("outertext")
   End Function
End Class
```

To use the above map table, we must use the following:

```
Dim oMapTable
Set oMapTable = New MappedHTMLTable

Call oMapTable.SetTableObject(Browser("X").WebElement(Desc("css=DIV.
maintile")))
Call oMapTable.SetRowsDesc(Desc("css=DIV.mainrow"))

oMapTable.AddColumn "Book", Desc("css=SPAN.book")
oMapTable.AddColumn "Author ", Desc("css=SPAN.author")
oMapTable.AddColumn "Order", Desc("css=DIV.bookcheck
input;micclass=WebCheckBox")

Msgbox oMapTable.GetCellData(1,"Book")
Msgbox oMapTable.GetCellData(1,"Author")

oMapTable.GetColumn(1,"Order").Set "ON"
```

Another advantage of this mapping technique is that because we can map columns directly to objects inside a cell, we can also map a column to a link, a textbox or any other object. We can then call the SetTableObject using the QTP WebTable object and treat different objects which may or may not reside in the same column as separate columns.

Localization Techniques and Design Patterns

Introduction

As applications become global, adapting them to specific cultures or locales becomes a massive task. You may have visited websites that provides its users to convert the base (local) text to the text of the locale chosen. For explanation and simplicity, this book uses a fixed HTML scheme for English and Spanish for the demonstration of techniques that can simplify localization testing.

Below is a list of some commonly used locales:

Locale Description	LCID (Locale ID)
Afrikaans	af
Arabic - United Arab Emirates	ar-ae
Chinese - China	zh-cn
Chinese - Hong Kong	zh-hk

Locale Description	LCID (Locale ID)
Chinese - Taiwan	zh-tw
English - Australia	en-au
English - Britain	en-gb
English - Canada	en-ca
English - India	en-in
English - Singapore	en-sg
English - United States	en-us
French - France	fr-fr
German - Germany	de-de
Hebrew	he
Hindi	hi
Russian	ru
Spanish - Spain (Modern)	es-es
Spanish - Mexico	es-mx
Swedish - Sweden	sv-se
Thai	th

Additional LCIDs can be found in the QTP Help file by entering LCID in the Index section.

As mentioned earlier, in this chapter we have used English (en-us) and Spanish (es-es) locales to demonstrate the testing of locales with QTP. It is possible that in your application, there is an even greater number of locales available. Even though only two locales have been included in this chapter, special consideration is given to cases where testing more than two locales is required. We will be using the below HTML to cover the localization techniques in this chapter.

ENGLISH.HTM -> LOCALE: ENGLISH - UNITED STATES (EN-US)

```
<html>
  <head>
    <title>Localization</title>
    <style>
      body {background-color: #FFFFEE; font-family:Calibri;}
      .header {border: 1px solid #CCCCCC;}
      .headerRow {background: #EEE;}
      .headerCell, .loginCell {padding:10px;}
      #submit {width:148px;height:50px;}
```

```
          .footerCell {padding:10px; font-size: 10pt;}
      </style>
  </head>
  <body>
    <table class="header">
      <tr class="headerRow">
        <td class="headerCell"><a href="#">About Us</a></td>
        <td class="headerCell"><a href="#">Contact Us</a></td>
        <td class="headerCell"><a href="#">Our Offices</a></td>
        <td class="headerCell"><a href="./spanish.htm">View in Spanish</
a></td>
      </tr>
    </table>
    <table>
      <tr>
        <td class="loginCell">UserName:</td>
        <td><input name="user" id="userName" /></td>
      </tr>
      <tr>
        <td class="loginCell">Password:</td>
        <td><input name="pass" id="password" /></td>
      </tr>
      <tr>
        <td></td>
        <td><input type="button" id="submit" value="Login" /></td>
      </tr>
    </table>
    <table>
      <tr>
        <td class="footerCell"><a href="#">Communication</a></td>
        <td class="footerCell"><a href="#">Privacy Policy</a></td>
        <td class="footerCell"><a href="#">Terms & Conditions</a></td>
      </tr>
    </table>
  </body>
</html>
```

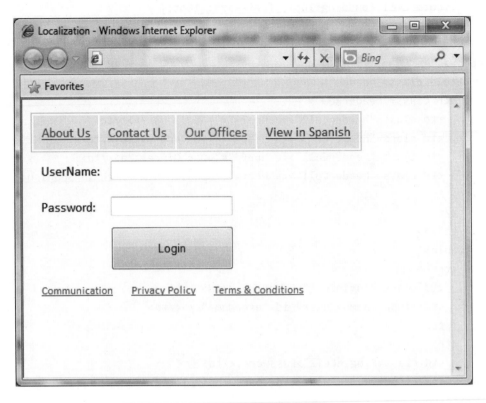

Figure 10.1 – English Locale AUT

SPANISH.HTM -> LOCALE: SPANISH — MODERN (ES-ES)

```html
<html>
  <head>
    <title>localización</title>
    <style>
      body {background-color: #FFFFEE; font-family:Calibri;}
      .header {border: 1px solid #CCCCCC;}
      .headerRow {background: #EEE;}
      .headerCell, .loginCell {padding:10px;}
      #submit {width:148px;height:50px;}
      .footerCell {padding:10px; font-size: 10pt;}
    </style>
  </head>
  <body>
    <table class="header">
      <tr class="headerRow">
```

```
        <td class="headerCell"><a href="#">Acerca de nosotros</a></td>
        <td class="headerCell"><a href="#">Contacte con nosotros</a></td>
        <td class="headerCell"><a href="#">nuestras Oficinas</a></td>
        <td class="headerCell"><a href="./english.htm">Ver en Inglés</a></
td>
      </tr>
    </table>
    <table>
      <tr>
        <td class="loginCell">Nombre de usuario:</td>
        <td><input name="user" id="userName" /></td>
      </tr>
      <tr>
        <td class="loginCell">contraseña:</td>
        <td><input name="pass" id="password" /></td>
      </tr>
      <tr>
        <td></td>
        <td><input type="button" id="submit" value="Login" /></td>
      </tr>
    </table>
    <table>
      <tr>
        <td class="footerCell"><a href="#">comunicación</a></td>
        <td class="footerCell"><a href="#">Política de Privacidad</a></td>
        <td class="footerCell"><a href="#">Términos y condiciones</a></td>
      </tr>
    </table>
  </body>
</html>
```

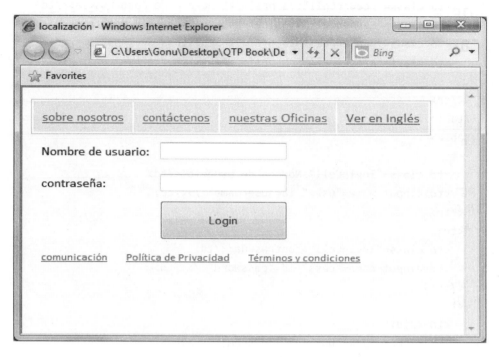

Figure 10.2 – Spanish Locale AUT

This chapter outlines the following localization techniques:

⦿ Using a Separate Function Library for each Locale.

⦿ Using an Extensible Scripting.Dictionary Approach.

⦿ Using an Excel based Locale Map.

⦿ Using OO Techniques and Delimited Scripting.Dictionary.

⦿ Using OO Techniques with a Centralized Delimited Scripting.Dictionary.

NOTE: All techniques outlined in this chapter work equally well with both Object Repository and programmatic descriptions. Special consideration has also been given to cases where more than 2 locales are being tested.

Using a Separate Function Library for each Locale

With this technique, a separate library is created for each locale, which is dependent upon the executing locale. Once the libraries are created, the test loads the correct libraries using either ExecuteFile or LoadFunctionLibrary (QTP 11.x onwards). Consider the two function libraries below for English and Spanish locales respectively:

```
''''en-us Login.vbs (OR style)''''
Sub LoginAction()
  With Browser("Localization").Page("Localization")
    .WebEdit("user").Set "John"
    .WebEdit("pass").Set "*****"
    .WebButton("Login").Click
    .Link("About Us").Click
    .Link("Contact Us").Click
    .Link("Our Offices").Click
  End With
End Sub
''''en-us Login (DP style)''''
Sub LoginAction()
  With Browser("Localization").Page("Localization")
    .WebEdit("name:=user").Set "John"
    .WebEdit("name:=pass").Set "*****"
    .Link("About Us").Click
    .Link("Contact Us").Click
    .Link("Our Offices").Click
    .Link("View in Spanish").Click
  End With
End Sub
''''es-es Login.vbs (OR style)''''
Sub LoginAction()
  With Browser("Localization").Page("localización")
    .WebEdit("user").Set "John"
    .WebEdit("pass").Set "*****"
    .Link("Acerca de nosotros").Click
    .Link("Contacte con nosotros").Click
    .Link("nuestras Oficinas").Click
```

```
      .Link("Ver en Inglés").Click
   End With
End Sub
''''es-es Login.vbs (DP style)''''
Sub LoginAction()
   With Browser("Localization").Page("localización")
      .WebEdit("name:=user").Set "John"
      .WebEdit("name:=pass").Set "*****"
      .Link("innertext:=Acerca de nosotros").Click
      .Link("innertext:=Contacte con nosotros").Click
      .Link("innertext:=nuestras Oficinas").Click
      .Link("innertext:=Ver en Inglés").Click
   End With
End Sub
```

During execution, depending upon which locale is to be executed, the test loads either of the two using these methods from the following directory structure:

- English: <root>\AppName\Libraries\Locale\en-us\Login.vbs

- Spanish: <root>\AppName\Libraries\Locale\es-es\Login.vbs

Even though we have shown libraries for the 2 locales in both OR and DP style, only one library for each must be used depending upon the approach being followed. In other words, if you are following an OR approach, you do not have to use the DP style library and vice versa.

Notice the difference in the folders above for each locale. This difference can be passed as an argument in our loading methods.

```
Sub LoadLocaleLib(ByVal fileName, ByVal locale)
   Dim path
   path = "<root>\AppName\Libraries\Locale\" & locale & "\" & fileName
   ExecuteFile path
End Sub
```

The LoadFunctionLibrary method was added in QTP 11 and this can be used to load the library instead. As opposed to ExecuteFile, LoadFunctionLibrary does offer the mechanism to debug libraries.

```
'QTP 11.x onwards
```

```
Sub LoadLocaleLib(ByVal fileName, ByVal locale)
  Dim path
  path = "<root>\AppName\Libraries\Locale\" & locale & "\" & fileName
  LoadFunctionLibrary path
End Sub
```

The following code will be used to load the login.vbs library with English locale:

```
LoadLocaleLib "login.vbs", "en-us" 'English
```

The code below will be used to load the login.vbs library with Spanish locale:

```
LoadLocaleLib "login.vbs", "es-es" 'Spanish
```

The above loading mechanism can either be stored in a test or in an associated function library (recommended).

Even though this technique is very easy to use, it has quite a high maintenance overhead because the same copy of the library (with different locales) exists in different locations. Changes made to the flow of the application will result in developers implementing the update in multiple places. However, a big maintenance overhead can be traded for a situation where changes in locale also results in the change of flow or overall UI design. In other words, this approach makes it easier to accomodate for situations where code logic changes from one locate to another.

Advantages

- ◉ Easy to use

- ◉ Provides flexibility in situations where flow differs from locale to locale

Disadvantages

- ◉ Poor maintenance: changes made to one library must be copied to all other libraries

- ◉ Creating libraries for each locale can be a time-consuming process

Using a Simple Locale Collection

An extensible Scripting.Dictionary is a very flexible and expandable approach which can be created using procedural methods or object-oriented. The crux of this approach is demonstrated by the following code snippet:

```
'If using function libraries, the variables below can be used as global
'If using Actions for each functionality, these can be local to the Action
Dim Locale, enLocale, spLocale

'Parent collection
Set LocaleCollection = CreateObject("Scripting.Dictionary")

'Child collections
Set enLocale = CreateObject("Scripting.Dictionary")
Set esLocale = CreateObject("Scripting.Dictionary")

'Add locale definitions: English
enLocale.Add "title", "Localization"
enLocale.Add "about-us", "About Us"

'Add locale definitions: Spanish
esLocale.Add "title", "localización"
esLocale.Add "about-us", "sobre nosotros"

'Add enLocale, esLocale to the parent collection
LocaleCollection.Add "en-us", enLocale
LocaleCollection.Add "es-es", esLocale
```

To simplify things further, the executing locale can be defined in a global scope. This will help in making a single change to enable testing any of the available locales.

```
'In function library associated with the test (global variable)
Public GlobalLocale : GlobalLocale = "en-us"
```

The parent dictionary (locale) above can be used to retrieve values for each locale-property combination (shown below):

```
GlobalLocale = "es-es"
MsgBox LocaleCollection(GlobalLocale)("title")
MsgBox LocaleCollection(GlobalLocale)("about-us")
```

Figure 10.3 – Output from LocaleCollection (es-es)

```
GlobalLocale = "en-us"
MsgBox LocaleCollection(GlobalLocale)("title")
MsgBox LocaleCollection(GlobalLocale)("about-us")
```

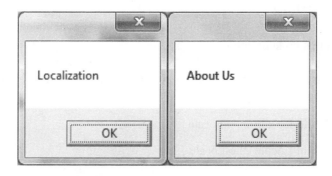

Figure 10.4 – Output from LocaleCollection (en-us)

However, it will not be a good approach to use it as-is because we have to provide GlobalLocale on each line a locale is called. A better approach is to use a function that does it for us and resides in a single function library. Finally, we need to add a function that will return the corresponding property value:

```
Function GetValue(ByVal sProperty)
  GetValue = LocaleCollection(GlobalLocale)(sProperty)
End Function
```

Usage:

```
'OR style (en-us)
Browser(GetValue("title")).Page(GetValue("title"))_
```

```
  .Link(GetValue("about-us")).Click
'OR style (es-es)
Browser(GetValue("title")).Page(GetValue("title"))_
  .Link(GetValue("about-us")).Click
'DP style (en-us)
Browser("name:=" & GetValue("title"))_
  .Link("innertext:=" & GetValue("about-us")).Highlight
'DP style (es-es)
Browser("name:=" & GetValue("title"))_
  .Link("innertext:=" & GetValue("about-us")).Highlight
```

Remember to release all dictionary instances at the end of the test.

```
Set LocaleCollection = Nothing
Set enLocale = Nothing
Set esLocale = Nothing
```

Let's understand this code in detail:

1. The locale is the parent collection containing all child locales: English, Spanish etc.

    a. Child Locale 1: enLocale

    b. Child Locale 2: esLocale

2. enLocale and esLocale contain definitions to object properties.

3. To get the correct property for any given locale, the code below is used:

```
GetValue("propertyName")
```

This approach is extensible because it can be used in both procedural- and object-oriented programming alike.

Advantages

⊙ It is only necessary to create a single library for all locales being tested

⊙ It is easy to implement

⊙ It will support both Object Repository and Descriptive Programming

Disadvantages

- It can become very difficult to maintain code if the number of locales increases

- The approach can cause bloated libraries as the locales increase. To counter this affect, use of separate library for each locale is recommended.

Using a Table-based Locale Map

This approach uses a data-source to store the locale definitions and uses a method to retrieve the use the correct locale depending on what is supplied as a global setting. This is data-driven localization handling!

Consider a data-source below containing locales for English and Spanish with a name assigned to each definition.

	A	B	C
1	Name	English	Spanish
2	title	Localization	localización
3	about-us	About Us	sobre nosotros
4	contact-us	Contact Us	contáctenos
5	our-offices	Our Offices	nuestras Oficinas
6	view-in-locale	View in Spanish	Ver en Inglés
7	communication	Communication	Comunicación
8	some-text	This is some text in english	Éste es un poco de texto en español

Figure 10.5 – Table of Localized Values

With the help of the data-source, the inline statements become extremely easy. The Name column is written in the inline statement whether you are using OR-style statements or DP.

This technique uses the following steps to implement localization:

1. The Locale is set in an associated library as a global variable.

2. Another global object (LocaleData) loads records from the data-source from a data builder (LoadLocaleData).

   a. The data builder runs a query against the data-source.

   b. All combinations are loaded against the Name column in key-item pairs.

3. QTP code uses inline descriptions calling the loaded global object (LocaleData) in either OR or DP format.

Let's begin by creating a global value for the locale being tested. Creating this value helps us make the change globally from a single place.

```
'1. Global settings variable
'This part goes in a function library
Public GlobalLocale : GlobalLocale = "Spanish"
```

Below is the function that is used to build data from the Excel file. Just like the previous approach with a dictionary object, this will also return a dictionary with key-value pairs. KEYS represents the entries in the Name column whereas VALUES represents the entries in either columns B (English) or C (Spanish).

```
'2a, 2b. LoadLocaleData runs a query against Excel and loads all data as
'          key-item pairs
'(This goes in a function library)
'
'Args:
' fileName As String: Excel file path
' sheet As Variant: Excel WorkSheet name or index
'Return: Scripting.Dictionary
Public Function LoadLocaleData(ByVal fileName, ByVal sheet)
  Dim adoConnection, sConnection, rstRecords, i, dic, sQuery, key, item
  Set LoadLocaleData = Nothing

  On Error Resume Next
    Set adoConnection = CreateObject("ADODB.Connection")

    'Connection string
    sConnection = "Provider=Microsoft.Jet.OLEDB.4.0;" &_
      "Data Source=" & fileName & ";" & _
      "Mode=1;" & _
      "Extended Properties=""Excel 8.0;HDR=YES;IMEX=1"";"

    adoConnection.Open sConnection

    If Err.Number > 0 Then
```

```
      Reporter.ReportEvent micFail, "LoadLocaleData", Err.Description
      Err.Clear : Exit Function
   End If


   Set rstRecords = CreateObject("ADODB.RecordSet")

   'Query to retrieve Name & Locale from Excel
   sQuery = "Select Name," & GlobalLocale & " from [" & sheet & "$]"

   rstRecords.Open sQuery, adoConnection, 1, 3, 1

   If Err.Number > 0 Then
      Reporter.ReportEvent micFail, "LoadLocaleData", Err.Description
      Err.Clear : Exit Function
   End If
 On Error Goto 0

 Set dic = CreateObject("Scripting.Dictionary")

 'Build the Scripting.Dictionary with data from Excel
 Do Until rstRecords.EOF
   For i = 0 To rstRecords.Fields.Count - 1
     key = rstRecords.Fields(i).Value
     item = rstRecords.Fields(rstRecords.Fields.Count - 1).Value
     dic.Add "" & key, "" & item

     Exit For
   Next

   rstRecords.MoveNext
 Loop

 Set LoadLocaleData = dic
End Function
```

The above function can be called in the following manner to make the collection live and ready for use:

```
'2. Global variable LocaleData created in function LoadLocaleData
```

```
'In test or associated library
Public LocaleData
Set LocaleData = LoadLocaleData(filename, sheet)
'Fail test if the Scripting.Dictionary was not created
If LocaleData Is Nothing Then ExitTest
```

Usage is shown below in both OR and DP styles:

```
'3. Inline statements use LocaleData to drive tests (OR style)
'Object Repository style
Browser(LocaleData("title")).Link(LocaleData("about-us")).Highlight
Browser(LocaleData("title")).WebElement(LocaleData("contact-us")).Highlight
Browser(LocaleData("title")).Link(LocaleData("communication")).Highlight
Browser(LocaleData("title")).Link(LocaleData("some-text")).Highlight
```

```
'3. Inline statements use LocaleData to drive tests (DP style)
'Programmatic Description style
Browser("title:=" & LocaleData("title"))_
  .Link("innertext:=" & LocaleData("about-us"), "index:=0").Highlight
Browser("title:=" & LocaleData("title"))_
  .WebElement("innertext:=" & LocaleData("contact-us")).Highlight
Browser("title:=" & LocaleData("title"))_
  .Link("innertext:=" & LocaleData("communication")).Highlight
Browser("title:=" & LocaleData("title"))_
  .Link("innertext:=" & LocaleData("some-text"), "index:=0").Highlight
```

This may look confusing, but it's quite a simple technique to grasp. Let's dig deeper to understand the details.

1. A global variable (GlobalLocale) determines against which locale testing is to be done.

2. A data-source (Excel in our case) houses the locale definitions with a name assigned to each.

    a. English (en-us)

        i. about-us -> About Us

        ii. contact-us -> Contact Us

        iii. communication -> Communication

      iv.   some-text -> This is some text in English

  b. Spanish (es-es)

      i.   about-us -> Nosotros

      ii.   contact-us -> Contacto

      iii.   communication -> Comunicación

      iv.   some-text -> Éste es un poco de texto en español

3. A method (LoadLocaleData) executes and loads the above key-item pairs.

4. Key-item pairs are passed to a global object (LocaleData) that is accessible by all actions of the QTP test.

5. QTP code uses the Name definitions stored in LocaleData to execute tests against the AUT.

This technique then is a more efficient approach in comparison to Technique 2 as it has all of its advantages, but none of the drawbacks. Also, because a unique name is assigned to each locale definition, it becomes easy to maintain data if there is a change to the UI. If there is a change in verbiage, simply changing the verbiage in the data-source will fix the test. If the element itself is removed, inline QTP statement can be removed from the code without having to manipulate the data-source.

Advantages

◉ It supports Ordinal Identifiers in descriptions, unlike Technique 2 above

◉ It works for both Object Repository and Descriptive Programming

◉ It is easy to maintain

Disadvantages

◉ Because using this approach adds a layer of dependency to the test suite, in the event of something happening to it can cause the affected tests to break. Good risk management can prevent this.

Using a Simple Class-based Delimited Collection

So far, we have covered procedural approach to handling localization. This technique uses an object-based approach and is a little different, so let's try to understand it at a high level before digging deeper into it. This is how localization is implemented here:

1. Create a Class module with the UI's functionality wrapped in it.

2. Create a Scripting.Dictionary with key-item pairs assigned to it (Content()):

    a. Similar to the approach with the Excel map

    b. key -> name

    c. item -> value of the property

3. The method with UI events (Run()) uses the description returned from the Scripting. Dictionary.

    a. The returned value depends upon the locale being tested.

    b. Localization Class is used to return locale definitions.

4. Locale.Define sets the locale to be tested against and it can changed any number of times to accommodate different locales at any given UI.

The code in this section shows two classes:

1. Localization Class

    a. Containing the mechanism for supplying the correct value associated with the locale.

    b. Based on indexes.

        i.   If the description is [English%Spanish], English = 0, Spanish = 1.

        ii. If the description is [Spanish%Japanese%English], Spanish = 0, Japanese = 1, English = 2.

2. LocalizationTest Class (MainPage)

    a. Containing UI events (.Set, .Click, .Highlight, .GetROProperty etc.).

    b. Containing locale definitions.

    c. May contain any other code deemed necessary to drive the events (not listed here).

        i.   Demonstrated in the Select...Case statement.

The class Localization below can be considered to be a parser for the running locale and contains the method to extract the correct definition for the executing locale. If another delimiter is to be used, it can be changed from within this code block, although if this is done, please remember to update the change in Content() above as well.

```
Class Localization
  Private locale_

  'Set the locale definition
  Public Property Let Define(ByVal Value)
    locale_ = Value
  End Property

  'Returns the word definition
  Public Default Property Get Definition(ByVal sItem)
    Dim arrItems

    arrItems = Split(sItem, Delimiter)

    Select Case locale_
      Case "en-us" : sItem = arrItems(0)
      Case "es-es" : sItem = arrItems(1)
    End Select

    Definition = sItem
  End Property

  Private Property Get Delimiter()
    Delimiter = "%"
  End Property
End Class

Public Locale
Set Locale = New Localization
```

A simple LocalizationTest Class for MainPage containing various locales is shown below. It contains two public methods: Run and ReleaseContent. The private method Content contains the definitions pertaining to the locales and is used by public Run().

```
Class MainPage
  Private locales_ 'Scripting.Dictionary containing delimited descriptions

  Public Default Function Run()
    With Browser(Content("title")) 'OR style object
      .Link("innertext:=" & Content("about-us")).Highlight 'DP style object
      .Link(Content("contact-us")).Highlight 'OR style object
      .Link(Content("communication")).Highlight 'OR style object
    End With

    ReleaseContent
  End Function

  Private Function Content(sItem)
    If Not TypeName(locales_) = "Dictionary" Then
      Set locales_ = CreateObject("Scripting.Dictionary")

      With locales_
        'Parent
        .Add "title", "Localization%localización"
        'Child
        .Add "about-us", "About Us%sobre nosotros"
        .Add "contact-us", "Contact Us%contáctenos"
        .Add "communication", "Communication%comunicación"
      End With
    End If

    Content = Locale.Definition(locales_(sItem))
  End Function

  Public Sub ReleaseContent
    Set locales_ = Nothing
  End Sub
End Class

Set main_Page = New MainPage
```

The following code can be used to execute a given module. The first statement defines the module being tested and the second statement executes the code-block that tests some functionality.

```
'Test: Action1
Locale.Define = "en-us"
main_Page.Run

Locale.Define = "es-es"
main_Page.Run
```

Unlike the previous approaches, this method does not use a global variable to define the locale to test against. This approach provides the flexibility to define the locale at any given time using Locale.Define.

Even though this approach is very much like the previous one with the data-source, it omits the need to create an external source to depend upon feeding the correct descriptions. This may be advantageous in environments where creating a standalone data-source does not work well (see the Disadvantages section of the previous approach, "Using a Table-based Locale Map"). All properties are stored within the same Class, and this enables a single location of maintenance for changes in flow as well as changes in locale verbiage. In addition, this approach also enables testing multiple locales on the same UI by simply changing the locale definition and running the correct module.

Advantages

- ◉ It supports testing multiple locales.

- ◉ All descriptions are stored within the library.

- ◉ It is object–based.

Disadvantages

- ◉ The engineer must be familiar with OO techniques to utilize it well.

- ◉ Because this technique also uses delimiters, as the number of locales increase, maintenance can become cumbersome in cases where locale strings are very long.

Using a Class-based Centralized Delimited Collection

This approach takes its inspiration from the previous technique where each functional class or PageObject (MainPage, Login, and Logout etc.) contains their respective localized definitions. The above approach can be modified to utilize a single object containing all localized definitions.

Using this method condenses our functional classes (MainPageClass and LoginPageClass) by taking out all the locale definitions as shown here:

```
Class MainPageClass
  'Scripting.Dictionary built from LocalizedRepository
  '@see BuildDefinitions
  Private Content

  Public Sub Action()
    Me.BuildDefinitions()
    With Browser("name:=" & Content("title")) 'OR style
      .Link("innertext:=" & Content("about-us")).Highlight 'DP style
    End With
  End Sub

  'builds the Dictionary from LocalizedRepository
  Public Sub BuildDefinitions()
    If Not TypeName(Content) = "Dictionary" Then
      Set Content = LocalizedRepository.MainPage()
    End If
  End Sub

  Private Sub Class_Terminate()
    Set Content = Nothing
  End Sub
End Class

Dim MainPage
Set MainPage = New MainPageClass

Class LoginPageClass
  'Scripting.Dictionary built from LocalizedRepository
  'see BuildDefinitions
  Private Content
```

```
  Public Sub Action()
    Me.BuildDefinitions()

    With Browser("name:=" & Content("title"))
      .Link("innertext:=" & Content("contact-us")).Highlight
      .Link("innertext:=" & Content("communication")).Highlight
      .Link("innertext:=" & Content("view-in")).Click
    End With
  End Sub

  'builds the Dictionary from LocalizedRepository
  Public Sub BuildDefinitions()
    If Not TypeName(Content) = "Dictionary" Then
      Set Content = LocalizedRepository.MainPage()
    End If
  End Sub

  Private Sub Class_Terminate()
    Set Content = Nothing
  End Sub
End Class

Dim LoginPage
Set LoginPage = New LoginPageClass
```

Below is how our functional class will be called. The locale will be set before running actions against the UI and followed by building the correct definitions for the locale.

```
'Test English
LocalizedRepository.CurrentLocale "en-us"

Call MainPage.Action()
Call LoginPage.Action()

'Test Spanish
LocalizedRepository.CurrentLocale "es-es"

Call MainPage.Action()
Call LoginPage.Action()
```

None of the locale text resides in our functional class. This streamlines our test code with events required to automate the UI and separates it with object management. The parsing occurs as soon as the class loads, making it ready to be fired with the correct locale definitions.

The private region variable 'Content' is loaded when BuildDefinitions() is called. 'Content' points to the MainPage function of the centralized repository containing all UI definitions only for the MainPage component. For all other components (and there can be many), separate implementations must be created as shown below (MainPage() and LoginPage()):

Because content is loaded in the BuildDefinitions routine of each functional class, it must be called every time new definitions are required and to avoid any errors during execution.

The centralized repository containing locale definitions is shown below:

```
Class CentralLocalizedRepository

  'Scripting.Dictionary containing locale definitions
  Private localeCollection_
  'Integer value pointing to the locale being tested
  Private currentLocale_

  'contains the localized definitions for Main page
  Public Function MainPage()
    Call Init()

    With localeCollection_
      .Add "title", "Localization%localización"></span>
      .Add "about-us", "About Us%sobre nosotros"
      .Add "contact-us", "Contact Us%contáctenos"
      .Add "communication", "Communication%comunicación"
      .Add "view-in", "View in Spanish% Ver en Inglés"
    End With

    Set MainPage = GetLocaleEx(localeCollection_)
  End Function

  'contains the localized definitions for Login page
  Public Function LoginPage()
```

```
    Call Init()

    With localeCollection_
      .Add "title", "Localization%localización"
      .Add "about-us", "About Us%sobre nosotros"
    End With

    Set LoginPage = GetLocaleEx(localeCollection_)
End Function

Private Sub Init()
    If TypeName(localeCollection_) = "Dictionary" Then
      localeCollection_.RemoveAll
    End If
End Sub

'Sets the value of currentLocale_
Public Sub CurrentLocale(ByVal Locale)
    Select Case Locale
      Case "en-us" : currentLocale_ = 0
      Case "es-es" : currentLocale_ = 1
    End Select
End Sub
' Replaces the ITEMS in the locale collection with the target locale  '

'   Call CurrentLocale("en-us")
'
'   collection.add "title", "Localization%localización"
'   collection.add "about-us", "About Us%sobre nosotros"
'
'   Set newLocale = GetLocaleEx(collection)
'
'   Output:
'     collection -> "title", "Localization"
'     collection -> "about-us", "About Us"
Private Function GetLocaleEx(ByVal collection)
    Dim keys, i

    keys = collection.keys
```

```
   For i = 0 To collection.Count - 1
      collection.Item(keys(i)) = Split(collection.Item(keys(i)), Delimiter)
(currentLocale_)
   Next

   Set GetLocaleEx = collection
 End Function

 Private Function Delimiter()
   Delimiter = "%"
 End Function

 'Create Scripting.Dictionary once only
 Private Sub Class_Initialize
   Set localeCollection_ = CreateObject("Scripting.Dictionary")
 End Sub

 Private Sub Class_Terminate
   If TypeName(localeCollection_) = "Dictionary" Then
     localeCollection_.RemoveAll
     Set localeCollection_ = Nothing
   End If
 End Sub
End Class


Public LocalizedRepository
Set LocalizedRepository = New CentralLocalizedRepository
```

As opposed to the previous technique, this brings all definitions of different functional classes under a single class, resulting in a more condensed functional class and forming single point of maintenance when changes in UI occur.

In this chapter, we have covered several approaches to performing localization testing with QTP. Because of the generic nature of some of these techniques, they can also be easily used with other technologies and test tools. After considering all techniques, it is quite obvious that the easiest to maintain in the long run, as the number of descriptions and locales grow, is the creation of an Excel Map.

Object Identification using XPath

Introduction

With QTP 11, HP launched several new web testing capabilities to provide engineers with greater flexibility when testing Web applications. One of the important additions was XPath for Object Identification, a query language for selecting nodes from an XML document. QTP automatically generates and assigns a XPath while recording objects on Web applications. However, this XPath is used in the background as a performance enhancement during test execution.

If QTP identifies the wrong object using the generated XPath, then it falls back to usual description properties. To force XPath based identification for an object, we need to add XPath as one of the description properties in the OR. To be able to use XPath based identification, having a sound understanding of XPath is highly recommended.

NOTE: The current XPath version is 2.0 but as per our observation QTP supports XPATH 1.0. QTP manual doesn't document this.

NOTE: Automatically-generated XPath Identifiers are NOT available through the Object Spy, the Add/Remove Properties dialog box, or the Object Identification dialog box.

NOTE: In the context of Web apps, XPath is an XML-based technique which is applied to HTML.

This first half of this section will provide an overview of XPath expressions, wildcards and operators.

To illustrate how XPath can identify target nodes, the following HTML source is used:

```html
<html>
  <head>
    <title>XPath</title>
    <style type='text/css'>
      body {background: #FFFFEE; font-family:Calibri, Corbel, Arial; font-size: 12px;}
      table {border: 1px solid #CCCCCC;}
      h4 {margin-bottom: -1px; font-variant: small-caps;}
      .row1 {background: #EEE;}
      .row2 {background: #DDD;}
      .row3 {background: #CCC;}
      .row4 {background: #BBB;}
      td {padding:5px;}
      .btn_blue {width: 75px; color: blue;}
```

```
      .btn_green {width: 75px; color: green;}
    </style>
  </head>
  <body>
    <h4>John Smith <input type=checkbox name="select" /></h4>
    <table id='table1'>
      <tr class='row1' id=BPT>
        <td>View ID</td>
        <td><input type='button' value='Button 1' class='btn_blue'
id='btnfirst'></td>
      </tr>
      <tr class='row2' id=QC>
        <td>View Address</td>
        <td><input type='button' value='Button 2' class='btn_blue'></td>
      </tr>
      <tr class='row3' id=QTP>
        <td>View Phone Number</td>
        <td><input type='button' value='Button 3' class='btn_green'></td>
      </tr>
    </table>
    <h4>Anne Anderson <input type="checkbox" name="select" checked=true
/></h4>
    <table id='table2'>
      <tr class='row1' id=BPT>
        <td>View ID</td>
        <td><input type='button' value='Button 4' class='btn_blue'></td>
      </tr>
      <tr class='row2' id=QC>
        <td>View Address</td>
        <td><input type='button' value='Button 5' class='btn_blue'></td>
      </tr>
      <tr class='row3' id=QTP>
        <td>View Phone Number</td>
        <td><input type='button' value='Button 6' class='btn_green'></td>
      </tr>
      <tr class='row4' id=QTP>
        <td>View Fax Number</td>
        <td><input type='button' value='Button 7' class='btn_green'> </td>
      </tr>
```

```
    </table>
  </body>
</html>
```

The output of the above HTML is shown below:

Figure 11.1 – XPath Demo web page

Automatic XPath – XPath Learned at Record Time

Using QTP 11 or later, it is possible to instruct QTP to automatically generate and store XPath values when learning web test objects. Note that, if during replay the automatically-learned XPath matches more than one object or matches a wrong object, the learned XPath will be ignored.

Automatically-generated XPath Identifiers are not available through the Object Spy, the Add/Remove Properties dialog box, or the Object Identification dialog box. In other words,

QTP doesn't show the generated XPath.

Options for automatic XPath Identifiers can be accessed from Tools > Options > Advanced tree.

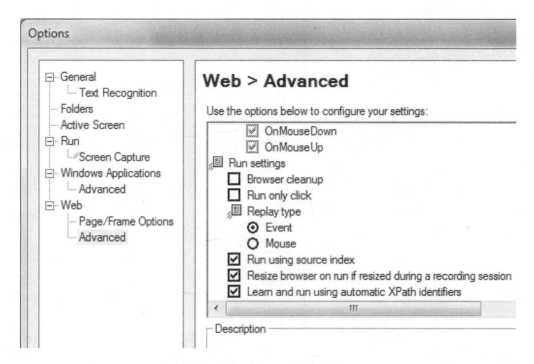

Figure 11.2 – Advanced Web Settings

Checking the 'Learn and run using automatic XPath identifiers' instructs QTP to generate an XPath for every web object and use it during replay.

NOTE: The Automatic XPath feature was added to QTP 11 to improve performance while replaying scripts.

Learning XPath on Firefox

Firefox provides different add-ons with which to test XPath on a currently open document.

To learn and explore XPath, we suggest that you install two important Firefox add-ons – Firebug and FirePath. The following image shows how the FirePath add-on works:

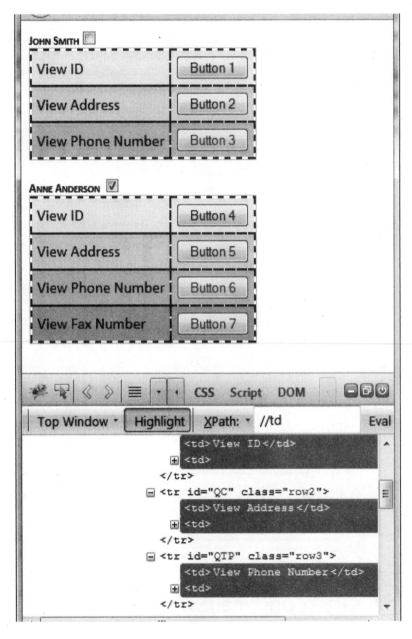

Figure 11.3 – FirePath Add-on for Firefox

The add-on highlights all objects that match the supplied XPath.

XPath Expressions, Wildcards, Operators and Functions

XPath can be used to select nodes in an XML or HTML document. In QTP with a web application, XPath expressions can be used to select target HTML nodes, which are simply test objects. Possible XPath expressions are described in this section.

Expression	Description	Expression	Description
node name	Selects all child nodes of the specified node.	`table`	Selects all TABLE nodes.
/	Selects from the root node.	`table/tr`	Selects all TR nodes that are children of the TABLE node.
//	Selects the named nodes, no matter where they appear in the document.	`//td`	Selects all TD nodes, no matter where they appear in the document.
.	Selects the current node.	`//h4[.='John Smith']`	Selects the H4 node which equals John Smith.
..	Selects the parent of the current node.	`tr/..`	Selects the parent node of TR node.
@	Selects by attribute.	`//input[@class='btn_blue']`	Selects the INPUT node where CLASS equals btn_blue.

Wildcards

There are instances in QTP where the target node (test object) is unknown at runtime and workarounds such as ChildObjects, ChildItem etc. are used to access it. The case of XPath is similar; it can drill down and select the target nodes with a combination of both Wildcards and Operators (next topic).

Wildcard	Description	Expresision with Wildcard	Description
*	Matches any element node.	/tr/td/*	Selects all child nodes of the TD element.
@*	Matches any node with an attribute.	//tr[@*]	Selects all TR nodes that have one or more attribute.

Operators

XPath Operators can be used to select nodes (test objects) based on certain conditions. They can also be used to return integers, strings or Boolean. The table below shows Operators available in XPath:

Operator	Description	Expression with Operator	Description
or	Or	age = 20 or age = 30	Returns a node-set of ages that equal 20 or 30. All other nodes will be discarded.
and	And	age > 20 and age < 30	Returns a node-set with ages 21 and 29. All other nodes will be discarded.
mod	Modulus (outputs the remainder of a division)	30 mod 20	Remainder 10
+	Addition	30 + 20	50
-	Subtraction	30 - 20	10
*	Multiplication	30 * 20	600
div	Division	100 div 20	5
|	Compute two node-sets	//name | //age	Returns a node-set of all name and age elements
=	Equal	age = 20	Returns a node-set with only age 20. All other nodes will be discarded.

Operator	Description	Expression with Operator	Description
!=	Not equal	`age != 20`	age not equal to 20. Nodes with age equal 20 will be discarded.
<	Smaller than	`age < 20`	Returns a node-set with ages less than 20. All other nodes will be discarded.
<=	Smaller than or equal to	`age <= 20`	Returns a node-set with ages less than or equal to 20. All other nodes will be discarded.
>	Greater than	`age > 20`	with ages more than 20. All other nodes will be discarded.
>=	Greather than or equal to	`age >= 20`	Returns a node-set with ages more than or equal to 20. All other nodes will be discarded.

XPath Functions

There are different sets of functions supported by XPath. For QTP's Object Identification however, we may require the following ones:

Function	Description	Example	Description
`contains(s1, s2)`	Returns true if s1 contains s2, els, returns false.	`//span[contains (text(),"book")]`	Selects the string element which contains the word "book".
`starts-with(s1,s2)`	Returns true if s1 starts with s2, otherwise returns false.	`//span[starts-with(text(),"b")]`	Selects the string element that starts with "b".
`ends-with(s1,s2)`	Returns true if s1 ends with s2, otherwise returns false.	`//span[ends-with(text(),"b")]`	Selects the string element that ends with "b".

In the next section, we will see how to put Wildcards, Operators and Functions into action.

Implementing XPath in QTP

In the previous section, we gave an introduction to XPath. Let's now use the Expressions, Operators and Wildcards in XPath to identify test objects in QTP.

Using XPath to identify specific nodes for our HTML example is shown below. Please note that some nodes can use more than one XPath for identification and several possible ways are shown in order to provide a deeper understanding.

NOTE: XPath Identifiers are so powerful that in QTP that they can completely remove the need to add more than a single property-value pair to identify objects.

NOTE: Do not confuse XPath with path to files or folders on a Windows system. A file-system path can have a slash at the end (C:\TestFolder\) but this is not true for XPath.

Selecting Nodes

In this section we will see how XPath can be used to select child nodes in a document.

Example 1: John Smith, Anne Anderson

Looking at the HTML at the beginning of this chapter, we know that both are H4 nodes. Let's first create some XPath to identify the John Smith WebElement. The HTML we need to consider is shown below followed by a few possible XPath selectors.

```
<body>
  <h4>John Smith <input type=checkbox name="select" /></h4>
```

Possible XPath	Comments
`//h4[contains(text(), 'John')]`	1. //h4 selects all the H4 nodes, no matter where they appear in the document. 2. The contains function then filters the selected H4 nodes that contain the word 'John'.
`//h4[text()='John Smith']`	//h4 selects all the H4 nodes where TEXT equals "John Smith".
`//h4[1]`	Selects the first H4 node.
`//body/h4[1]`	Selects the first H4 node that is the CHILD node of BODY.

Similarly, to select Anne Anderson, the following XPath can be used:

```
<body>
<!-- Other HTML -->
<h4>Anne Anderson <input type="checkbox" name="select" checked=true /></h4>
```

Possible XPath	Comments
`//h4[contains(text(), 'Anne')]`	1. //h4 selects the H4 nodes, no matter where they appear in the document. 2. The contains function then filters the selected H4 nodes that contain the word 'John'.
`//h4[2]`	//h4 selects all the H4 nodes and with text as "John Smith".
`//body/h4[2]`	Selects the first H4 node.

The above XPath will be written in QTP in the following manner:

```
'Selecting John Smith
Browser("XPath").WebElement("xpath:=//h4[1]").Click
'Selecting Anne Anderson

Browser("XPath").WebElement("xpath:=//h4[contains(text(), 'Anne')]").Click
```

233

NOTE: XPath property doesn't support Regular Expressions. It is not required to escape any of the special characters in the DP code as shown above. Functions such as 'contains' can be used as a replacement instead.

Example 2: View Address

This may be a bit more difficult as View Address appears twice in the document; both times, it is located in the first cell of the second row as shown in Figure 11.4. Let's see how we can distinguish between the two occurrences.

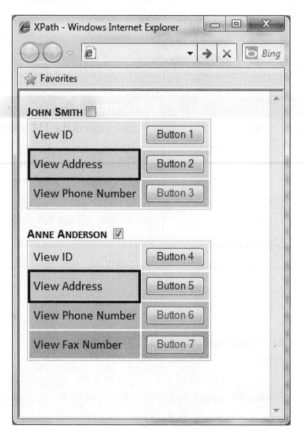

Figure 11.4 – XPath View Address demo page

```
<tr class='row2' id=QC>
  <td>View Address</td>
  <td><!-- Button 2 --></td>
```

Possible XPath for the first occurrence of View Address from the HTML source are shown below:

Possible XPath	Comments
`(// td[contains(text(),'Address')]) [1]`	`(//td[contains(text(),'Address')])` statement selects all TD nodes (collection) with TEXT containing Address. Ending the statement with [1] selects the first occurrence of the collection. Notice the parenthesis around //td. Without the parenthesis, the statement will fail to work. i. `(//td[contains(text(),'Address')])[1]` will work. ii. `//td[contains(text(),'Address')][1]` will not work.
`(//tr[@class='row2']/td[1])[1]`	Select the first item in the collection where TD is the first CHILD of TR with the attribute CLASS equals ROW2.

A few possible XPath expressions for the second occurrence are shown below:

1. `(//td[contains(text(),'Address')])[2]`

2. `(//tr[@class='row2']/td[1])[2]`

3. `(//tr[@id='QC']/td[1])[2]`

The above XPath will be written in QTP in the following way:

```
'Selecting 1st View Address
Browser("XPath").WebElement("xpath:=(//tr[@class='row2']/td[1])[1]").Click

'Selecting 2nd View Address
Browser("XPath")_
  .WebElement("xpath:=(//td[contains(text(),'Address')])[2]").Click
```

235

Example 3: View Fax Number

The WebElement View Fax Number appears only once in the document in the second TABLE. The HTML we need to consider to select this node is shown below:

```
<tr class='row4' id=QTP>
  <td>View Fax Number</td>
  <td> <input type='button' value='Button 7' class='btn_green'> </td>
</tr>
```

Possible XPath	Comments
`//td[contains(text(),'View Fax Number']`	Selects the TD node containing text View Fax Number.
`//tr[@class='row4']/td[1]`	1. `//tr[@class='row4']`: Selects all TR nodes with attribute CLASS equals row4. 2. `td[1]`: Using the collection, drill down to the first TD tag.

Example 4: Button 1

Let's see how XPath can be used to select this INPUT node. HTML and possible XPath for Button 1 are as follows:

```
<table id='table1'>
  <tr class='row1' id=BPT>
    <td>View ID</td>
    <td><input type='button' value='Button 1' class='btn_blue'
id='btnfirst'></td>
  </tr>
```

Possible XPath	Comments
`//input[@value='Button 1']`	Selects the INPUT node with the attribute VALUE equals Button 1.
`//input[@value='Button 1' and @class='btn_blue']`	Searches the INPUT node with the attribute VALUE equals Button 1 AND attribute CLASS equals btn_blue.
`//input[@id='btnfirst']`	Selects the INPUT node with the attribute ID equals btnfirst.

Possible XPath	Comments
`//td/input[@id='btnfirst']`	Selects the TD node with child equals INPUT which has the attribute ID equals btnfirst.
`(//table[@id='table1']/*/*)` `[1]/*[2]/input`	1. `//table[@id='table1']/*`: Searches all TABLE nodes with ID equals 'table1'. 2. `(//table[@id='table1']/*/*)[1]`: Drills down to all possible children (TR) and points to the first child node TR. 3. `/*[2]`: Drills down to all children (TD) of previously-selected TR node and points to the 2nd TD node. 4. `/input`: Finally, selects the INPUT node.

The above XPath is written in QTP in the following way:

```
'Selecting Button 1
Browser("XPath").WebButton("xpath:=//td/input[@id='btnfirst']").Click
```

```
'Selecting Button 1
Browser("XPath").WebButton("xpath:=(//table[@id='table1']/*/*)[1]/*[2]/
input").Click
```

Selecting Parent Nodes using Children

So far, we have seen how PARENT nodes can be used to drill down to select CHILDREN. This section shows how target nodes can be used to drill upwards to select PARENT nodes.

Example 1: Select the PARENT table of Button 6

HTML and possible XPath:

```
<table id='table2'>
  <tr class='row1' id=BPT>
    <td>View ID</td>
    <td><input type='button' value='Button 4' class='btn_blue'></td>
  </tr>
  <tr class='row2' id=QC>
    <td>View Address</td>
```

```
    <td><input type='button' value='Button 5' class='btn_blue'></td>
  </tr>
  <tr class='row3' id=QTP>
    <td>View Phone Number</td>
    <td><input type='button' value='Button 6' class='btn_green'></td>
  </tr>
```

Possible XPath	Comments
((//INPUT[@value='Button 6'])[1])/../../..	1. ((//INPUT[@value='Button 6'])[1]): Selects the INPUT tag with attribute VALUE equals Button 6. 2. /..: Climbs up once to select the TD node. 3. /..: Climbs up once from the selected TD node to select the TR node. 4. /..: Climbs up once from the selected TR node to select the TABLE node.

NOTE: There is a better and more flexible way of selecting neighboring nodes by the use of XPath Axes. We will look at these later in the chapter.

The above XPath will be written in QTP in the following way:

```
'Select the PARENT table of Button 6
Browser("XPath").WebElement("xpath:=((//INPUT[@value='Button 6'])
[1])/../../..").Click
```

Using Manual XPath with Object Repository

Using the concepts described in the tables above (Expressions, Wildcards and Operators), we have already seen how manual XPath can be used with Descriptive Programming. To use the same XPath using the Object Repository, follow these steps:

1. In the Object Repository, point to the target object and click the Add Properties button.

2. Select xpath from the list and click OK (as shown below):

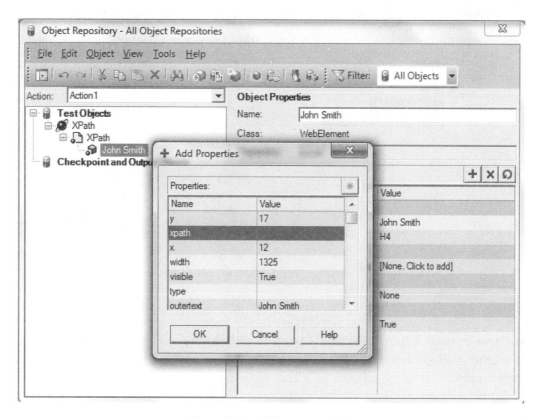

Figure 11.5 – Add Properties dialog

3. Add //h4[1] for the newly-added property and use Highlight in Application (John Smith would be highlighted).

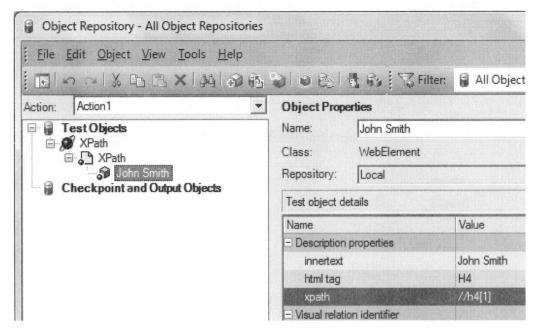

Figure 11.6 – Adding XPath property to object description

The above steps sum up how to use manual (user-defined) XPath with Object Repository.

We have covered XPath Wildcards, Operators and Functions in much detail. Yet there is another important aspect of XPath that can prove extremely important in Object Identification. This is the concept of XPath Axes. It can be used in the same fashion as Visual Relational Identifiers.

XPath Axes

An XPath axis can be used to identify nodes using a relationship between them. An axis defines the path relative to the current node.

AxisName	Description
ancestor	Selects all parent nodes (ancestors: parent, grandparent etc) of the current node.
ancestor-or-self	Selects all parent nodes (ancestors: parent, grandparent etc) of the current node and the node itself.
attribute	Contains all attributes of the current node.

AxisName	Description
child	Contains the children of the current node.
descendant	Contains all children of the current node.
descendant-or-self	Contains all children of the current node and the node itself.
following	Select all nodes in the document that come after the current node.
following-sibling	Contains all the following siblings of the current node. Note: Siblings are the same level nodes as the current node.
parent	Select the parent of the current node.
preceding	Contains all nodes that come before the current node.
preceding-sibling	Contains all siblings before the current node. Note: Siblings are the same level nodes as the current node.

Axes usage is shown below:

```
'without predicate
axisname::node_test
'with predicate
axisname::node_test[predicate]
```

Usage in QTP is as follows:

```
Browser("name:=Working with XPath.*")_
 .WebElement("xpath:=target/axisname::node_text[predicate]").Click
Browser("name:=Working with XPath.*")_
 .WebElement("xpath:=(//tr[@class='row2'])[1]/descendant::td[1]").Click
```

Understanding XPath Axes

To understand how the outlined axes work, let's now take into consideration the following HTML:

```
<html>
  <body>
    <div id="forsomereason">
      <span>This is before table</span><br/>
    </div>
    <table border="1">
```

241

```
        <tr>
          <TD>
            <span>Row1 span1</span><br/>
            <span id="selectednode">Row1 span2 <!-- target -->
              <p>TEST</p>
              <p>REST</p>
            </span><br/>
            <span>Row1 span3</span><br/>
          </TD>
        </tr>
        <tr>
          <TD>
            <span>Row2 span1</span><br/>
            <span>Row2 span2</span><br/>
            <span>Row2 span3</span><br/>
          </TD>
        </tr>
      </table>
      <div id="fornoreason">
        <span>This is after table</span>
      </div>
    </body>
</html>
```

The SPAN node with ID value of 'selectednode' will be used as a target. The groups of nodes selected that are selected are in bold and underlined format. The target (selectednode) is italicized.

ancestor

XPath selector: //SPAN[@id='selectednode']/ancestor::*

```
<html>
  <body>
    <div id="forsomereason">
      <span>This is before table</span><br/>
    </div>
    <table border="1">
      <tr>
```

```
    <td>
      <span>Row1 span1</span><br/>
      <span id="selectednode">Row1 span2 <!-- target -->
        <p>TEST</p>
        <p>REST</p>
      </span>
```

ancestor-or-self

XPath selector: //SPAN[@id='selectednode']/ancestor-or-self::*

```
<html>
  <body>
    <div id="forsomereason">
      <span>This is before table</span><br/>
    </div>
    <table border="1">
      <tr>
        <td>
          <span>Row1 span1</span><br/>
          <span id="selectednode">Row1 span2 <!-- target -->
            <p>TEST</p>
            <p>REST</p>
          </span><br/>
```

child

XPath selector: //SPAN[@id='selectednode']/child::*

```
<span id="selectednode">Row1 span2 <!-- target -->
  <p>TEST</p>
  <p>REST</p>
</span>
```

descendant

XPath selector: //SPAN[@id='selectednode']/descendant::*

```
<span id="selectednode">Row1 span2 <!-- target -->
  <p>TEST</p>
```

```
    <p>REST</p>
</span>
```

descendant-or-self

XPath selector: //SPAN[@id='selectednode']/descendant-or-self::*

```
<span id="selectednode">Row1 span2 <!-- target -->
    <p>TEST</p>
    <p>REST</p>
</span>
```

following

XPath selector: //SPAN[@id='selectednode']/following::*

```
            <span id="selectednode">Row1 span2 <!-- target -->
              <p>TEST</p>
              <p>REST</p>
            </span><br/>
            <span>Row1 span3</span>
            <br/>
          </TD>
      </tr>
      <tr>
        <td>
          <span>Row2 span1</span>
          <br/>
          <span>Row2 span2</span>
          <br/>
          <span>Row2 span3</span>
          <br/>
        </TD>
      </tr>
    </table>
    <div id="fornoreason">
      <span>This is after table</span>
    </div>
  </body>
```

```
</html>
```

following-sibling

XPath selector: //SPAN[@id='selectednode']/following-sibling::*

```
<span id="selectednode">Row1 span2 <!-- target -->
  <p>TEST</p>
  <p>REST</p>
</span>
<br/>
<span>Row1 span3</span>
<br/>
```

parent

XPath selector: //SPAN[@id='selectednode']/parent::*

```
<td>
  <span>Row1 span1</span><br/>
  <span id="selectednode">Row1 span2 <!-- target -->
    <p>TEST</p>
    <p>REST</p>
  </span><br/>
  <span>Row1 span3</span><br/>
</td>
```

preceding

XPath selector: //SPAN[@id='selectednode']/preceding::*

```
<html>
  <body>
    <div id="forsomereason">
      <span>This is before table</span>
      <br/>
    </div>
    <table border="1">
      <tr>
        <TD>
```

```
<span>Row1 span1</span>
<br/>
<span id="selectednode">Row1 span2 <!-- target -->
```

 NOTE: Preceding selects all tags that begin and end before the target.

preceding-sibling

XPath selector: //SPAN[@id='selectednode']/preceding-sibling::*

```
<span>Row1 span1</span>
<br/>
<span id="selectednode">Row1 span2 <!-- target -->
   <p>TEST</p>
   <p>REST</p>
</span><br/>
<span>Row1 span3</span><br/>
```

Let's now cover some examples, taking into consideration the HTML source at the beginning of this chapter.

Example 1: Use Button 3 to climb up to its TABLE

This is similar to the example we saw in the section 'Selecting Parent Nodes using Children' but instead of using the XPath expression /.., we will use axes. The target HTML and XPath axis is shown below:

```
<table id='table1'> "!-- destination -->
  <tr class='row1' id=BPT>
    <td>View ID</td>
    <td><input type='button' value='Button 1' class='btn_blue'
id='btnfirst'></td>
  </tr>
  <tr class='row2' id=QC>
    <td>View Address</td>
    <td><input type='button' value='Button 2' class='btn_blue'></td>
```

```
  </tr>
  <tr class='row3' id=QTP>
    <td>View Phone Number</td>
    <td><input type='button' value='Button 3' class='btn_green'></td>
  </tr>
</table>
```

Following are the 2 possible XPath axes used to move up from the button (<input>) to its parent Table:

```
1. //input[@value='Button 3']/parent::td/parent::tr/parent::tbody/
parent::table
2. (//input[@value='Button 3'])[1]/ancestor::table
```

The above XPath will be written in QTP as shown below:

```
'Use Button 3 to climb up to its TABLE
Browser("XPath").WebElement("xpath:=(//input[@value='Button 3'])[1]/
ancestor::table").Click
```

Example 2: Use TR[@CLASS=ROW4] row to identify preceding rows

This example shows how one anchor row can be used to identify neighboring rows.

```
<tr class='row1' id=BPT> <!-- destination -->
  <td>View ID</td>
  <td><input type='button' value='Button 4' class='btn_blue'></td>
</tr>
<tr class='row2' id=QC> <!-- destination -->
  <td>View Address</td>
  <td><input type='button' value='Button 5' class='btn_blue'></td>
</tr>
<tr class='row3' id=QTP> <!-- destination -->
  <td>View Phone Number</td>
  <td><input type='button' value='Button 6' class='btn_green'></td>
</tr>
<tr class='row4' id=QTP> <!-- target -->
  <td>View Fax Number</td>
  <td> <input type='button' value='Button 7' class='btn_green'> </td>
```

```
</tr>
```

1. Identify the first row with attribute ROW1: (//tr[@class='row4']/preceding-
   sibling::tr)[1]

2. Identify the second row with attribute ROW2: (//tr[@class='row4']/preceding-
   sibling::tr)[2]

3. Identify the third row with attribute ROW3: (//tr[@class='row4']/preceding-
   sibling::tr)[3]

The above XPath will be written in QTP as follows:

```
'1. Identify the first row with attribute ROW1
Browser("XPath").WebElement("xpath:=(//tr[@class='row4']/preceding-
sibling::tr)[1]").Click
```

Example 3: Use View ID to identify Button 1

This example is a little different from the previous ones we have seen. Here we show how to use View ID (TD node) to move to the sibling TD node and drill down once to select the CHILD node:

```
<td>View ID</td> <!-- target -->
<td>
  <input type='button' value='Button 1' class='btn_blue' id='btnfirst'> <!--
destination -->
</td>
```

1. (//td[.='View ID'])[1]/following-sibling::td/child::input

The above XPath will be written in QTP in the following way:

```
Browser("XPath").WebButton("xpath:=(//td[.='View ID'])[1]/following-
sibling::td/child::input").Click
```

Example 4: Use View ID to identify Button 4

```
<td>View ID</td> <!-- target -->
<td>
  <input type='button' value='Button 4' class='btn_blue'> <!-- destination
-->
</td>
```

1. `(//td[.='View ID'])[2]/following-sibling::td/child::input`

The above XPath will be written in QTP as below:

```
Browser("XPath").WebElement("xpath:=(//td[.='View ID'])[2]/following-
sibling::td/child::input").Click
```

Example 5: Use View Address row to identify its TD cells

```
<tr class='row2' id=QC> <!-- target -->
  <td>View Address</td> <!-- destination -->
  <td> <!-- destination -->
    <input type='button' value='Button 2' class='btn_blue'>
  </td>
</tr>
```

Resulting XPath using axes:

1. First cell: `(//tr[@class='row2'])[1]/descendant::td[1]`

2. Second cell: `(//tr[@class='row2'])[1]/descendant::td[2]`

The following code shows how the above XPath will be written in QTP:

```
'First cell
Browser("XPath")_
  .WebElement("xpath:=(//tr[@class='row2'])[1]/descendant::td[1]").Click
```

XPath Limitations and Unsupported XPath in QTP

A few limitations of XPath are outlined in this section. It may sometimes be difficult to tell if the XPath supplied is incorrect or if QTP does not support it.

XPath to identify multiple objects

XPath can be used to identify different type of objects using a single XPath expression. Consider this XPath expression:

```
//H4 | //td//input
```

This statement will identify all H4 nodes present on the HTML page as well as all input controls present inside a table cell. The following image shows which controls the XPath will match:

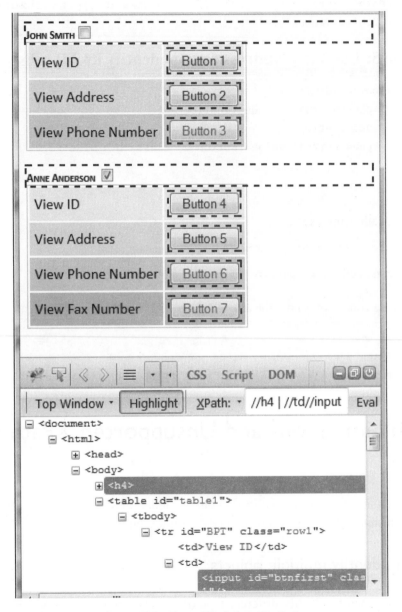

Figure 11.7 – Target XPath from FirePath

Let's put the same XPath in action inside QTP using the description object:

```
Dim oDesc
Set oDesc = Description.Create
oDesc("xpath").value = "//H4 | //td//input"
Set allObjects = Browser("Browser").Page("Page").ChildObjects(oDesc)
For i = 0 to allObjects.Count - 1
  Print "Type = " & allObjects(i).GetTOProperty("micclass") & _
    ", HTML = " & allObjects(i).GetROProperty("outerhtml")
Next
```

When we run the above code, the following output is produced:

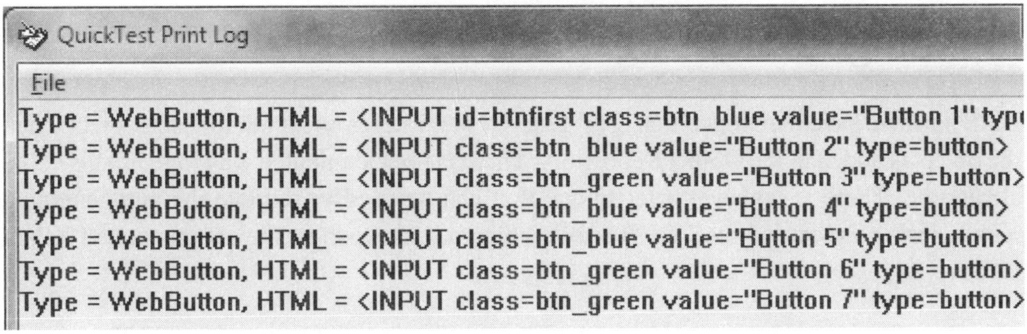

Figure 11.8 – Output without oDesc("micclass").Value = "WebElement"

Now the surprising thing is that none of the H4 elements are present in the output. So let's update our code and add an additional line oDesc("micclass").value = "WebElement". After running the code again we will find that the output is as expected.

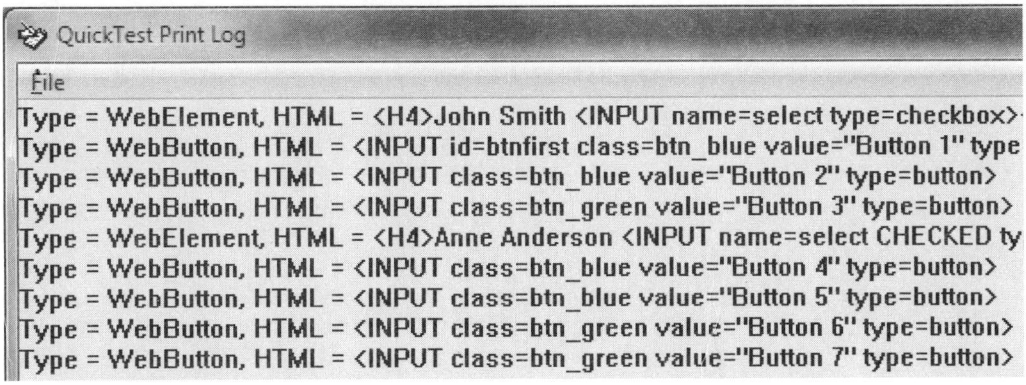

Figure 11.9 – Output with oDesc("micclass").Value = "WebElement"

This happens because ChildObjects requires micclass to be assigned as WebElement when searching for objects which will be represented as WebElement.

 NOTE: For more information on ChildObjects, see Chapter 5.

Fetching the QTP-generated XPATH

Until now, we have mentioned that QTP generates and stores an XPath for each object when the object is added to the Object Repository. There is no documented way to fetch this value at runtime. There is however a technique that can be used to retrieve the autogenerated XPath during a recorded session. The following code shows how the autogenerated XPath is retrieved:

```
sXPath = Browser("Browser").WebEdit("Search").GetTOProperty("_XPath")
```

Object Identification using CSS

As we saw in the XPath chapter, Object Identification can be made very flexible, even offering the ability to utilize the unique elements to identify the non-unique ones. Just like with XPath, we will use CSS Selectors to identify objects by directly locating the target node and also by using a neighboring node as an anchor.

This is going to be a familiar topic for a web developer or anyone who has experience styling web-pages. A CSS Selector is used to style an element by pointing to its tag in conjunction with any attributes associated with that tag. The syntax of using a CSS Selector in QTP is similar to using any other property-value pair in the Object Identification separated by the := delimiter.

The following code statement shows CSS selector usage for a WebButton with the HTML TAG equals INPUT and CLASS equals btnTarget.

```
Browser("CSS Chapter").WebButton("css:=input.btnTarget").Click
```

To understand how CSS Selectors work, let's use the following web page as an example:

```html
<html>
  <head>
    <title>CSS</title>
    <style type='text/css'>
      body {background: #FFFFEE; font-family:Calibri, Corbel, Arial; font-size: 12px;}
      table {border: 1px solid #CCCCCC;}
      h4 {margin-bottom: -1px; font-variant: small-caps;}
      .row1 {background: #EEE;}
      .row2 {background: #DDD;}
      .row3 {background: #CCC;}
      .row4 {background: #BBB;}
      td {padding:5px;}
      .btn_blue {width: 75px; color: blue;}
      .btn_green {width: 75px; color: green;}
    </style>
  </head>
  <body>
    <h4>John Smith <input type=checkbox name="select" /></h4>
    <table id='table1'>
      <tr class='row1' id=BPT>
        <td>View ID</td>
        <td><input type='button' value='Button 1' class='btn_blue' id='btnfirst'></td>
      </tr>
      <tr class='row2' id=QC>
        <td>View Address</td>
        <td><input type='button' value='Button 2' class='btn_blue'></td>
      </tr>
      <tr class='row3' id=QTP>
        <td>View Phone Number</td>
        <td><input type='button' value='Button 3' class='btn_green'></td>
      </tr>
    </table>
    <h4>Anne Anderson <input type="checkbox" name="select" checked=true /></h4>
    <table id='table2'>
```

```
    <tr class='row1' id=BPT>
      <td>View ID</td>
      <td><input type='button' value='Button 4' class='btn_blue'></td>
    </tr>
    <tr class='row2' id=QC>
      <td>View Address</td>
      <td><input type='button' value='Button 5' class='btn_blue'></td>
    </tr>
    <tr class='row3' id=QTP>
      <td>View Phone Number</td>
      <td><input type='button' value='Button 6' class='btn_green'></td>
    </tr>
    <tr class='row4' id=QTP>
      <td>View Fax Number</td>
      <td><input type='button' value='Button 7' class='btn_green'> </td>
    </tr>
  </table>
  </body>
</html>
```

The output from the above HTML is shown here:

Figure 12.1 – CSS Demo web page

Some of the important CSS patterns are described below:

Pattern	Description
*	Matches any node.
p	Matches any P (paragraph) node.
table tr	Matches any TR node that is the descendant of TABLE node.
table > tr	Matches any TR node that is the child of TABLE node.
h4 + table	Matches any TABLE node that is preceded by H4.

In the next table, possible CSS Selectors are provided along with examples.

 NOTE: The CSS expressions in the examples below come from the HTML source at the beginning of this chapter.

Selector	Description	Example	Description
.class	Selects all elements with the supplied CLASS (CSS1).	.row1	Selects all elements where CLASS = row1.
#id	Selects the element with the supplied ID (CSS1).	#table1	Selects the element with ID = table1.
*	Selects all elements (CSS2).	*	Selects all elements.
element	Selects the supplied elements (CSS1).	Input	Selects all <input> elements.
[attribute]	Selects all elements with the supplied attribute (CSS2).	[id]	Selects all elements with the ID attribute.
[attribute=value]	Selects all elements with the supplied attribute where ATTRIBUTE equals VALUE (CSS2).	[class=btn_blue]	where the CLASS attribute equals btn_blue.

Selector	Description	Example	Description
[attribute~=value]	Selects the element whose ATTRIBUTE is a list of whitespace-separated values, one of which is exactly equal to VALUE (CSS2).	[innertext~=John]	Selects the element where the INNERTEXT is a list of whitespace-separated values, one of which is exactly equal to JOHN.
[attribute^=value]	Selects all elements where ATTRIBUTE value begins with VALUE (CSS3).	[class^=btn]	Selects all elements where the CLASS attribute begins with btn.
[attribute$=value]	Selects all elements where ATTRIBUTE value ends with VALUE (CSS3).	[class$=green]	Selects all elements where the CLASS attribute ends with green.
[attribute*=value]	Selects all elements where ATTRIBUTE value contains the substring VALUE (CSS3).	[class*=w4]	Selects all elements where the CLASS attribute contains the substring w4.
:first-of-type	Selects every element that is the first child of its parent (CSS3).	input:first-of-type	Selects every INPUT element that is the first INPUT element of its parent.
:last-of-type	Selects every element that is the last child of its parent (CSS3).	input:last-of-type	Selects every INPUT element that is the last INPUT element of its parent.
:only-of-type	Selects every element that is the only child of its parent (CSS3).	input:only-of-type	Selects every INPUT element that is the only INPUT element of its parent.
:nth-child(n)	Selects every element that is the nth child of its parent (CSS3).	input:nth-child(1)	Selects every INPUT element that is the first child of its parent.

Selector	Description	Example	Description
:nth-of-type(n)	Selects every specified element that is the nth element of its parent (CSS3).	input:nth-of-type(1)	Selects every INPUT element that is the first INPUT element of its parent.
:nth-last-of-type(n)	Selects every specified element that is the nth element of its parent, counting from the last child (CSS3).	input:nth-last-of-type(1)	Selects every INPUT element that is the first element of its parent, starting from the last child.

The next table details the CSS pseudo-classes.

Pseudo-Class	Description	Example	Description
:last-child	Selects every element that is the child of its parent (CSS3).	td:last-child	Selects every TD element that is the last child of its parent.
:root	Selects the document root element (CSS3).	:root	Selects the document root element.
:enabled	Selects every specified element that is enabled (CSS3).	input:enabled	Selects every enabled INPUT element.
:disabled	Selects every specified element that is disabled (CSS3).	input:disabled	Selects every disabled INPUT element.
:checked	Selects every specified element that is checked (CSS3).	input:checked	Selects every checked INPUT element.

Testing CSS Selectors with FirePath

As shown in the XPath chapter, we can use the following two Firefox add-ons to test CSS selectors: Firebug, FirePath. After installing the add-ons, select CSS as the target Selector.

Figure 12.2 – Selecting CSS Option from FirePath

The next figure shows how the FirePath add-on works with a CSS selector. The first <H4> tag is highlighted when the h4:first-of-type CSS selector is supplied to FirePath.

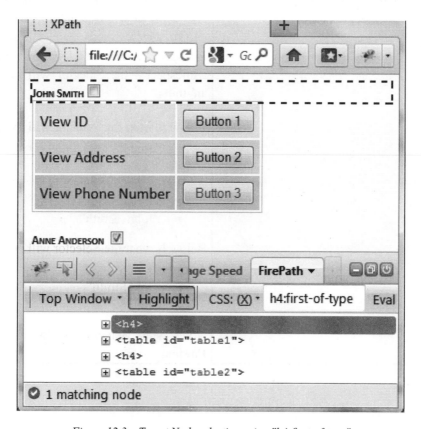

Figure 12.3 – Target Node selection using "h4:first-of-type"

Implementing CSS Selectors in QTP

In the table, an introduction to several CSS selectors has been provided. Let's use the CSS concepts along with the defined Selectors to identify test objects using the sample HTML source above.

Example 1: John Smith

John Smith is within the H4 tag. Its TEXT value is used to implement Object Identification in this example. Below is the target HTML used:

```
<body>
  <h4>John Smith <input type=checkbox name="select" /></h4>
```

CSS Expression	Comments
h4[innertext~='John']	This Selector will match only the complete text, a list of whitespace-separated values, one of which exactly equals John (notice the spaces). Also, if 'John' contains any whitespaces, the Selector will not match anything.
	Below is what the Selector will match:
	• "John"
	• " John"
	• "John "
	• " John "
	• "John Smith"
	Below is what the Selector will not match:
	• "J ohn"
	• "JohnSmith"
	• "JohnS."
	Note: This Selector works in IE, not Firefox.

CSS Expression	Comments
h4:first-of-type	The first-of-type pseudo-class allows the selection of the first sibling of its type. This Selector will select the first H4 (John Smith) to appear in the document.
h4[innertext*='John'] h4[innertext*='ohn S'] h4[innertext*='John S']	Matches any string that contains any of the following: • "John" • "ohn S" • "John S"
h4[innertext$='Smith']	Matches any string that ends with Smith. It will also match any string that ends with: • "mith" • "John Smith" • " Smith" • "n Smith"

Example 2: Table with attribute ID='table2'

The target HTML for the table in question is shown below:

```
<body>
  <h4>John Smith <input type=checkbox name="select" /></h4>
  <table id='table1'>
    <!--other nodes -->
  <h4>Anne Anderson <input type="checkbox" name="select" checked=true /></
h4>
  <table id='table2'>
```

CSS Expression	Comments
table + h4 + table	This pattern will select any sibling TABLE (table2) node preceded by H4 where H4 is preceded by a sibling TABLE (table1)'.
table#table2	The # symbol is used to select an element by its ID. This statement will select a TABLE node that has ID equals table2.

CSS Expression	Comments
table:last-of-type	The last-of-type pseudo-class allows selection of the last sibling of its type. This Selector will select the last TABLE node to appear in the document. In our example, the target table is last to appear in the document.
table:nth-of-type(2)	The use of nth-of-type(n) pseudo-class will point to the NODE that occurs Nth time in the document.

NOTE: When working with CSS Selectors, the first item will start at 1, not 0.

Example 3: Button 2 of Table 1

In the previous two examples, we have seen how to identify a heading and a table node. In this example, let's see how to identify the below INPUT node.

```
<td><input type='button' value='Button 2' class='btn_blue'></td>
```

CSS Expression	Comments
input[value='Button 2']	Selects the WebButton where the VALUE attribute equals Button 2.
td > input[value='Button 2']	Selects the WebButton drilling down from its parent TD which has attribute VALUE equals Button 2.
input[value='Button 2'] [class='btn_blue']	Uses multiple attributes to identify Button 2. Selects any INPUT tag which has the attribute VALUE equals Button 2 and the attribute CLASS equals btn_blue.

Example 4: Identify the Checkbox in 'checked' state

The checkbox in question is beside the Anne Anderson H4 tag. The target HTML to consider is the following:

```
<h4>Anne Anderson <input type="checkbox" name="select" checked=true /></h4>
```

CSS Expression	Comments
`h4 > input:checked`	Matches any CHECKED INPUT node that is the child of H4.
`input:checked`	Selects every checked INPUT node.

Example 5: Identify the Checkbox in 'unchecked' state

In the previous example, we saw how to identify the checkbox in its checked state. Even though we are working with a checkbox, there are different ways of identifying the target using CSS. Below is the HTML for the checkbox:

```
<h4>John Smith <input type=checkbox name="select" /></h4>
```

Note that this checkbox is the first to appear in the HTML.

CSS Expression	Comments
`h4:first-child > input`	Points to the first H4 child of BODY node. Then selects the INPUT child node.
`h4:first-child :nth-child(1)`	Points to the first H4 child of BODY node. Then selects the first child node.

nth-child(n) Pseudo-Class

For the next example, let's examine the list shown below:

```
<title>CSS Chapter</title>
<!-- HTML -->
<ol id="nameslist" name="names">
  <li>John</li>
  <li>Anne</li>
  <li>Mary</li>
  <li>Will</li>
  <li>Joseph</li>
</ol>
```

CSS selectors can also be used to separate each list item using the nth-child(x) pseudo-class. To first select the target list, its ID property can be used as shown below:

```
Browser("CSS Chapter").WebElement("css:=#nameslist").Highlight
```

```
Browser("CSS Chapter").WebElement("css:=ol#nameslist").Highlight
```

To find the items of the list, nth-child(x) can be used:

```
'First item in the list
Browser("CSS Chapter").WebElement("css:=#nameslist :nth-child(1)").
Highlight
```

 NOTE: When working with CSS Selectors, unlike zero-based VBScript, the first item will start at 1, not 0.

For the second to the fifth items in the list, the following index may be used for the pseudo-class:

```
css:=#nameslist :nth-child(2)
css:=#nameslist :nth-child(3)
css:=#nameslist :nth-child(4)
css:=#nameslist :nth-child(5)
```

ObjectRepositoryUtil

QTP provides an Object Repository Automation API called ObjectRepositoryUtil. This API provides a set of functions that can be used to read and/or write contents to a Shared Object Repository (SOR). It can be used to update an external Object Repository except the one already loaded in the memory.

There is a common misconception that this API can be used to add objects dynamically to their script. This understanding is incorrect. It is possible, however, to create an OR using the API and load it in the script using the RepositoriesCollection utility object.

Before proceeding further, it would be beneficial to list all the methods supported by ObjectRepositoryUtil. These are listed in the following table:

Method Name	Description
AddObject	Adds the specified object to the Object Repository under the specified parent object.
Convert	Converts the specified Object Repository file (version 8.2.1 or earlier) to the current format.
CopyObject	Creates a copy of the specified object in the Object Repository.
ExportToXML	Exports the specified Object Repository to the specified XML file.
GetAllObjects	Retrieves all objects under the specified parent object.
GetAllObjectsByClass	Retrieves all objects of the specified class under the specified parent object.
GetChildren	Retrieves all direct children of the specified parent object.
GetChildrenByClass	Retrieves all direct children of the specified class under a specified parent.
GetLogicalName	Retrieves the name of the specified object.
GetObject	Retrieves the object according to the specified path.
GetObjectByParent	Retrieves the object according to the specified parent object and object name.
ImportFromXML	Imports the specified XML file to the specified Object Repository.
Load	Loads the specified Object Repository file.
RemoveObject	Removes the specified object from the Object Repository.
RenameObject	Renames the specified object in the Object Repository.
Save	Saves any changes made while running an Object Repository Automation script.
UpdateObject	Updates the Object Repository with any changes made to the specified object.

Converting Between TSR Files and XML Files

We can use the ExportToXML method to convert a TSR file to XML file.

```
Set ORUtil = CreateObject("Mercury.ObjectRepositoryUtil")
ORUtil.ExportToXML "C:\Temp\SharedOR.tsr", "C:\Temp\XMLSharedOR.XML"
```

NOTE: The method cannot export BDB files, which is the format for the Local Object Repository.

NOTE: If the destination file already exists, the method will throw an error.

Similarly we can use the ImportFromXML method to create a TSR file from an XML file:

```
ORUtil.ImportFromXML "C:\Temp\XMLSharedOR.XML", "C:\Temp\ObjectRepository.
tsr"
```

Converting Files from Previous Format to the Latest Format

In case we have an OR which was created in an earlier version of QTP and we want to convert it to the latest version, we can use the convert method

```
ORUtil.Convert "C:\Temp\QTP9OR.tsr", "C:\Temp\QTP11OR.tsr"
```

NOTE: The format/version of the new OR will depend on the QTP version installed on the machine where the code is executed. We cannot convert a QTP 9 format OR to a QTP 11 format OR when the system on which we execute the code has QTP 10 installed.

Printing Names of the WebTables in the OR

We can use the GetAllObjectsByClass method to get all objects that belong to a particular class.

```
Dim ORUtil
'Create the object repository automation API
Set ORUtil = CreateObject("Mercury.ObjectRepositoryUtil")

'Load the object repository
ORUtil.Load "C:\temp\SharedOR.tsr"

'Get all the objects with class as WebTable
Set allTableObjects = ORUtil.GetAllObjectsByClass ("WebTable")

'Print their logical name
For i = 0 to allTableObjects.Count - 1
 Print ORUtil.GetLogicalName(allTableObjects.item(i))
Next

'Destroy the object
Set ORUtil = Nothing
```

Now if we look at the supported methods we will see that there is no way to get the parent object for the object we have in the loop, which is important if we want to display the full name of the object. The code below demonstrates how we can get the type of the object, its parent and full name.

```
Function GetObjectFullName(ORUtil, Obj)
  Dim parentObject
```

```
    Dim sObjectType
    Dim sLogicalName

    'Type of the object
    sObjectType = obj.GetTOProperty("micclass")

    'Get the logical name of the object
    sLogicalName = ORUtil.GetLogicalName(obj)

    'If Empty is returned by GetTOProperty then there is no parent
    If IsEmpty(obj.GetTOProperty("parent")) Then
      'No more parent
      GetObjectFullName = sObjectType & "(""" & sLogicalName & """)"
    Else
      Set parentObject = obj.GetTOProperty("parent")
      GetObjectFullName = GetObjectFullName(ORUtil, parentObject) &"." _
          & sObjectType & "(""" & sLogicalName & """)"
    End If
End Function
```

We can then modify the loop to print the full name of the object:

```
'Print the full object path
For i = 0 to allTableObjects.Count - 1
  Print GetObjectFullName(ORUtil, allTableObjects.item(i))
Next
```

Retrieving an Object Directly and Modifying its Properties

We can use the GetObject method to retrieve an object and then use SetTOProperty to change its identification properties:

```
Set Obj = ORUtil.GetObject("Browser(""Browser"")")

'Update one of the properties
Obj.SetTOProperty "title", "this is set using API"
```

```
'Update the object we have changed
ORUtil.Update obj

'Save the object repository changes
ORUtil.Save

Set Obj = Nothing
```

Although there are other methods, the majority of them are self-explanatory and can be used in the above manner.

Working with QTP XML OR

Shared Object Repositories (SORs) can be exported to XML files, but cannot be directly loaded in a QTP script using the XML format. However, we can load an SOR in the TSR file format as we saw earlier in the "Chapter 2 – Object Repository".

Here we will explore how to use these exported XMLs and get complete object descriptions from the XML. Consider the following Object Repository in QTP:

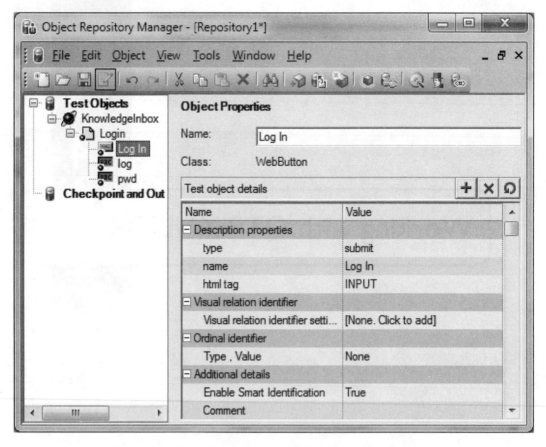

Figure 14.1 – Object Repository for KnowledgeInbox demo login page

The above Object Repository contains five objects: KnowledgeInbox (Browser), Login (Page), Log In (WebButton), log (WebEdit) and pwd (WebEdit), all of which have some identifications properties in the OR. If we export the Repository to a file using the File->Export to XML option, we will get the following XML file (partial file shown):

```
<qtpRep:ObjectRepository xmlns:qtpRep="http://www.mercury.com/qtp/ObjectRepository">
 <qtpRep:Objects>
  <qtpRep:Object Class="Browser" Name="KnowledgeInbox">
   <qtpRep:Properties>
    <qtpRep:Property Name="title" Hidden="1" ReadOnly="1" Type="STRING">
     <qtpRep:Value RegularExpression="0"><![CDATA[KnowledgeInbox Login]]></qtpRep:Value>
    </qtpRep:Property>
```

```
</qtpRep:Properties>
<qtpRep:BasicIdentification>
 <qtpRep:PropertyRef>micclass</qtpRep:PropertyRef>
 <qtpRep:OrdinalIdentifier Type="creationtime">
  <qtpRep:Value>0</qtpRep:Value>
 </qtpRep:OrdinalIdentifier>
</qtpRep:BasicIdentification>
<qtpRep:ChildObjects>
 <qtpRep:Object Class="Page" Name="Login">
  <qtpRep:Properties>
  </qtpRep:Properties>
  <qtpRep:BasicIdentification>
   <qtpRep:PropertyRef>micclass</qtpRep:PropertyRef>
  </qtpRep:BasicIdentification>
  <qtpRep:SmartIdentification Algorithm="Mercury.TolerantPriority" Active="1">
   <qtpRep:BaseFilter>
    <qtpRep:PropertyRef>micclass</qtpRep:PropertyRef>
   </qtpRep:BaseFilter>
   <qtpRep:OptionalFilter>
    <qtpRep:PropertyRef>title</qtpRep:PropertyRef>
    <qtpRep:PropertyRef>url</qtpRep:PropertyRef>
   </qtpRep:OptionalFilter>
  </qtpRep:SmartIdentification>
  <qtpRep:LastUpdateTime>Sunday, June 13, 2010 10:54:44</qtpRep:LastUpdateTime>
  <qtpRep:ChildObjects>
   <qtpRep:Object Class="WebEdit" Name="pwd">
    <qtpRep:Properties>
     <qtpRep:Property Name="micclass" Hidden="1" ReadOnly="1" Type="STRING">
      <qtpRep:Value RegularExpression="0"><![CDATA[WebEdit]]></qtpRep:Value>
     </qtpRep:Property>
    </qtpRep:Properties>
    <qtpRep:BasicIdentification>
     <qtpRep:PropertyRef>micclass</qtpRep:PropertyRef>
     <qtpRep:PropertyRef>_xpath</qtpRep:PropertyRef>
     <qtpRep:PropertyRef>type</qtpRep:PropertyRef>
     <qtpRep:PropertyRef>name</qtpRep:PropertyRef>
     <qtpRep:PropertyRef>html tag</qtpRep:PropertyRef>
    </qtpRep:BasicIdentification>
    <qtpRep:LastUpdateTime>Sunday, June 13, 2010 10:54:48</qtpRep:LastUpdateTime>
```

```
  <qtpRep:ChildObjects>
  </qtpRep:ChildObjects>
 </qtpRep:Object>
 <qtpRep:Object Class="WebEdit" Name="log">
  <qtpRep:Properties>
   <qtpRep:Property Name="micclass" Hidden="1" ReadOnly="1" Type="STRING">
    <qtpRep:Value RegularExpression="0"><![CDATA[WebEdit]]></qtpRep:Value>
   </qtpRep:Property>
  </qtpRep:Properties>
  <qtpRep:BasicIdentification>
   <qtpRep:PropertyRef>micclass</qtpRep:PropertyRef>
   <qtpRep:PropertyRef>_xpath</qtpRep:PropertyRef>
   <qtpRep:PropertyRef>type</qtpRep:PropertyRef>
   <qtpRep:PropertyRef>name</qtpRep:PropertyRef>
   <qtpRep:PropertyRef>html tag</qtpRep:PropertyRef>
  </qtpRep:BasicIdentification>
  <qtpRep:SmartIdentification Algorithm="Mercury.TolerantPriority" Active="1">
   <qtpRep:BaseFilter>
    <qtpRep:PropertyRef>micclass</qtpRep:PropertyRef>
    <qtpRep:PropertyRef>type</qtpRep:PropertyRef>
    <qtpRep:PropertyRef>html tag</qtpRep:PropertyRef>
   </qtpRep:BaseFilter>
   <qtpRep:OptionalFilter>
    <qtpRep:PropertyRef>name</qtpRep:PropertyRef>
    <qtpRep:PropertyRef>html id</qtpRep:PropertyRef>
    <qtpRep:PropertyRef>max length</qtpRep:PropertyRef>
    <qtpRep:PropertyRef>default value</qtpRep:PropertyRef>
    <qtpRep:PropertyRef>class</qtpRep:PropertyRef>
    <qtpRep:PropertyRef>rows</qtpRep:PropertyRef>
    <qtpRep:PropertyRef>visible</qtpRep:PropertyRef>
   </qtpRep:OptionalFilter>
  </qtpRep:SmartIdentification>
  <qtpRep:LastUpdateTime>Sunday, June 13, 2010 10:54:44</qtpRep:LastUpdateTime>
  <qtpRep:ChildObjects>
  </qtpRep:ChildObjects>
 </qtpRep:Object>
 <qtpRep:Object Class="WebButton" Name="Log In">
  <qtpRep:Properties>
   <qtpRep:Property Name="micclass" Hidden="1" ReadOnly="1" Type="STRING">
```

```
    <qtpRep:Value RegularExpression="0"><![CDATA[WebButton]]></qtpRep:Value>
   </qtpRep:Property>
  </qtpRep:Properties>
 <qtpRep:BasicIdentification>
 <qtpRep:PropertyRef>micclass</qtpRep:PropertyRef>
 <qtpRep:PropertyRef>_xpath</qtpRep:PropertyRef>
 <qtpRep:PropertyRef>type</qtpRep:PropertyRef>
 <qtpRep:PropertyRef>name</qtpRep:PropertyRef>
 <qtpRep:PropertyRef>html tag</qtpRep:PropertyRef>
 </qtpRep:BasicIdentification>
 <qtpRep:LastUpdateTime>Sunday, June 13, 2010 10:54:53</qtpRep:LastUpdateTime>
 <qtpRep:ChildObjects>
 </qtpRep:ChildObjects>
   </qtpRep:Object>
  </qtpRep:ChildObjects>
 </qtpRep:Object>
 </qtpRep:ChildObjects>
 </qtpRep:Object>
 </qtpRep:Objects>
</qtpRep:ObjectRepository>
```

This XML has everything we need to identify an object. We will now look at the key aspects or attributes of the XML.

- ⊙ <qtpRep:Objects> node represents the root node of the OR.

- ⊙ <qtpRep:Object Class="Browser" Name="KnowledgeInbox"> each object node represents an object in the OR. The Class attribute signifies the TestObject type and the Name attribute signifies the logical name.

- ⊙ <qtpRep:Properties> represents the set of properties associated with the object.

- ⊙ <qtpRep:Property Name="user-input in post data" Hidden="1" ReadOnly="1" Type="STRING"><qtpRep:Value RegularExpression="0"><![CDATA[]]></qtpRep:Value></qtpRep:Property> represents the individual property values. The Hidden attribute signifies whether or not the property is being used for identification. A value "1" indicates that the value is not used. These values are stored by QTP for implementation of the SMART Identification algorithm.

- ⊙ The <qtpRep:Value RegularExpression="0"><![CDATA[]]></qtpRep:Value> represents the value of the given property. Attribute RegulerExpression="1" signifies that the value is a pattern and "0" signifies a literal value.

- If an object has some child objects the <qtpRep:Object> node will have a non-blank child node <qtpRep:ChildObjects>.

Now we will use the above information to come up with an XMLORManager class which would allow us to extract information from this XML and use it in our test. We will use "Microsoft.XMLDOM" as the XML parser. To start with we need to create a class and initialize our parser:

```
Class XMLORManager
  Private xmlDoc

  Sub Class_Initialize()
    Set xmlDoc = CreateObject("Microsoft.XMLDOM")
  End Sub

  Sub Class_Terminate()
    Set xmlDoc = Nothing
  End Sub
End Class
```

When instantiated, the above class will create the "Microsoft.XMLDOM" objects and destroy the same when the object is set to Nothing. The next step is to load the XML into the parser. For this we can add a method to the class:

```
Sub LoadORXML(ByVal XMLFilePath)
  xmlDoc.Async = False

  'Load the XMLfile into memory
  xmlDoc.Load(XMLFilePath)

  'Use XPATH in selectNodes and not the tag names
  xmlDoc.SetProperty "SelectionLanguage", "XPath"

  'Set the NameSpace else it will raise unknown namespace 'qtpRep' error
  xmlDoc.SetProperty "SelectionNamespaces", "xmlns:qtpRep=""http://www.
mercury.com/qtp/ObjectRepository"""
End Sub
```

To load the XML we first need to create the class object and the call LoadORXML method on the object of the class. The code below shows the same:

```
'Create the XMLORManager object
Set XMLOR = New XMLORManager
'Load the XML file
XMLOR.LoadORXML "C:\RepoTest.xml"
```

Finding Root Object Names

To get all the objects at the root, we would need to extract all direct <qtpRep:Object> children of the <qtpRep:Objects> node. This can be done by adding the following function:

```
Function GetRootObjectNames()
  Dim oNodeList

  'Get all XML nodes at the start
  Set oNodeList = xmlDoc.selectNodes("//qtpRep:Objects/qtpRep:Object")

  Dim arrRootNames
  ReDim arrRootNames(oNodeList.Length - 1)

  Dim i

  'Populate the name of the objects
  For i = 0 to oNodeList.Length - 1
    arrRootNames(i) = oNodeList(i).attributes.getNamedItem("Name").Value
  Next

  'Return the array of names
  GetRootObjectNames = arrRootNames
End Function
```

The oNodeList object contains all the objects at root. "oNodeList(i).attributes" gives access to attributes of the node and we are interested in extracting the Name attribute of the node. For this we can use the getNamedItem method of the attributes collection.

Finding Object Nodes using Names

If we need to extract a node using the name of the object, we can use the match criteria in XPATH.

```
sObjectName = "Log In"
sXPath = "//qtpRep:Object[@Name='" & sObjectName &"']"
Set NodeList = xmlDoc.selectNodes(sXPath)
```

Above code selects all nodes with the Name as "Log In". If we want to limit the test object types as well, we can use the following:

```
sObjectName = "Log In"
sObjectType = "WebButton"
sXPath = "//qtpRep:Object[@Name='" & sObjectName & "'][@Class='" &
sObjectType & "']"
Set NodeList = xmlDoc.selectNodes(sXPath)
```

The code above is case-sensitive; if we change "Log In" to "log in", the code won't return any result. To overcome this, we can use the translate function of XPATH:

```
sObjectName = "Log In"
sXPath = "//qtpRep:Object[translate(@Name,'abcdefghijklmnopqrstuvwxyz','ABC
DEFGHIJKLMNOPQRSTUVWXYZ')='" & Ucase(sObjectName) &"']"
Set NodeList = xmlDoc.selectNodes(sXPath)
```

This translate method will convert all the lower-case characters to upper-case and we can then search for the object name. In this way the code can be made case-insensitive.

The above code returns all the objects with the given name. If we want only those objects which have no child objects, we can add another criterion by adding "[not(qtpRep:ChildObjects/qtpRep:Object)]" to the end of the XPATH. In case we want only objects which have child objects then the XPATH at the ending would be: "[(qtpRep:ChildObjects/qtpRep:Object)]".

Getting Object Descriptions from Names

We know how to get the object node from the name of the object and now we will find out how to extract the object description string using the OR logical names. The function below allows us to extract the object description by passing the XML node object:

```
Function GetObjectDescFromNode(objNode)
  Dim objName, objClass
  Dim objDesc

  'Get the object name
  objName = objNode.attributes.getNamedItem("Name").Value

  'Get the test object type
  objClass = objNode.attributes.getNamedItem("Class").Value

  'We need to return the description with logical name
  objDesc = objClass & "(""" & objName & """)"

  'Get to the parent node
  Set oParent = objNode.parentNode.parentNode

  If oParent.nodeName = "#document" or oParent.nodeName =
"qtpRep:ObjectRepository"Then
    'This is last parent root node
    GetObjectDescFromNode = objDesc
  Else
    'There is some parent object
    GetObjectDescFromNode = GetObjectDescFromNode(oParent, bDPProperties) &
"." & objDesc
  End If
End Function
```

Using this function for the Log In object will return the object description as:

```
Browser("KnowledgeInbox").Page("Login").WebButton("Log In")
```

However, this will only work if the Object Repository is associated with the test. Repositories cannot be associated using the XML format but can be by using the TSR files. This approach creates the limitation of needing to have the XML as well as the TSR file for a Repository. To overcome this, we can instead get the DP identification properties rather than the logical name of the object. To do so we need to look at the <qtpRep:Property> which has the hidden property set as "0". If there are no properties which have a hidden set as "0" then we can use the "micclass" parameter as the object type. In order to do this, we must add another parameter to the function:

```
Function GetObjectDescFromNode(objNode, ByVal bDPProperties)
  Dim objName, objClass
  Dim objDesc

  'Get the object name
  objName = objNode.attributes.getNamedItem("Name").Value

  'Get the test object type
  objClass = objNode.attributes.getNamedItem("Class").Value

  If Not bDPProperties Then
    'We need to return the description with logical name
    objDesc = objClass & "(""" & objName & """)"
  Else
    Set oProps = objNode.selectNodes("qtpRep:Properties/qtpRep:Property[@
Hidden='0']")
    If oProps.Length = 0 Then
      'There are no properties with Hidden set as 0, use the micclass
instead
      objDesc = objClass & "(""micclass:=" & objClass &""")"
    Else
      'There are properties, loop through all of them
      ReDim arrProp(oProps.Length - 1)
      Dim i: i = 0

      'Get each property as Name:=Value
      For each oProp in oProps
            arrProp(i) = oProp.attributes.getNamedItem("Name").Value
        arrProp(i) = arrProp(i) & ":=" & oProp.selectNodes("qtpRep:Value")
(0).nodeTypedValue
        i = i + 1
      Next

      'Join the type and properties for description
      objDesc = objClass & "(""" & Join(arrProp,""",""") & """)"
    End If
```

```
   End If

   'Get to the parent node
   Set oParent = objNode.parentNode.parentNode

   If oParent.nodeName = "#document" or oParent.nodeName =
"qtpRep:ObjectRepository"Then
      'This is last parent root node
      GetObjectDescFromNode = objDesc
   Else
      'There is some parent object
      GetObjectDescFromNode = GetObjectDescFromNode(oParent, bDPProperties) &
"." & objDesc
   End If
End Function
```

Using the above function on the Log In node will result in the following output:

```
Browser("micclass:=Browser").Page("micclass:=Page").WebButton("type:=submit
","name:=Log In","html tag:=INPUT")
```

Getting Object Description using Path

Earlier we extracted object descriptions using the name of the object. But using just the name could lead to multiple matches. Fortunately, we can also use Path to access the object, which uses the logical names of the objects before the final object. To get the object Path for:

```
Browser("KnowledgeInbox").Page("Login").WebButton("Log In")
```

We can have various possible paths: KnowledgeInbox\\Log In, Login\\Log In, Log In and KnowledgeInbox\\Login\\Log In. The advantage to this approach is that we don't need to specify all the objects in the path, but by specifying a partial path, we can still get the object. Additionally, if we know or want to enforce the object type, we can do that by specifying the ObjectType parameter:

```
Function GetObjectDescFromPath(ByVal ObjectPath, ByVal ObjectType)
   'Support path with names seperate by \\ or //
   ObjectPath = Replace(ObjectPath, "\\", "//")
```

```
'Split the path into array
ObjectPath = Split(ObjectPath, "//")
Dim i

Dim sXPathPreFix
sXPathPreFix = "//qtpRep:Object[translate(@Name,'abcdefghijklmnopqrstuvwx
yz','ABCDEFGHIJKLMNOPQRSTUVWXYZ')='"
'Get the XPATH for each node
For i = 0 to UBound(ObjectPath)
  ObjectPath(i) =  sXPathPreFix  & Ucase(ObjectPath(i)) &"']"
Next

If ObjectType <> "" Then
  'In the last XPath we can enfornce the object type
  ObjectPath(i) = ObjectPath(i) & "[@Class='" & ObjectType & "']"
End If

'Join the XPATH to impose the full path
ObjectPath = Join(ObjectPath, "")

Dim oNodeList

'Get all XML nodes at the start
Set oNodeList = xmlDoc.selectNodes(ObjectPath)

'Return the object description
GetObjectDescFromPath = GetObjectDescFromNode(oNodeList(0), FALSE)
End Function
```

Finding String Descriptions for Child Objects

Child Objects can be accessed by getting the <qtpRep:Object> node from the
<qtpRep:ChildObjects> node. We can access direct child as well as all children nodes.

```
Function GetChildObjects(objNode, ByVal bDPProperties, ByVal bDirectChilds)
  If  bDirectChilds Then
    'Get only direct childs
```

```
      Set oChilds = objNode.selectNodes("qtpRep:ChildObjects/qtpRep:Object")
   Else
      'Get all the child objects
      Set oChilds = objNode.selectNodes("qtpRep:ChildObjects//qtpRep:Object")
   End If

   'Declare array for  object descriptions
   ReDim arrObjectDesc(oChilds.Length - 1)

   For i = 0 to oChilds.Length - 1
      'Get the description of the object
      arrObjectDesc(i) = GetObjectDescFromNode(oChilds(i), bDPProperties)
   Next

   'Return the array of description
   GetChildObjects = arrObjectDesc
End Function
```

Getting the Object from the Description

All our functions so far have returned the string description of the object and not the object itself. To convert the string to its actual object we must use the Eval method of VBScript:

```
sObjectDesc = GetObjectDescFromNode(oNode, TRUE)
Set oObject = Eval(sObjectDesc)
Msgbox oObject.Exist(0)
```

This approach has several advantages over normal DP OR implementations:

- ◉ Objects can be used without specifying the full hierarchy. This creates shorter and more efficient code.

- ◉ The OR can be created, updated and maintained through Object Repository Manager UI. This makes it easier to add objects and also is less prone to errors.

Using ORPath to Shorten Code

We have just seen how to use the Path to get an object from XML. We can utilize this technique to implement a unique way of using test objects without losing the IntelliSense in the QTP IDE. This approach lets us achieve the following types of statement in QTP scripts:

```
WebButton("ORPath:=KnowledgeInbox\\Log In").Click
```

In order for the above code to work, we have to carry out further actions:

- ◉ The Click event has to be captured in our code because WebButton cannot be identified with our custom ORPath property.

- ◉ The WebButton object doesn't exist, so its corresponding object needs to found in the XML.

To use this approach, it is necessary to override every single method for which we intend to use ORPath.

```
Dim XMLOR
Set XMLOR = New XMLORManager
XMLOR.LoadORXML "C:\Temp\QTPObjects.xml"

'Register and capture the new click events
RegisterUserFunc "WebButton", "Click", "ProcClick"

Function ProcClick(Obj)
  Dim sORPath

  sORPath = Obj.GetTOProperty("ORPath")

  If sORPath <> "" Then
    'Get the object type
    sObjType = Obj.GetTOProperty("micclass")

    'ORPath is not blank. We need to get the object from XML
    Set Obj = Eval(XMLOR.GetObjectDescFromPath(sORPath, sObjType))
  End If

  Obj.Click
End Function
```

When we execute the following line of code:

```
WebButton("ORPath:=KnowledgeInbox\\Log In").Click
```

QTP finds that WebButton's Click event is to be routed to ProcClick. In the ProcClick method the Obj object receives the object "WebButton("ORPath:=KnowledgeInbox\\Log In")". Since the object is not valid, the only thing we can do is to access its test object properties. We extract ORPath and check if it is specified or not. If it is, we get the object from the XML; if not, we directly use the object. This method uses a Custom DP hybrid and OR approach. The only shortcoming is that every method that we want to use needs to be overridden using RegisterUserFunc. The huge advantage is the IntelliSense in the QTP IDE and the ability to get objects using a shorter path. We can also shorten the ORPath as below, in case the object name and type combination is unique:

```
WebButton("ORPath:=Log In").Click
```

NOTE: When the Click method is called, it always gets called twice. This happens because when we use Eval to get the new object from the XML and use obj.Click, the Click method is again re-routed using RegisterUserFunc. The re-routed method will not find the ORPath parameter specified and will perform the actual click. If we use some kind of logging code in such a function, we need to make sure that the event is not reported twice.

Testing Web Services

Introduction

As web services become key areas of enterprise applications, the focus on testing them has become increasingly important. A web service is used to provide a response to a client's request. The request and response are sent and received respectively using the Simple Object Access Protocol (SOAP). To test a web service, an automation engineer must carry out the following steps:

1. Define the parameters to supply to the web service.

2. Send the request with the defined input parameters.

3. Parse response to verify expected versus actual values.

The process of sending a request and receiving a response is shown below:

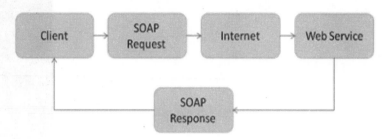

Figure 15.1 – Web Service Send/Receive Process

The client sends a SOAP request to the web service. Where QTP is used to test a web service, QTP itself is the client. If it's a valid request, the web service sends a SOAP response back to the client. Below is a sample request and response for a service that computes the arithmetic formula $10 + 5 * 4$:

```
http://qtp.arithmeticservice.demo/api/xml?10&%plus%&5&%multiply%&4
```

```xml
<?xml version="1.0" encoding="UTF-8"?>
<QTPArithmeticServiceDemo>
  <status>OK</status>
  <entry>
    <input>10 + 5 * 4</input>
    <value>30</value>
  </entry>
</QTPArithmeticServiceDemo>
```

Notice the URL string above. To request the output for 10+5*4, the parameters have been formulated in the request URL and separated by '&'. Please note that this is not always what the request will look like and that the above URL is used only for the purpose of explanation.

The output contains the status of the request, as well as the input and output values computed by the web service. The output from the web service is 30.

This brings us back to the three-step process of sending and receiving a response from a web service. We have defined the input parameters, sent the request and parsed the response for the output. However, our first example was visual and there was no code involved. This will be demonstrated further within the chapter.

Since QTP offers a web service add-in, this chapter will be demonstrating testing web services using:

1. The Web service add-in.

2. Programmatically using: XMLHTTPRequest, XMLUtil and XMLDOM.

A Simple Temperature Conversion Web Service

For this section, a simple temperature conversion web service has been used. It takes the following two parameters as its input:

```
Conversion(double Degrees, string Unit)
```

- ◉ Degrees (integer)

- ◉ Unit: Celsius (C), Fahrenheit (F), Kelvin (K) or Rankine (R)

Below is the C# code used to create our sample web service:

```csharp
namespace RelevantCodes.TestingWebServices
{
  using System;
  using System.Web.Services;
  using System.Xml;
  using System.Xml.Serialization;
  using System.Text;
  [WebService(Namespace = "localhost")]
  [WebServiceBinding(ConformsTo = WsiProfiles.BasicProfile1_1)]
  [System.ComponentModel.ToolboxItem(false)]
  [Serializable]
  public class Temperature : WebService
  {
    private double Degrees;
    private string Unit;

    [WebMethod]
    public XmlDocument Conversion(double Degrees, string Unit)
    {
```

```
      Unit = Unit.ToUpper();

      this.Degrees = Degrees;
      this.Unit = Unit;

      StringBuilder stringBuilder = new StringBuilder();

      using (XmlWriter xmlWriter = XmlWriter.Create(stringBuilder))
      {
        XmlWriter newXmlWriter = Conversion(xmlWriter);
        XmlDocument xmlDocument = new XmlDocument();
        xmlDocument.LoadXml(stringBuilder.ToString());

        return xmlDocument;
      }
  }

  private XmlWriter Conversion(XmlWriter xmlWriter)
  {
    Scale scale = new Scale();

    switch (Unit)
    {
      case "K":
        scale.Celsius = Degrees - 273.15; break;
      case "R":
        scale.Celsius = (Degrees - 491.67) * 5 / 9; break;
      case "F":
        scale.Celsius = (Degrees - 32) * 5 / 9; break;
      default:
        scale.Celsius = Degrees; break;
    }

    scale.Degrees = Degrees;
    scale.Unit = Unit;
    scale.Fahrenheit = scale.Celsius * 1.8 + 32;
    scale.Kelvin = scale.Celsius + 273.15;
    scale.Rankine = (scale.Celsius + 273.15) * 1.8;
```

```
    xmlWriter.WriteStartDocument();
    xmlWriter.WriteStartElement("Conversion");

    xmlWriter.WriteStartElement("Input");
    xmlWriter.WriteElementString("Degrees", Degrees.ToString());
    xmlWriter.WriteElementString("Unit", Unit);
    xmlWriter.WriteEndElement();

    xmlWriter.WriteStartElement("Output");
    xmlWriter.WriteAttributeString("Time", DateTime.Now.ToString());
    xmlWriter.WriteElementString("Celsius", scale.Celsius.ToString());
    xmlWriter.WriteElementString("Fahrenheit", scale.Fahrenheit.
ToString());
    xmlWriter.WriteElementString("Kelvin", scale.Kelvin.ToString());
    xmlWriter.WriteElementString("Rankine", scale.Rankine.ToString());
    xmlWriter.WriteEndElement();

    xmlWriter.WriteEndElement();
    xmlWriter.WriteEndDocument();

    xmlWriter.Flush();

    return xmlWriter;
  }

  public struct Scale
  {
    public double Degrees;
    public string Unit;
    public double Celsius;
    public double Kelvin;
    public double Rankine;
    public double Fahrenheit;
  }
 }
}
```

Invoking the web service takes us to the single WebMethod conversion. As stated earlier, it takes two inputs: degrees and unit. A value of -10 is specified for degrees (integer) and

Celsius (C) for the unit (string).

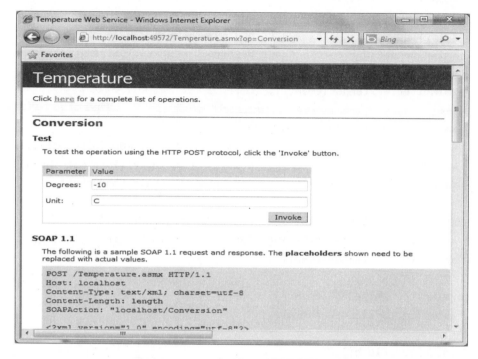

Figure 15.2 – Sample Temperature Web Service

The snapshot below is the output from invoking the WebMethod:

```
<?xml version="1.0" encoding="utf-8" ?>
- <Conversion>
   - <Input>
       <Degrees>-10</Degrees>
       <Unit>C</Unit>
     </Input>
   - <Output Time="7/24/2012 12:12:29 PM">
       <Celsius>-10</Celsius>
       <Fahrenheit>14</Fahrenheit>
       <Kelvin>263.15</Kelvin>
       <Rankine>473.67</Rankine>
     </Output>
  </Conversion>
```

Figure 15.3 – Sample WebMethod Input and Output

Testing Web Services using the Web Service Add-in

With the help of the Web Service Add-in, web services can be tested without the need for extensive knowledge of your web service architecture. For example, you can use QTP to invoke the operations of your web service and verify returned XML data using CheckPoints and special functionality designed for web services. The Web Service Add-in can be used in conjunction with other add-ins as well, enabling you to test multiple components at the same time.

Installation

If you do not already have the Web Service Add-in installed, you can do so by using the installation media. Open the Setup.exe file and click QuickTest Professional Setup.

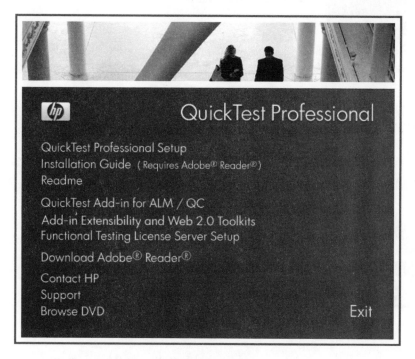

Figure 15.4 – QuickTest Professional Setup

Select Modify and click Next. From the list of add-ins, select Web Services Add-in and click Next.

Figure 15.5 – QuickTest Professional setup Add-ins

Installation will begin and the add-in will be installed.

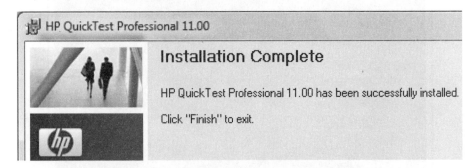

Figure 15.6 – Installation complete confirmation

Once the installation is complete, an Additional Installation Requirements window will be displayed. Click Run to install all required settings.

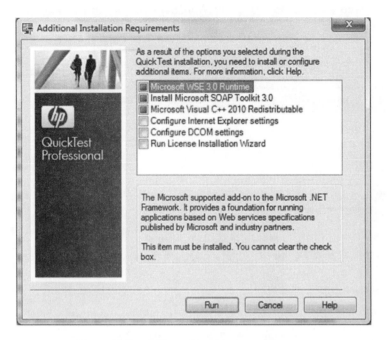

Figure 15.7 – Additional installation requirements

After this process is complete, start QTP. You should now see Web Services under the list of installed add-ins:

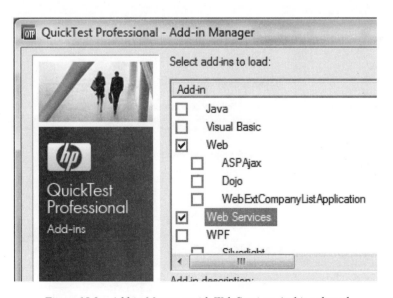

Figure 15.8 – Add-in Manager with Web Services Aad-in selected

To work with web services in QTP, the Web Services Wizard can be found under the Automation menu.

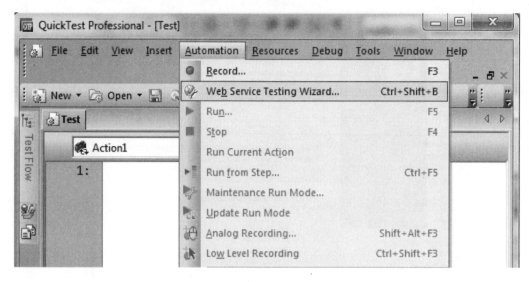

Figure 15.9 – Web Service Testing Wizard

Additional web service settings are available from File > Settings > Web Services.

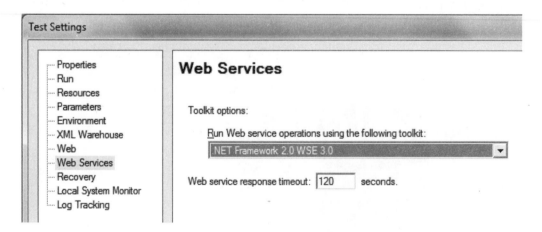

Figure 15.10 – Web Services Settings

Toolkit and WS-I options are available from Tools > Options > Web Services.

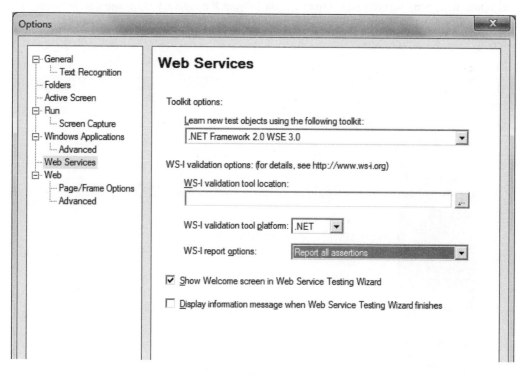

Figure 15.11 – Web Services Options

Web Services Testing Wizard

The Web Service Add-in Object Wizard enables you to automatically create a WebService test object and then add steps manually. It also enables you to automatically generate checkpoints for the added steps. The Web Services Testing Wizard can be started from the Automation menu. Alternatively, CTRL+SHIFT+B can be used. When you start the Web Services Testing Wizard, you will see a welcome screen which provides an overview of the Wizard's steps.

NOTE: QuickTest includes Maintenance Run Mode, which is not supported for applications such as web services as they do not have a user interface.

Click Next. The Specify WSDL for Scanning Screen will appear. This is used to select the source of the test object (web service) you want to include. The selection can be a URL, a file path or a web service test object in the Object Repository. The sample web service is used and a URL is specified: http://localhost:49572/WebService1.asmx?WSDL. After entering the URL, click Navigate.

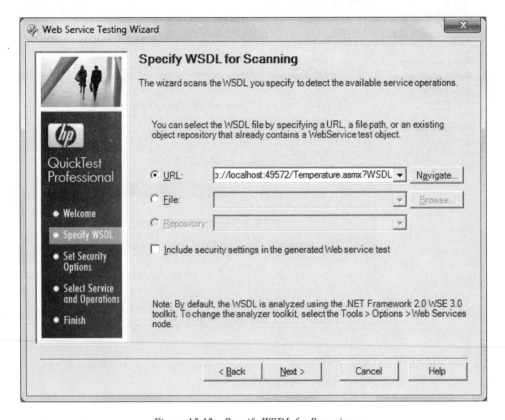

Figure 15.12 – Specify WSDL for Scanning

If you have selected 'Include security settings in the generated web service test', the following window will appear:

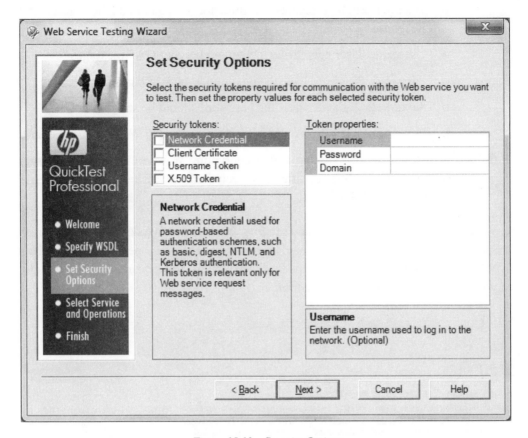

Figure 15.13 – Security Options

This screen enables you to select any security tokens required for communicating with the web service under test. 4 types of Security tokens are described above:

- ◉ Network Credential: Used for password-based authentication schemes, such as basic, digest, NTLM, and Kerberos authentication and is relevant only for Web service request messages. It includes the following properties to log-in to the network: Username, Password and Domain.

- ◉ Client Certificate: Used when a client uses the SSL3.0/PCT1 protocol to connect to a server, and the server requires client certificates for mutual authentication. It uses a StoreType property which indicates whether the certificate is located in the file system or installed on the computer.

- ◉ Username Token: Contains information regarding Username and Password security credentials. It includes the following properties:

- o TokenDirection: Indicates the direction of communication: Request or Response

- o Username: User name used to sign or encrypt SOAP messages

- o Password: Password used to sign or encrypt SOAP messages

- o SendMode: Indicates how the password should be sent

- o ProtectionMode: Protection mode to be applied to Web service operations

- ⊙ X.509 Token: Used for signing and/or encrypting Web service request messages when a server's public certificate is required. It includes two properties: TokenDirection and StoreType.

Our sample web service does not use any security tokens, so we've skipped this screen. On the Specify WSDL for Scanning screen, click Navigate. This will open the WSDL schema of your test object. When the schema opens, click Capture. The schema window will close and your WSDL is also verified by the tool.

Figure 15.14 – Capture and verify WSDL

Click Next. The Select Service and Operations screen will appear. This enables selecting the WSDL services that are to be tested and the service operations that will be included in the generated test. Our sample service only provides a single operation: Conversion. We select this and click Next.

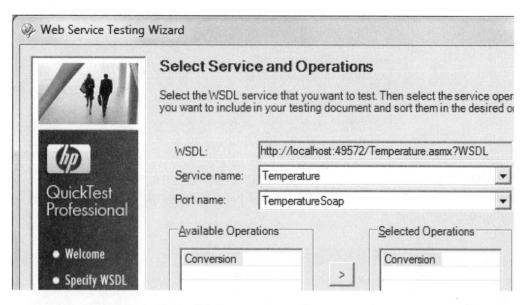

Figure 15.15 – Web Service service and operations selection

Finally, the Summary screen appears, displaying a summary of the selections made on the previous screens. On this screen, you can select whether you would like to add CheckPoints after each relevant operation step; we have selected this option. After clicking Finish, the Wizard will generate the web service test.

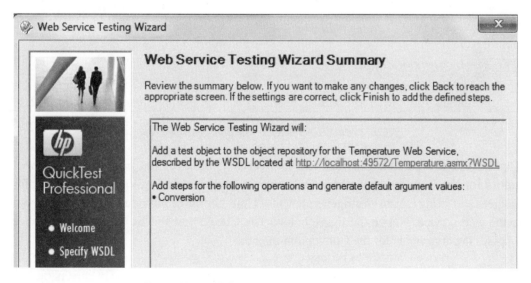

Figure 15.16 – Web Service Testing Wizard Summary

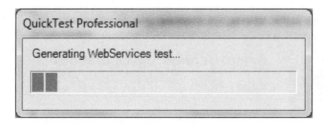

Figure 15.17 – Generating test dialog

The following code was generated after completing the above process. Notice that our input for Degrees (double) and Unit (string) have been substituted by 0 and "string Autogenerated".

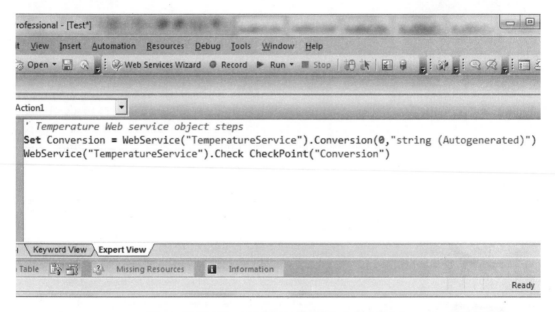

Figure 15.18 – Generated test with auto-generated code

This auto-generated code provides just an overview, but does not provide correct input values for the Conversion method. Only the 'value types' are provided: integer (0) for Degrees and string (string (Autogenerated)) for Unit. Let's now provide some relevant input to the web service. Notice the figure below. The CheckPoint for the TemperatureService displays the arguments for the Conversion method.

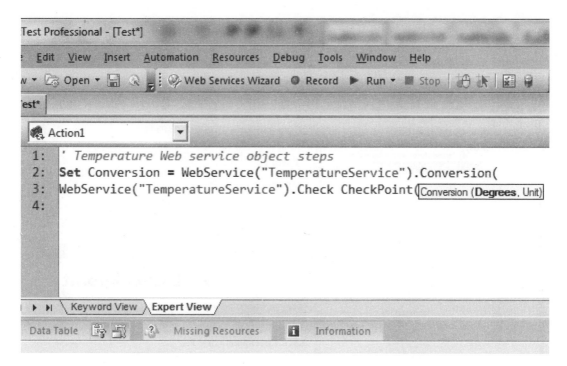

Figure 15.19 – Web Service Conversion +-method arguments

We have used -10 for Degrees and "C" (Celsius) for the Unit.

```
'Temperature Web service object steps
Set Conversion = WebService("TemperatureService").Conversion(-10, "C")
WebService("TemperatureService").Check CheckPoint("Conversion")
```

This is pretty much all the creation involved with the Web Services Wizard. The above code can now be run and our web service under test be verified. However, there is one element of this process still remaining which we discover after the above script completes. The following output is received:

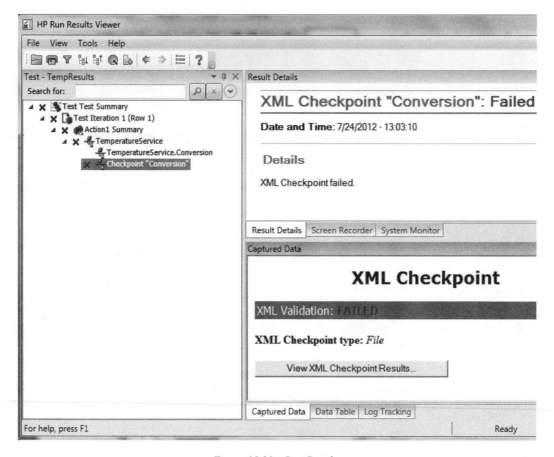

Figure 15.20 – Run Results

Our test has failed. By digging further into the Results Viewer, we find something interesting:

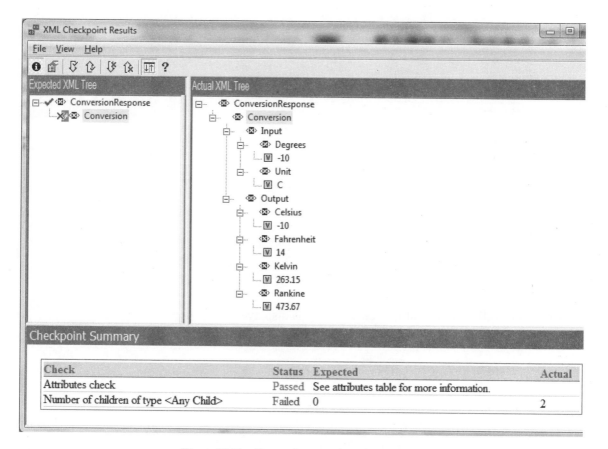

Figure 15.21 – Expected vs actual result

The number of expected children for Conversion is 0, whereas the actual number of children from the response is 2 (Input and Output elements). Our expected value is incorrect. To correct the expected value for the request, we can open the CheckPoint properties and modify the expected children for Conversion from 0 to 2.

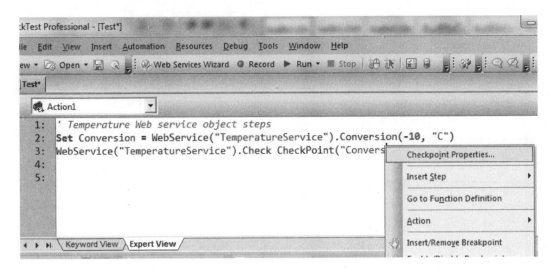

Figure 15.22 – XML CheckPoint properties

The XML Checkpoint Properties dialog is displayed:

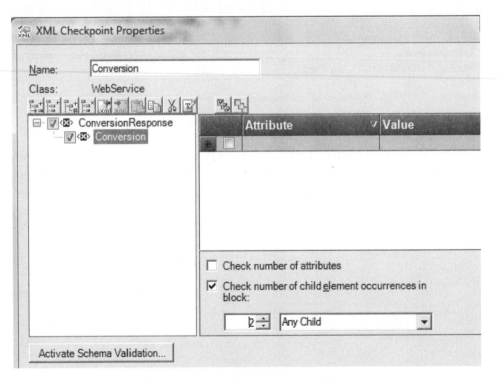

Figure 15.23 – XML CheckPoint Properties dialog

This should fix the error. At runtime, our test will expect two Conversion children. After executing the script, we can see in the Results Viewer that the test has now passed:

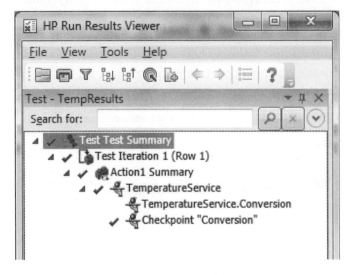

Figure 15.24 – Run Results Viewer

The SOAP request and response can also be viewed from the Results Viewer:

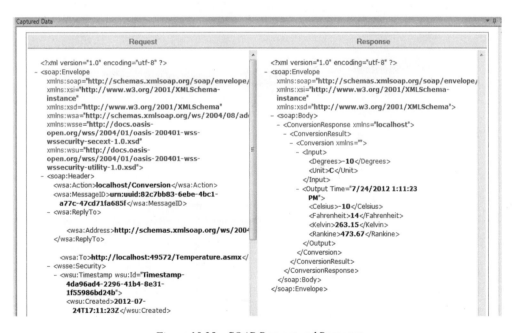

Figure 15.25 – SOAP Request and Response

Verifying XML Response Values

The CheckPoint for the WebService object can be used to verify values from the SOAP response. In the response above, the values for Celsius, Fahrenheit, Kelvin and Rankine are 10, 14, 263.15 and 473.67 respectively. This can be verified at a granular level using the CheckPoint. At Run-time, besides checking all child-nodes, QTP will also check for their values and validate whether or not the system provides the correct ones. There are two ways in which to do this:

1. By manually adding the nodes and values for verification.

2. By manually supplying the XML.

Technique 1: Manually adding the nodes and values for verification

The Add Child ⊞ button can be used to add child elements for a given node. Below, all child nodes for Conversion have been added with the INPUT values to verify during Run-time:

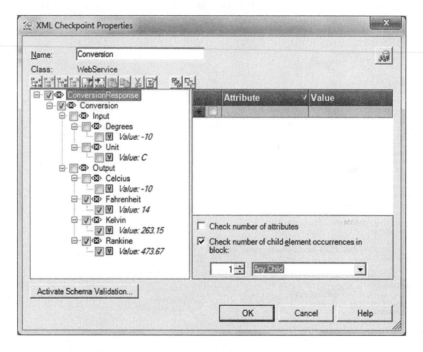

Figure 15.26 – XML CheckPoint Properties dialog

Technique 2: Manually supplying the XML

The same effect as shown above can be achieved by supplying the XML text and clicking the Edit XML as Text ⬛ button:

```
Edit XML as Text                                          X

Modify the XML string and click OK. Your string will replace all sub-nodes of the node you
selected in the XML tree. Note that you cannot modify the root element name.

<ConversionResponse>
    <Conversion>
        <Input>
            <Degrees>-10</Degrees>
            <Unit>C</Unit>
        </Input>
        <Output Time="04/26/2012 9:26:38 AM">
            <Celcius>-10</Celcius>
            <Fahrenheit>14</Fahrenheit>
            <Kelvin>263.15</Kelvin>
            <Rankine>473.67</Rankine>
        </Output>
    </Conversion>
</ConversionResponse>
```

Figure 15.27 – Edit XML as Text Window

WebService Object Methods

To provide more out-of-the-box functionality, QTP also provides several methods for the WebService object as shown below:

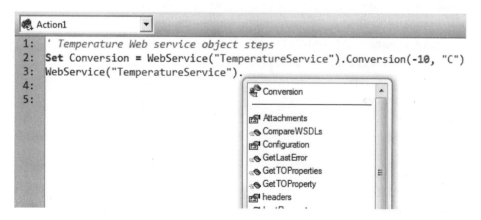

Figure 15.28 – WebService object methods displayed via IntelliSense

We can use WebService object methods to drill deeper into the web service under test. For example, the LastRequest and LastResponse methods provide the following output:

```
Print WebService("TemperatureService").LastRequest
Print WebService("TemperatureService").LastResponse
```

Request

```
<?xml version="1.0" encoding="utf-8"?>
<soap:Envelope xmlns:soap="http://schemas.xmlsoap.org/soap/envelope/"
xmlns:xsi="http://www.w3.org/2001/XMLSchema-instance" xmlns:xsd="http://
www.w3.org/2001/XMLSchema" xmlns:wsa="http://schemas.xmlsoap.org/
ws/2004/08/addressing" xmlns:wsse="http://docs.oasis-open.org/wss/2004/01/
oasis-200401-wss-wssecurity-secext-1.0.xsd" xmlns:wsu="http://docs.oasis-
open.org/wss/2004/01/oasis-200401-wss-wssecurity-utility-1.0.xsd">
  <soap:Header>
    <wsa:Action>localhost/Conversion</wsa:Action>
    <wsa:MessageID>urn:uuid:abbcb3c2-1950-45bb-8956-8bc46f37d667</
wsa:MessageID>
    <wsa:ReplyTo>
      <wsa:Address>
        http://schemas.xmlsoap.org/ws/2004/08/addressing/role/anonymous
      </wsa:Address>
    </wsa:ReplyTo>
    <wsa:To>http://localhost:49499/WebService1.asmx</wsa:To>
    <wsse:Security>
      <wsu:Timestamp wsu:Id="Timestamp-520608d7-69e4-4150-91cf-
60fb90e23516">
        <wsu:Created>2012-04-26T12:25:46Z</wsu:Created>
        <wsu:Expires>2012-04-26T12:30:46Z</wsu:Expires>
      </wsu:Timestamp>
    </wsse:Security>
  </soap:Header>
  <soap:Body>
    <Conversion xmlns="localhost">
      <Degrees>-10</Degrees>
      <Unit>C</Unit>
    </Conversion>
  </soap:Body>
```

```
</soap:Envelope>
```

Response

```xml
<?xml version="1.0" encoding="utf-8"?>
<soap:Envelope xmlns:soap="http://schemas.xmlsoap.org/soap/envelope/"
xmlns:xsi="http://www.w3.org/2001/XMLSchema-instance" xmlns:xsd="http://
www.w3.org/2001/XMLSchema">
  <soap:Body>
    <ConversionResponse xmlns="localhost">
      <ConversionResult>
        <Conversion xmlns="">
          <Input>
            <Degrees>-10</Degrees>
            <Unit>C</Unit>
          </Input>
          <Output Time="4/26/2012 8:25:46 AM">
            <Celsius>-10</Celsius>
            <Fahrenheit>14</Fahrenheit>
            <Kelvin>263.15</Kelvin>
            <Rankine>473.67</Rankine>
          </Output>
        </Conversion>
      </ConversionResult>
    </ConversionResponse>
  </soap:Body>
</soap:Envelope>
```

 NOTE: A CheckPoint or an Output Value of a step that returns a multi-dimensional array will be parsed to display only one dimension of the array.

Testing Web Services Programmatically

In the previous section, we saw the QTP approach to working with web services. It is a largely visual approach and can make it easier for Automation teams to work with web services without using much code. But although using the web service add-in will provide the same output as compared to its programmatic counterpart, it may not always provide the same level of flexibility or performance.

This section will show how to work with web services using XMLHTTPRequest, XMLUtil and XMLDOM. In practice, engineers only need to use either XMLUtil or XMLDOM as they are both parsers and will provide the same output. There is one key difference though, which is that XMLUtil works in an environment with QTP installed whereas XMLDOM will work on any Microsoft OS.

XMLHTTPRequest

The XMLHTTPRequest object belongs to Microsoft XML Core Services (MSXML) and provides support for communicating with HTTP servers. It is used to send a HTTP request and receive the response, thus making it a client-side protocol. Because this communication is asynchronous, XMLHTTP makes it possible to create web applications that do not require a page refresh to display incoming (new) data.

XMLHTTP methods and properties are detailed in the following tables:

Method	Description
open(method, URL) open(method,URL,async) open(method,URL,async,username) open(method,URL,async,username,password)	Specifies the arguments and other optional attributes of a request. Method parameter can be one of the following, or other HTTP methods: ⊙ DELETE ⊙ GET ⊙ HEAD ⊙ POST ⊙ PUT Async parameter specifies whether the request is asynchronous or not. Possible values: ⊙ true: asynchronous (continue without waiting for response) ⊙ false: not asynchronous (wait for response)

Method	Description
abort()	Cancels the request.
getAllResponseHeaders()	Returns all HTTP headers as string.
getResponseHeader(headerName)	Returns the value of headerName.
send(content)	Send the request with or without content.
setRequestHeader(label,value)	Add a label/value pair to the HTTP header.

Property	Description
readyState	Returns the state of the Request object with one of the following values: ⊙ 0 = uninitialized, open() not yet called ⊙ 1 = open, send() not yet called ⊙ 2 = request sent, headers and status available ⊙ 3 = receiving or downloading responseText but holds only partial data ⊙ 4 = finished
responseText	Returns the response as a string.
Status	Returns the HTTP status code: 200, 301, 302, 404 etc.
statusText	Returns the status as a string. That is, returns the string equivalent of the HTTP status code.

As stated above, XMLHTTP can be used to communicate between the client and the server. The code below shows just that. Unlike the example using the Web Service Wizard above, the arguments (and corresponding values) are specified using the SEND method.

```
url = "http://localhost:49499/WebService1.asmx/Conversion"
unitsToConvert = "Degrees=-10&Unit=C"

Set oRequest = CreateObject("Microsoft.XMLHTTP")

'oRequest.open method, URL, async
oRequest.open "GET", url, False

'oRequest.setRequestHeader label,value
oRequest.setRequestHeader "Content-Type", "application/x-www-form-
urlencoded"
```

```
'oRequest.send content
oRequest.send(unitsToConvert)

'Response
sResponseText = oRequest.responseText

Print sResponseText

Print "oRequest.status -> " & oRequest.status
Print "oRequest.statusText -> " & oRequest.statusText

Set oRequest = Nothing
```

Output: Response Text

```
<?xml version="1.0" encoding="utf-8"?>
<Conversion>
  <Input>
    <Degrees>10</Degrees>
    <Unit>C</Unit>
  </Input>
  <Output Time="4/26/2012 7:41:41 AM">
    <Celsius>10</Celsius>
    <Fahrenheit>14</Fahrenheit>
    <Kelvin>263.15</Kelvin>
    <Rankine>473.67</Rankine>
  </Output>
</Conversion>
```

Response → Status, StatusText

oRequest.status → 200
oRequest.statusText → OK

The code above shows how a request is sent to a URL using XMLHTTP. If the request is valid, the responseText will return the values for the request. If it is invalid, there will be no response and the STATUS will not return HTTP code 200.

After receiving some data in the form of XML, there is a need to now parse it to retrieve some necessary information. There are two ways to parse XML files and extract required information from them: XMLUtil (QTP) and XMLDOM (VBScript). Both techniques are detailed in the next two sections.

Parsing Response with XMLUtil

XMLUtil is a QTP object used to access and return XML objects. It exposes two methods that can be used to parse XML files and extract the required information from them:

- CreateXML
- CreateXMLfromFile

Since the response is coming in the form of XML through localhost, we do not need to load an XML file and therefore, the CreateXML method will be used to initialize an instance of type XMLData.

```
'XMLData
Set oXMLUtil = XMLUtil.CreateXML

'Initialize using the XML string sResponseText
oXMLUtil.Load(sResponseText)

Fahrenheit = oXMLUtil.GetRootElement.GetValueByXPath("Output/Fahrenheit")
MsgBox "Fahrenheit: " & Fahrenheit

Kelvin = oXMLUtil.GetRootElement.GetValueByXPath("//Kelvin[1]")
MsgBox "Kelvin: " & Kelvin

Rankine = oXMLUtil.GetRootElement.GetValueByXPath("//Rankine")
MsgBox "Rankine: " & Rankine

Set oXMLUtil = Nothing
```

GetValueByXPath is used to extract values for Fahrenheit, Kelvin and Rankine. Note that different types of XPath above are used for this. For more information on XPath, refer to the XPath section of this book. Another method that can be used to extract information from XML is ChildElementsByPath, shown below:

```
Set oXMLUtil = XMLUtil.CreateXML

oXMLUtil.Load(sResponseText)

Set FahrenheitTag = oXMLUtil.GetRootElement.ChildElementsByPath("Output/
Fahrenheit")
MsgBox "Fahrenheit: " & FahrenheitTag.Item(1).Value

Set KelvinTag = oXMLUtil.GetRootElement.ChildElementsByPath("Output/
Kelvin")
MsgBox "Kelvin: " & KelvinTag.Item(1).Value

Set RankineTag = oXMLUtil.GetRootElement.ChildElementsByPath("Output/
Rankine")
MsgBox "Rankine: " & RankineTag.Item(1).Value

Set oXMLUtil = Nothing
```

Parsing Response with XMLDOM

XMLDOM stands for eXtensible Markup Language Document Object Model. The Document Object Model for XML defines a set of commands for the parser that make data available from XML documents. The XMLDOM object is exposed via a set of standard COM interfaces defined in MSXML.dll. To create a new instance of the parser, CreateObject can be used.

```
Set XMLDOM = CreateObject("Microsoft.XMLDOM")
```

The example below shows how the ResponseText from XMLHTTP is used to retrieve the required information:

```
Set XMLDOM = CreateObject("Microsoft.XMLDOM")

XMLDOM.loadXML(sResponseText)

'Output -> Time attribute
Set OutputTag = XMLDOM.getElementsByTagName("Output")(0)
```

```
timeAttribute = OutputTag.getAttribute("Time")
MsgBox "Output->Time Attribute: " & timeAttribute

'Fahrenheit
Set FahrenheitTags = XMLDOM.getElementsByTagName("Fahrenheit")
MsgBox "Fahrenheit: " & FahrenheitTags(0).text

'Kelvin
Set KelvinTags = XMLDOM.getElementsByTagName("Kelvin")
MsgBox "Kelvin: " & KelvinTags(0).text

'Rankine
Set RankineTags = XMLDOM.getElementsByTagName("Rankine")
MsgBox "Rankine: " & RankineTags(0).text

Set XMLDOM = Nothing
```

The LoadXML method is used to load the response from the server. Once it is loaded, the getElementsByTagName and getAttribute methods are used to extract information. The output values for Time, Fahrenheit, Kelvin and Rankine are shown below:

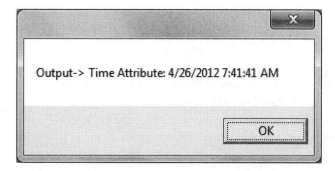

Figure 15.29

Figure 15.30 – Output using XMLDOM Object

In the example above, getElementsByTagName is used to extract information. Similarly, selectSingleNode and selectNodes can also be used to provide exactly the same result.

```
Set XMLDOM = CreateObject("Microsoft.XMLDOM")

XMLDOM.loadXML(sResponseText)

Set FahrenheitTags = XMLDOM.documentElement.selectSingleNode("Output/
Fahrenheit")
MsgBox "Fahrenheit: " & FahrenheitTags.text

Set KelvinTags = XMLDOM.documentElement.selectSingleNode("Output/Kelvin")
MsgBox "Kelvin: " & KelvinTags.text

Set RankineTags = XMLDOM.documentElement.selectSingleNode("Output/Rankine")
MsgBox "Rankine: " & RankineTags.text
Set XMLDOM = Nothing
```

Figure 15.31 – Output from XMLDOM (selectSingleNode Method)

The next example shows usage of selectNodes:

```
Set XMLDOM = CreateObject("Microsoft.XMLDOM")

XMLDOM.loadXML(sResponseText)

Set FahrenheitTags = XMLDOM.documentElement.selectNodes("Output/
Fahrenheit")(0)
MsgBox "Fahrenheit: " & FahrenheitTags.text

Set KelvinTags = XMLDOM.documentElement.selectNodes("Output/Kelvin")(0)
MsgBox "Kelvin: " & KelvinTags.text

Set RankineTags = XMLDOM.documentElement.selectNodes("Output/Rankine")(0)
MsgBox "Rankine: " & RankineTags.text

Set XMLDOM = Nothing
```

Figure 15.32 – Output from XMLDOM (selectNodes Method)

Notes

1. When working with a .NET web service, you may encounter the following error: "The selected WSDL resource has no defined services." If this occurs, make sure you have appended the address of the URL with "?wsdl".

2. Currently, the actual support toolkit options with the Web Services Add-in are:

    a. .NET Web Service: .NET Framework 1.1 WSE 2.0 and .NET Framework 2.0 WSE 3.0

    b. Java Web Service: Axis 1.x

3. Sometimes, the SOAP header needs to be customized for the message to be sent. In this case, the AddSOAPHeader method may be used.

Testing SOAP Request and Response

Similarly to what has been shown earlier in this chapter, the same test can also be performed using a SOAP request. For the temperature web service used in this chapter, here is the format for the SOAP request:

```
<?xml version="1.0" encoding="utf-8"?>
<soap:Envelope xmlns:xsi="http://www.w3.org/2001/XMLSchema-instance"
xmlns:xsd="http://www.w3.org/2001/XMLSchema" xmlns:soap="http://schemas.
xmlsoap.org/soap/envelope/">
  <soap:Body>
    <Conversion xmlns="localhost">
      <Degrees>double</Degrees>
      <Unit>string</Unit>
    </Conversion>
  </soap:Body>
</soap:Envelope>
```

The Figure 15.33 shows the same. Below is the code used to test the temperature web service using a SOAP request:

```
request = "<?xml version=""1.0"" encoding=""utf-8""?>" & _
"<soap:Envelope xmlns:xsi=""http://www.w3.org/2001/XMLSchema-instance""
xmlns:xsd=""http://www.w3.org/2001/XMLSchema"" xmlns:soap=""http://schemas.
xmlsoap.org/soap/envelope/"">" & _
  "<soap:Body>" & _
    "<Conversion xmlns=""localhost"">" & _
      "<Degrees>10</Degrees>" & _
      "<Unit>C</Unit>" & _
    "</Conversion>" & _
  "</soap:Body>" & _
"</soap:Envelope>"

url = "http://localhost:49572/Temperature.asmx?op=Conversion"
```

```
Set oRequest = CreateObject("Microsoft.XMLHTTP")
oRequest.open "POST", url, False
oRequest.setRequestHeader "Content-Type", "text/xml; charset=utf-8"
oRequest.Send request
```

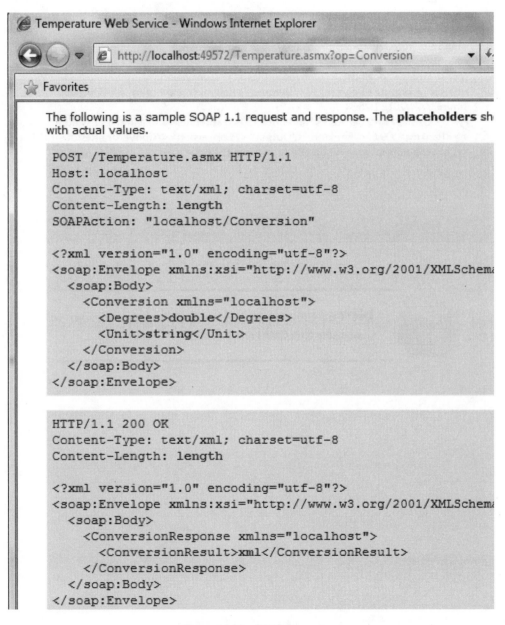

Figure 15.33 – SOAP Request

The response from the above operation is as follows:

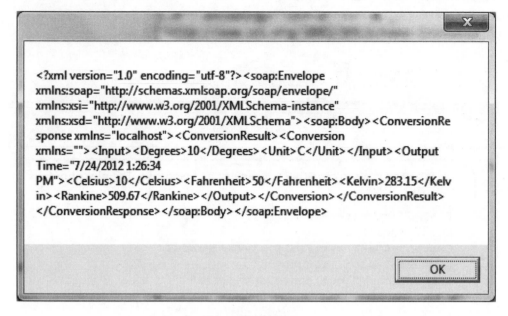

```
<?xml version="1.0" encoding="utf-8"?><soap:Envelope
xmlns:soap="http://schemas.xmlsoap.org/soap/envelope/"
xmlns:xsi="http://www.w3.org/2001/XMLSchema-instance"
xmlns:xsd="http://www.w3.org/2001/XMLSchema"><soap:Body><ConversionRe
sponse xmlns="localhost"><ConversionResult><Conversion
xmlns=""><Input><Degrees>10</Degrees><Unit>C</Unit></Input><Output
Time="7/24/2012 1:26:34
PM"><Celsius>10</Celsius><Fahrenheit>50</Fahrenheit><Kelvin>283.15</Kelv
in><Rankine>509.67</Rankine></Output></Conversion></ConversionResult>
</ConversionResponse></soap:Body></soap:Envelope>
```

Figure 15.34 – Output

NOTE: The same parsing mechanism as shown earlier will work using XMLDOM and XMLUtil.

Coding Scripts in .NET

There are times when advanced users want the ability to code QTP scripts in a different scripting language than VBScript. A few such instances include the need for better exception handling (using Try-Catch-Finally), designing forms for user interaction, Object-Oriented features, need for Optional Parameters and better support for Win32 APIs (VBScript's support through the Extern object is very limited) etc. It is not possible to use any language except VBScript inside QTP, yet it is still possible to create a COM-based bridge for languages that support COM. We will be demonstrating such a bridge in this chapter built in C# and Visual Basic using .NET Framework 4.0. Before we see how the bridge is created, there are few concepts that we need to understand.

QTP's Communication with an Out-of-Process COM Object

Consider the following code:

```
Set oXlApp = CreateObject("Excel.Application")
oXLApp.Visible = True
Set oXLBook = oXLApp.WorkBooks.Open("C:\Test.xls")
Set oXLSheet = oXLBook.WorkSheets(1)
oXLSheet.Cells(1,1) = "Anshoo"
oXLSheet.Cells(2,2) = "Tarun"
```

In this code an oXLSheet.Cells object is used to pass a value to an Excel Worksheet. Even though Excel runs as a separate process in the system, we can still pass values to it. This is called out-process communication. It works through use of a proxy object in the caller process, which routes the call using Remote Procedure Call (RPC) as shown in the figure below:

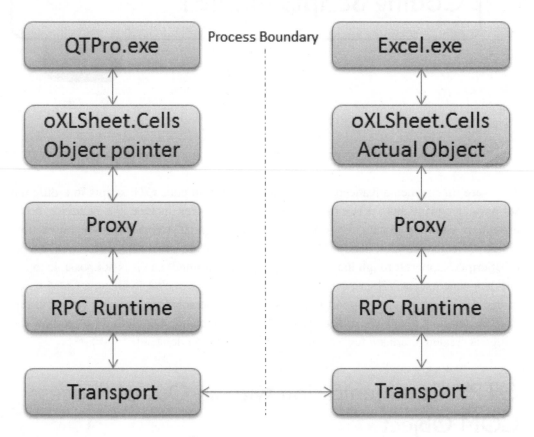

Figure 16.1 – Out-Process Communication

Every Object in QTP is a COM Object

Every object used in QTP is a COM object. Every COM object has a default interface, wherein each interface allows accessing methods and properties of this object. Consider the following code statement:

```
Reporter.ReportEvent micPass, "Pass", "This is a pass statement"
```

In the above statement, Reporter is a QTP-specific object. It is also a COM object, which means it can be passed to an outside process or COM DLL as we saw in the previous Excel example.

QTP .NET COM Bridge

Let's build a small COM Bridge that can be used to code QTP-related statements. SharpDevelop is an open source tool for .NET development and we will use SharpDevelop IDE to develop this bridge. The tool can be downloaded from: http://www.icsharpcode. net/.

Install and launch the Sharp Develop IDE. Choose from the menu File -> New -> Solution. In the New Solution dialog, select Class Library, name the Solution as QTPCOMBridge and click the Create button as shown in Figure 16.2

Remove the MyClass.cs file added by default before right-clicking on the project and choosing New -> Item. Select Class and name it as QTPCOMBridge.cs, as shown in Figure 16.3

Add the class code as follows:

```
public class QTPCOMBridge
{
  public QTPCOMBridge()
  {
    private dynamic Browser;
    private dynamic SystemUtil;
    private dynamic Reporter;
  }
}
```

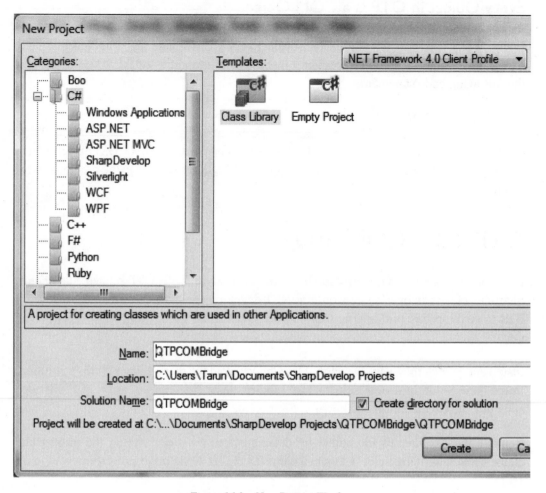

Figure 16.2 – New Project Window

We have created three variables with dynamic data-type (the dynamic type was introduced in of .NET Framework 4.0) and will use these variables to store object reference from QTP. Now we need to add a method to initialize these objects:

```
public void InitObjects(dynamic _Browser, dynamic _SystemUtil, dynamic _
Reporter)
{
 Browser = _Browser;
 SystemUtil = _SystemUtil;
 Reporter = _Reporter;
}
```

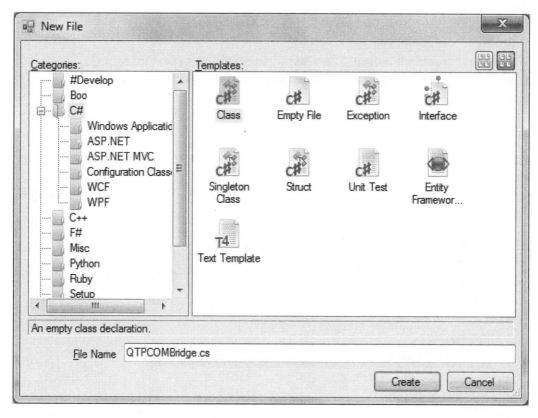

Figure 16.3 – New File Window

Alternatively, we can also add two constructors to the object; one that takes arguments and another that doesn't.

```
public QTPCOMBridge(dynamic _Browser, dynamic _SystemUtil, dynamic _
Reporter)
{
  InitObjects(_Browser, _SystemUtil, _Reporter);
}
public QTPCOMBridge()
{
}
```

Now we will create a function to launch a Browser and perform a search on Google.com:

```
public void SearchOnGoogle(String textToSearch)
```

```
{
  SystemUtil.Run("iexplore.exe", "http://www.google.com");
  Browser("creationtime:=0").Sync();
  Browser("creationtime:=0").WebEdit("name:=q").Set(textToSearch);
  Browser("creationtime:=0").WebButton("name:=Google Search").Click();
  Browser("creationtime:=0").Sync();
  Reporter.ReportEvent(0, "Google search launched", "Launched using C# QTP
Bridge");
}
```

Right-click on the project and add a reference to "Microsoft.CSharp" as shown in the next figure:

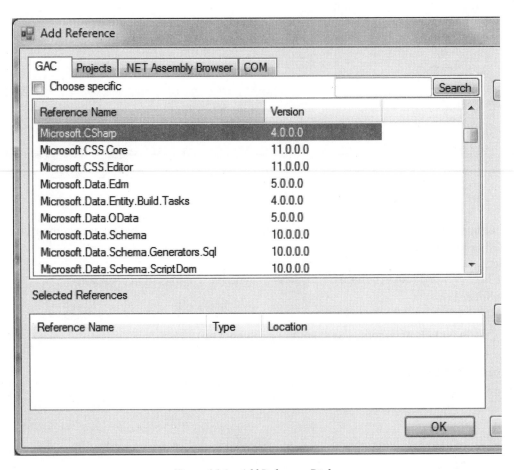

Figure 16.4 – Add Reference Dialog

Build the project and DLL will be created in the project path. Then copy the DLL file to C:\. After that, open QTP and execute the following code in the test:

```
Set oQTPCOMBridge = DotNetFactory.CreateInstance("QTPCOMBridge.
QTPCOMBridge", "C:\QTPCOMBridge.dll",Browser, SystemUtil, Reporter)
oQTPCOMBridge.SearchOnGoogle
```

When we run the test we get the following error:

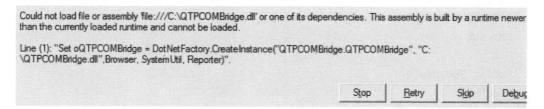

Could not load file or assembly 'file:///C:\QTPCOMBridge.dll' or one of its dependencies. This assembly is built by a runtime newer than the currently loaded runtime and cannot be loaded.

Line (1): "Set oQTPCOMBridge = DotNetFactory.CreateInstance("QTPCOMBridge.QTPCOMBridge", "C:\QTPCOMBridge.dll",Browser, SystemUtil, Reporter)".

| Stop | Retry | Skip | Debug |

Figure 16.5 – Run Error Dialog

This error occurs because DotNetFactory was created with a previous .NET framework and we are using .Net 4. There are two possible options for us to choose to workaround this situation:

- The first option is to use a lower version of .NET framework. Doing this in C# will make the coding difficult, as dynamic data-type is not available. So we can switch to VB.NET instead of C#. DotNetFactory supports .NET 3.5 amd below with QTP 11.0.

- The second option is to make our C# class accessible as a COM object.

We will look at both of these options.

VB.NET COM Bridge

The class code for our QTP COM bridge in VB.NET will change to:

```
Imports System
Imports System.Collections.Generic

Public Class QTPCOMBridge
    Private Browser
    Private SystemUtil
```

```
   Private Reporter

   Public Sub InitObjects(_Browser, _SystemUtil, _Reporter)
     Browser = _Browser
     SystemUtil = _SystemUtil
     Reporter = _Reporter
   End Sub

   Public Sub New(_Browser, _SystemUtil, _Reporter)
     InitObjects(_Browser, _SystemUtil, _Reporter)
   End Sub

   Public Sub New()
   End Sub

   Public Sub SearchOnGoogle(ByVal textToSearch As String)
     SystemUtil.Run("iexplore.exe", "http://www.google.com")
     Browser("creationtime:=0").Sync()
     Browser("creationtime:=0").WebEdit("name:=q").[Set](textToSearch)
     Browser("creationtime:=0").WebButton("name:=Google Search").Click()
     Browser("creationtime:=0").Sync()
     Reporter.ReportEvent (0, "Google search launched", "Launched using
VB.NET QTP Bridge")
   End Sub
End Class
```

In QTP we will be able to run the following code, making sure we compile the DLL with the .NET 3.5 framework:

```
Set oQTPCOMBridge = DotNetFactory.CreateInstance("QTPCOMBridgeVB.
QTPCOMBridge", "C:\Temp\QTPCOMBridgeVB.dll", Browser, SystemUtil, Report)
oQTPCOMBridge.SearchOnGoogle "Tarun Lalwani"
```

This solution cannot run without QTP as all the pointers we pass (Browser, SystemUtil, Report) will only be valid until the test is running in QTP.

Upgrading the Code to a COM Project

There are a few tasks that need to be performed to expose the class as a COM class:

1. Right-click on the project name and select the Properties option. Go to the Compiling Tab and mark the Register for COM Interop checkbox:

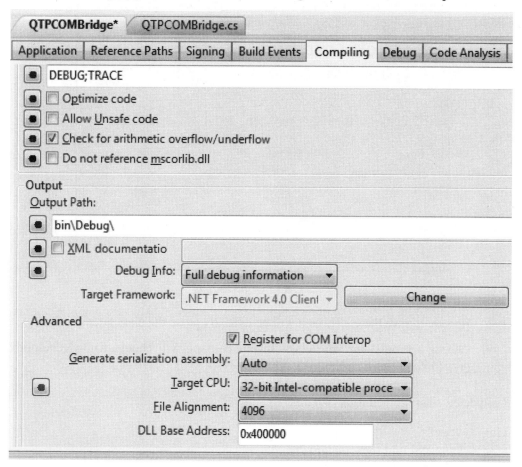

Figure 16.6 – QTPCOMBridge checking 'Register for COM Interop' option

2. The next step is to generate a GUID for the class. This can be done in different ways, including going to http://www.guidgen.com or downloading the Microsoft GUIDGen tool to use to generate a new GUID as shown here:

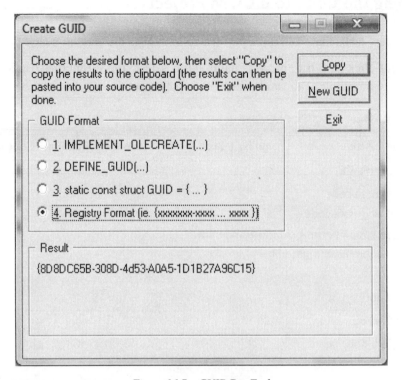

Figure 16.7 – GUIDGen Tool

Be sure to save the GUID as it will be used to update the class later.

3. Choose a ProgID for your class. In this case we will choose KnowledgeInbox. QTPCOMBridge.

The updated class file will look like this:

```
using System;
using System.Collections.Generic;
using System.Runtime.InteropServices;

namespace QTPCOMBridge
{
  /// <summary>
  /// Description of QTPCOMBridge.
  /// </summary>
  [Guid("8D8DC65B-308D-4d53-A0A5-1D1B27A96C15")]
  [ProgId("KnowledgeInbox.QTPCOMBridge")]
```

```
[ComVisible(true)]
public class QTPCOMBridge
{
  private dynamic Browser;
  private dynamic SystemUtil;
  private dynamic Reporter;

  public void InitObjects(dynamic _Browser, dynamic _SystemUtil, dynamic
_Reporter)
  {
    Browser = _Browser;
    SystemUtil = _SystemUtil;
    Reporter = _Reporter;
  }

  public QTPCOMBridge(dynamic _Browser, dynamic _SystemUtil, dynamic _
Reporter)
  {
    InitObjects(_Browser, _SystemUtil, _Reporter);
  }

  public QTPCOMBridge() { }

  public void SearchOnGoogle(string textToSearch)
  {
    SystemUtil.Run("iexplore.exe", "http://www.google.com");
    Browser("creationtime:=0").Sync();
    Browser("creationtime:=0").WebEdit("name:=q").Set(textToSearch);
    Browser("creationtime:=0").WebButton("name:=Google Search").Click();
    Browser("creationtime:=0").Sync();
    Reporter.ReportEvent(0, "Google search launched", "Launched using C#
QTP Bridge");
  }
 }
}
```

Compile the project and now run the following code in QTP:

```
Set oQTPCOMBridge = CreateObject("KnowledgeInbox.QTPCOMBridge")
```

```
oQTPCOMBridge.InitObjects Browser, SystemUtil, Reporter
oQTPCOMBridge.SearchOnGoogle "Tarun Lalwani"

Set oQTPCOMBridge = Nothing
```

Running the above code will launch the Google site with the search performed. The results file will also show the events we had reported.

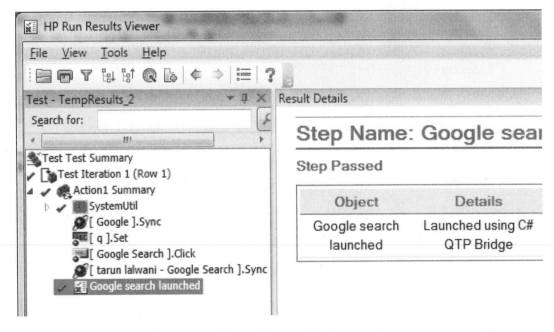

Figure 16.8 – Run Results

One thing to notice is that when we use the oQTPCOMBridge object there is no IntelliSense provided by QTP, as opposed to other COM objects.

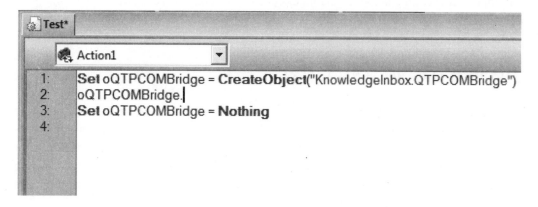

Figure 16.9 – Calling QTPCOMBridge in QTP (no IntelliSense)

This happens when the class is generated in C#. To be able to get IntelliSense, we need to add another attribute [ClassInterface(ClassInterfaceType.AutoDual)] of System.Runtime. InteropService namespace to the class.

```
[Guid("8D8DC65B-308D-4d53-A0A5-1D1B27A96C15")]
[ProgId("KnowledgeInbox.QTPCOMBridge")]
[ComVisible(true)]
[ClassInterface(ClassInterfaceType.AutoDual)]
public class QTPCOMBridge
```

This will fix the issue and give us IntelliSense in QTP as well.

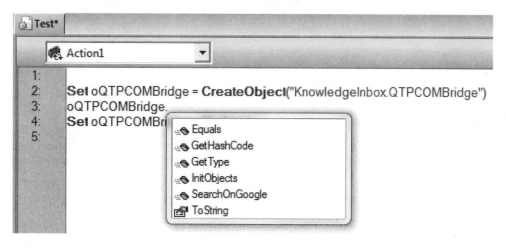

Figure 16.10 – Calling QTPCOMBridge in QTP (with IntelliSense)

The approach of coding in .NET languages opens new doors where a user can even integrate UI and other complex activities which are just not possible to achieve with QTP alone.

IntelliSense in .NET IDE

In the previous section, we saw how to create IntelliSense for our .NET custom class in QTP. However, IntelliSense cannot be viewed while building the test, since all our types (Browser, SystemUtil and Reporter) are dynamic. It is possible to view IntelliSense for these objects and this can be done by adding the relevant reference to the IDE by selecting the DLL containing the Interface of each type. It is still recommended to use Browser as a dynamic type but for other objects, the following references must be added:

- ◉ Reporter
    - o ContextManager Type Library
    - o ContextManager.dll
    - o Directive: using CONTEXTMANAGERLib
- ◉ SystemUtil
    - o Standard Windows Environment
    - o StdPackage.dll
    - o Directive: using STDPACKAGELib;

By adding these references and providing the correct directive for each, it becomes possible to view IntelliSense for QTP's reserved objects in the IDE of your choice. Our new code is shown here:

```
using System;
using System.Collections.Generic;
using System.Runtime.InteropServices;
using CONTEXTMANAGERLib;
using STDPACKAGELib;

namespace QTPCOMBridge
{
  /// <summary>
  /// Description of QTPCOMBridge.
  /// </summary>
```

```
[Guid("8D8DC65B-308D-4d53-A0A5-1D1B27A96C15")]
[ProgId("KnowledgeInbox.QTPCOMBridge")]
[ComVisible(true)]
public class QTPCOMBridge
{
    private dynamic Browser;
    private SystemUtil SystemUtil;
    private ILogger5 Reporter;
    public void InitObjects(dynamic _Browser, SystemUtil _SystemUtil,
ILogger5 _Reporter)
    {
        Browser = _Browser;
        SystemUtil = _SystemUtil;
        Reporter = _Reporter;
    }

    public QTPCOMBridge(dynamic _Browser, SystemUtil _SystemUtil, ILogger5
_Reporter)
    {
        InitObjects(_Browser, _SystemUtil, _Reporter);
    }

    public QTPCOMBridge() { }

    public void SearchOnGoogle(string textToSearch)
    {
        SystemUtil.Run("iexplore.exe", "http://www.google.com");
        Browser("creationtime:=0").Sync();
        Browser("creationtime:=0").WebEdit("name:=q").Set(textToSearch);
        Browser("creationtime:=0").WebButton("name:=Google Search").Click();
        Browser("creationtime:=0").Sync();
        Reporter.ReportEvent(0, "Google search launched", "Launched using C#
QTP Bridge");
    }
  }
}
```

Below is a snapshot of IntelliSense for the SystemUtil Reserved object. It was simply done by adding the correct reference, the directive STDPACKAGELib and declaring the type

SystemUtil as SystemUtil (STDPACKAGELib.SystemUtil) instead of dynamic.

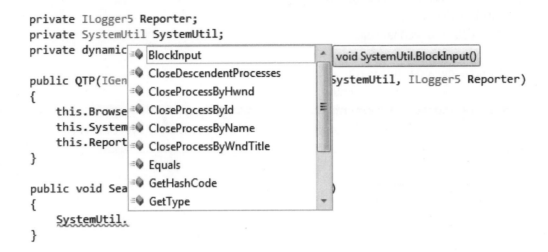

Figure 16.11 – IntelliSense for QTP Objects

This addition to your .NET project will give you an added capability to create your tests quickly.

Even though this feature makes development easy, remember that with every new version of QTP, the interface implementation may change and even a new interface may be created. The interface ILogger5 for Reporter, for example, is currently in its fifth iteration and with the new version of QTP (12.0), ILogger6 may be added. Make sure to update your test by updating the interface in your test or you may not get the full benefit of the new methods added to the ContexManager class.

NOTE: A new interface roll-out will not break your tests if ILogger5 is still found in the assembly.

NOTE: This approach of using .NET should be used with care. The dependency for compiling and registering the DLL can require regular maintenance for frequent code changes. Moreover, debugging a hybrid of VBScript and .NET can be challenging.

17

Web Extensibility

Introduction

The Web Extensibility Add-in coupled with the Extensibility Accelerator for HP Functional Testing provides a platform that enables Automation Engineers to extend support for custom web controls and toolkits.

A compelling case to opt for Extensibility is in a situation where some web controls which are not supported out-of-the-box are recognized as generic WebElements; these generic objects may implement the behavior of a TextBox, Link, Button or List etc. Since the Web Add-in does not recognize their specific behavior, QTP maps them to the WebElement class. Every such generic object thus ends up supporting the functions/methods/events of the WebElement class.

This is where the web add-in Extensibility plays an important role because a control can be mapped to that test object class instead of a generic class. The mapped test object can utilize methods required for it to run a successful test.

Another case where Web Extensibility Add-in could play a crucial role is where a custom control is built from a collection of test objects – similar WebTables with N number of numeric links (as shown in this chapter's example). The WebTables can be extended using the Web Extensibility Add-in to treat each WebTable as a group. This can make code more descriptive and even more robust, as shown in this chapter by building a custom WebExtTable control and implementing custom methods for it.

NOTE: There is a common misconception that even WinObjects, or objects not recognized as a standard web class can be identified when using Web Extensibility. This notion is incorrect. An object that is not mapped to a standard or generic web test object class is not a candidate for Web Extensibility.

An application with DIV and SPAN elements that builds the overall layout and controls of a web application is also a good candidate when deciding to use Extensibility. This is because QTP identifies DIV and SPAN elements as generic WebElements but in some cases these controls can offer the functionality of other classes. The concepts covered in the chapter "Testing Complex HTML Tables" shows such behavior and its DIV table can be implemented using Web Extensibility.

With the Extensibility Accelerator for HP Functional Testing, Automation Engineers and Developers can utilize a Visual Studio-like IDE to easily design, develop and deploy support for custom controls. The IDE can be used to add new test objects and define their operations and properties. It can also provide a point-and-click mechanism to map test object classes. Unlike QTP though which uses VBScript, the Extensibility Accelerator uses JavaScript to create support toolkits.

To know when to use Extensibility, a good initial measure is to understand the application under test (AUT) from the QuickTest perspective. Navigate around the application and instruct QTP to either learn controls or use the Object Spy to understand how QTP sees them.

The Company List Application

In this chapter, we are going to use a simple Company List Application to demonstrate the Web Add-in Extensibility utilizing the Extensibility Accelerator. The HTML source for the table below makes up the Company List Application.

```html
<html>
  <head><title>Company List Application</title>
    <style>
      body{font-family:Consolas;}
      .company{border:1px solid #69C;margin:25px;border-collapse:
collapse;text-align:left;}
      .companyName{font-size:16pt;text-align:center;}
      #heading{padding:16px;border-bottom:1px solid #69C;}
      .entry{padding:16px;}
      .value{padding:16px;}
    </style>
  </head>
  <body>
    <table class='company'>
      <tr class='companyName'>
        <th colspan=2 id='heading'>CompanyOne</td>
      </tr>
      <tr>
        <td class='entry'>Employee Count</td>
        <td class='value'><a href="./cmp1_employee.htm"
name="empCount">100</a></td>
      </tr>
      <tr>
        <td class='entry'>Patent Count</td>
        <td class='value'><a href="./cmp1_patents.htm"
name="patentCount">50</a></td>
      </tr>
    </table>
    <table class='company'>
      <tr class='companyName'>
        <th colspan=2 id='heading'>CompanyTwo</td>
      </tr>
```

```
        <tr>
          <td class='entry'>Employee Count</td>
          <td class='value'><a href="./cmp2_employee.htm"
name="empCount">200</a></td>
        </tr>
        <tr>
          <td class='entry' >Patent Count</td>
          <td class='value'><a href="./cmp2_patents.htm"
name="patentCount">10</a></td>
        </tr>
      </table>
    </body>
</html>
```

Figure 17.1 – Company List demo web page

The Company List application contains two tables which are similar in many ways. Both have the name of the company as their heading. Both also have Employee and Patent Count fields and a number associated with them. It is possible to extend the table with the Extensibility add-in with the help of the Accelerator. In this chapter, we will extend this collection of tables into a custom WebExtTable class and create support for the following methods:

- GetEmployeeCount

- GetPatentCount

- GotoEmployeeList

- GotoPatentList

When recording against this control, the following code will be used to perform the above actions:

```
empCount = Browser("Company List Application") _
  .WebExtTable("CompanyOne").GetEmployeeCount()
patentCount = Browser("Company List Application") _
  .WebExtTable("CompanyOne").GetPatentCount()
Browser("Company List Application") _
  .WebExtTable("CompanyOne").GotoEmployeeList()
Browser("Company List Application") _
  .WebExtTable("CompanyOne").GotoPatentList()
```

The same can be used for CompanyTwo:

```
empCount = Browser("Company List Application") _
  .WebExtTable("CompanyTwo").GetEmployeeCount()
patentCount = Browser("Company List Application") _
  .WebExtTable("CompanyTwo").GetPatentCount()
Browser("Company List Application") _
  .WebExtTable("CompanyTwo").GotoPatentList()
Browser("Company List Application") _
  .WebExtTable("CompanyTwo").GotoPatentList()
```

Notice the new ClassName WebExtTable. Once created, it will support any method defined for it using Extensibility. Moreover, when adding this object to the Repository or even using it in a DP-style statement, it will be learned as a WebExtTable instead of as a standard WebTable. The custom WebExtTable will also support all methods of WebTable if WebTable is used as the BaseClass. This means, just as with a normal WebTable, that the GetCellData method would be supported (along with all other WebTable methods) for WebExtTable when data is to be retrieved.

```
cellData = Browser("Company List Application") _
  .WebExtTable("CompanyOne").GetCellData(1, 1)
```

Extensibility can be used to create custom controls that not only contain custom methods but can also be configured to support methods from their base class. The use of Web Extensibility far exceeds our simple example above and will be covered in the coming sections.

Installation

The two available options to install Extensibility Accelerator are:

- QuickTest Professional Media (Setup) > Add-in Extensibility and Web 2.0 Toolkit option.

- www.hp.com/go/functionaltestingWeb2 > Sign in or Register.

From the Installer window shown below, click Add-in Extensibility and Web 2.0 toolkits.

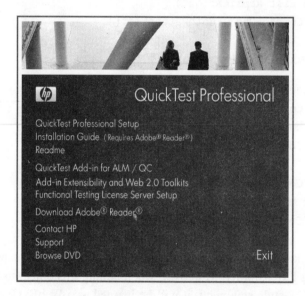

Figure 17.2 – QuickTest Professional Setup

A new Browser window will be launched. From the list of installation links, click 'Web 2.0 Toolkit Support Setup'.

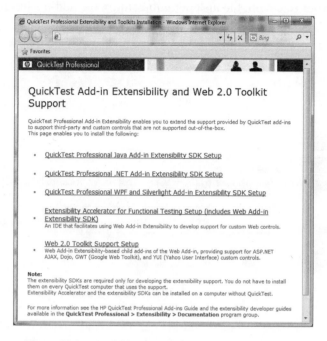

Figure 17.3 – Available extensibility toolkits for installation

Follow the steps and once you reach the Toolkits Selection window, select the add-ins you would like to be installed. The choices here depend upon your environment and the toolkit(s) used in your AUT. Click Install after making your choices.

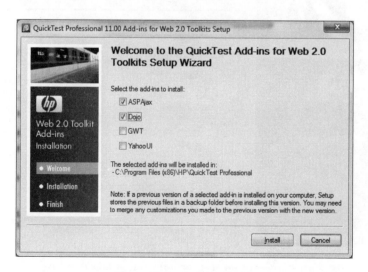

Figure 17.4 – Toolkit selection

Once you make your selection, the installer will confirm the add-ins installed.

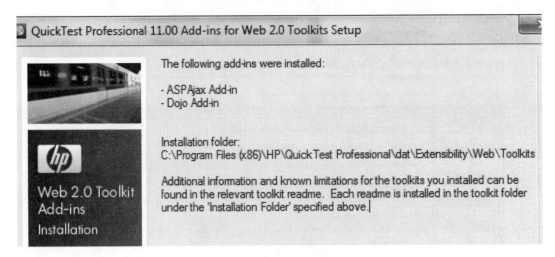

Figure 17.5 – Toolkits installed confirmation

Once QTP is restarted, the installed add-ins can be found under Web. We had selected ASPAjax and Dojo so that's what we see in the list:

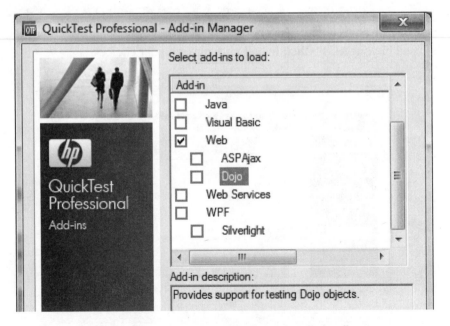

Figure 17.6 – Add-in Manager displaying installed toolkits

The installation also creates the following directory:

```
%Profile%\Documents\ExtAccTool
```

In addition, it installs a sample Book application, which we will use in this chapter to further explore Extensibility. The path of the Book application is:

```
%Profile%\Documents\ExtAccTool\Samples\WebExtSample\Application\Book.htm
```

Installing the Web 2.0 Toolkit support also installs child add-ins with some pre-built support from HP for ASP.NET AJAX, GWT, YUI, and Dojo.

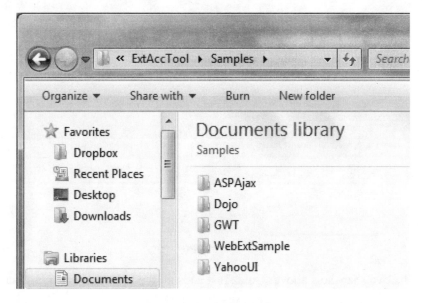

Figure 17.7 – Toolkit Folders

Recording a Test Without Web Add-in Extensibility

In order to better understand the difference between using and not using Extensibility, let's consider a test against the Company List application. The following code snippet shows Keyword and Expert views of the recorded test against the two tables of the Company List application:

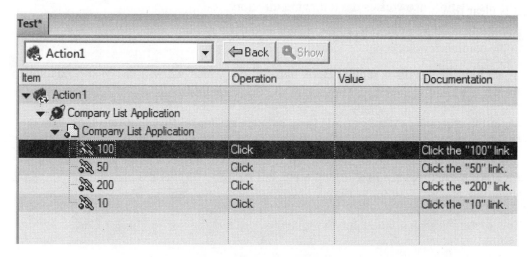

Figure 17.8 – Keyword view

Figure 17.9 – Expert view

Notice in the two snapshots above: QuickTest adds all the links during record but it is not clear which link belongs to what Company (CompanyOne or CompanyTwo). Let's cover this in a bit more detail. Look at the events performed against the link in the two snapshots. It is very difficult to differentiate between the links – it may seem as if they belong to the same table, which is certainly not the case.

Consider an extension of this application where hundreds of such tables (CompanyThree, CompanyFour etc.) exist. With the huge numbers involved, distinguishing between the associations of links and elements with the target companies would be a mammoth task. Also, assume a situation where each company has more than two rows and many other links. Now, to add another layer of complexity, what if each company had a different number of rows? What if attributes such as "Employee Count" and "Patent Count" were dynamic (present only for a few companies)?

It is clear that building and maintaining a test with such dynamic content can become an extremely difficult task. This is where Extensibility plays a crucial role which we will see in the coming few sections.

Developing Toolkit Support Set with Extensibility Accelerator

To understand how Extensibility can be used when working with a large number of situations, we will create a custom WebExtCompanyTable test object class.

This section will be divided into the following groups:

A. Creating a new project in Extensibility Accelerator.

B. Configuring general test object settings from the Extensibility Accelerator.

C. Mapping the custom control.

D. Defining operations to be supported by the custom control.

E. Defining properties of the custom control.

F. Deploying the solution to QuickTest.

G. Using the custom control with QTP.

H. Deploying the solution on other machines.

A. Creating a New Project in Extensibility Accelerator

The following steps show how to create a new project in Extensibility Accelerator:

1. Start HP Extensibility Accelerator.

2. From the File Menu > New > Project.

3. Name the Solution 'WebExtCompanyListApplication'.

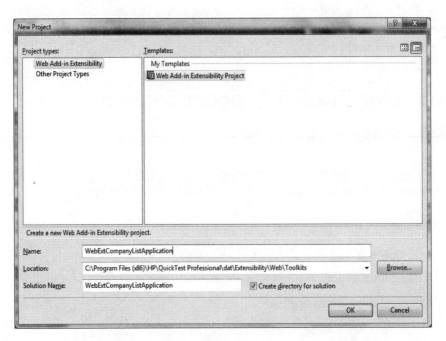

Figure 17.10 – Extensibility Accelerator - New Project dialog

NOTE: The path of the solution is C:\Program Files (x86)\
HP\QuickTestProfessional\dat\Extensibility\Web\Toolkits.

4. Click OK. The new project will be created.

Completion of the above steps ensures that a new project has been created. Let's now configure the general test object settings.

B. Configuring General test object settings from the Extensibility Accelerator

Once the solution is created, the following view will be displayed:

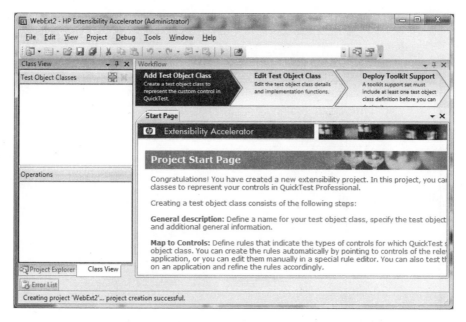

Figure 17.11 – Extensibility Accelerator - New Solution created view

1. Click 'Add Test Object Class' from the Project menu or double-click the 'Add Test Object Class' element under the Workflow label.

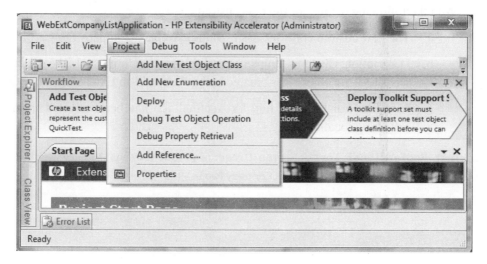

Figure 17.12 – Add New Test Object Class

The following view will be displayed:

351

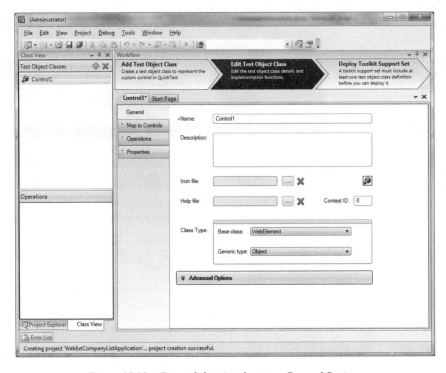

Figure 17.13 – Extensibility Accelerator - General Settings

2. Add the following details for the new custom control:

    a. The new custom control class (*Name): WebExtCompanyTable.

    b. Description: Custom Company List Table for the Company List Application website. This object was created using Web Add-in Extensibility for QTP.

    c. Icon file: For the icon file, ExtAccShell.ico has been selected from the following location:

```
<QuickTest Professional Installation Directory>\dat\Extensibility\Web\
Toolkits\WebExtCompanyTable\WebExtCompanyTable\Res
```

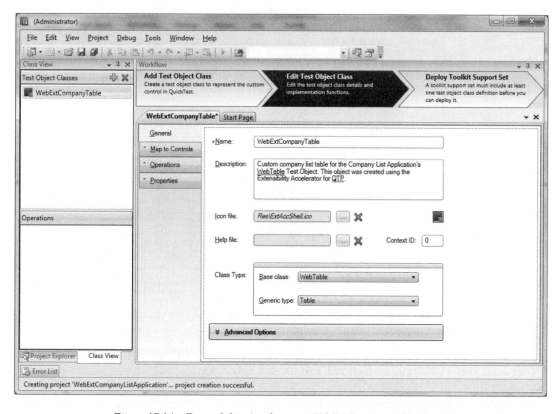

Figure 17.14 – Extensibility Accelerator - WebExtCompanyTable details

3. For the ClassType, we would like our custom test object to inherit all methods of the WebTable class. In other words, the standard WebTable will become the BaseClass of WebExtCompanyTable class. Select the following options:

    a. Base class: WebTable (will enable WebExtCompanyTable to inherit all methods of the WebTable class)

    b. Generic type: Table

4. Select Advanced Options for further configuration.

5. Under Filter Options, Select 'No' for 'Learn test object's children'. This will prevent QTP from automatically learning all child objects of WebExtCompanyTable class. In this example, we are not learning the child elements because they will be accessed with our custom operations: GetEmployeeCount, GetPatentCount, GotoEmployeeList and GotoPatentList.

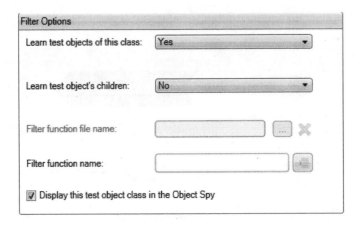

Figure 17.15 – Filter Options

C.   Mapping the Control

In this section, we will use the Extensibility Accelerator to map our custom control against the target control (or set of controls) in the AUT. During record and replay, the mapped control is identified by QTP as having the same methods and properties of the BaseClass (see section B - Configuring General Test Object Settings).

Click Map to Controls in the left pane; the view as shown in the next figure will be displayed.

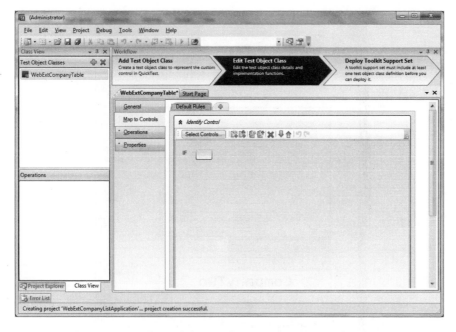

Figure 17.16 – Extensibility Accelerator - Map to Controls settings

1. Click the 'Select Controls' button (see Figure 17.16) to select the custom test object class from the AUT. A tab will appear (at the top of your Desktop-view) with the Create Rules and Cancel buttons, as shown below:

Figure 17.17 – Create Rules

2. Navigate to the Company List Application window and point to the CompanyOne table as shown in the next figure. This enables creation of rules that will instruct QTP to work with the custom control during both record and replay.

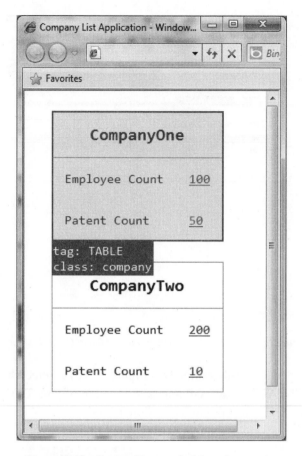

Figure 17.18 – Target object marked for rules creation

NOTE: You must cancel the ActiveX warning if displayed to successfully identify the control.

3. Once the required control is selected, click it. The following hierarchy will be displayed within the AUT:

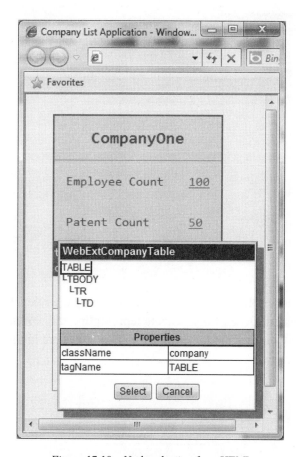

Figure 17.19 – Node selection from HTML

4. Select TABLE and click Select to create custom rules for our control. Once the rule is created, the HP Extensibility Accelerator displays the mapped rule in Map to Controls view.

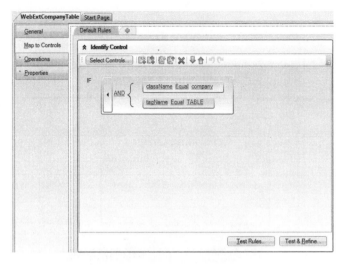

Figure 17.20 – Node selection rules

5. To verify whether the correct object is specified by the rule, click Test Rules. If the rule was created successfully, objects representing the selected properties will be highlighted (CompanyOne and CompanyTwo tables are highlighted below).

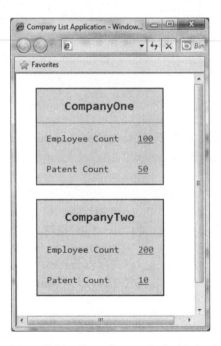

Figure 17.21 – Test rules - nodes highlighted

These steps conclude the section. We have successfully mapped our custom control with the target TABLE in the AUT. In the next section, we will define operations that our custom control will support.

D.   Defining Operations to be Supported by the Custom Control

To define operations, click the Operations button in the left pane. The following view will be displayed:

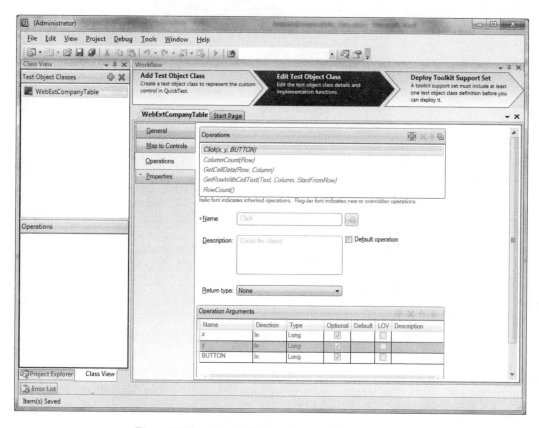

Figure 17.22 – Extensibility Accelerator - Operations view

1. To add a new operation, click the ➕ button.

2. To retrieve the number of employees in the company, we can create a new operation (method) called GetEmployeeCount().

3. For the description, enter the following: "Retrieve the count of employees from the custom WebExtCompanyTable class".

4. Select the Return type value as 'Variant'.

5. To define the logic for the GetEmployeeCount() method/operation, click the control next to the operation name to define the implementation code.

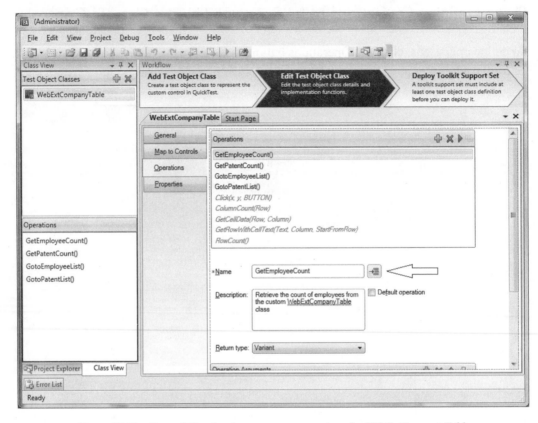

Figure 17.23 – Extensibility Accelerator - new operations for WebExtCompanyTable

The Extensibility Accelerator has powerful IntelliSense and as you type, all methods supported by _elem (the target object represented by the custom test object class) are displayed:

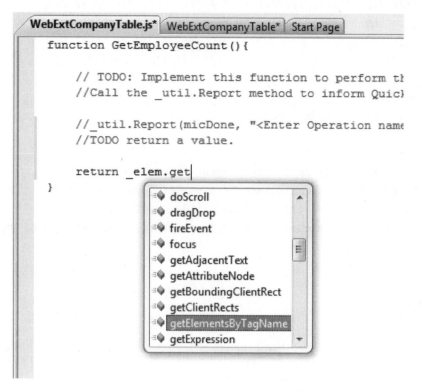

Figure 17.24 – Extensibility Accelerator IntelliSense for _elem

NOTE: The _elem object is a reserved object that QuickTest uses to refer to the HTML control currently being handled.

NOTE: IntelliSense for _elem is only available once the Test Rules command from the Map to Controls tab selects the correct object.

6. To retrieve the employee count associated with the company table, we will use the following code:

```
//////////////////////////////////////////////////////////////
// Retrieve the count of employees from the custom WebExtCompanyTable class
// Returns: Variant
//////////////////////////////////////////////////////////////
function GetEmployeeCount() {
  var innerText = "";
  var tr = _elem.getElementsByTagName('tr');

  try {
    for (var cell = 1; cell < tr.length - 1; cell++) {
      if (tr[cell].firstChild.innerText == "Employee Count") {
        innerText = tr[cell].childNodes[1].innerText;
        _util.Report(micDone, "GetEmployeeCount", toSafeArray(new Array()),
innerText);
        break;
      }
    }
  }
  catch (e) {
    _util.Report(micFail, "GetEmployeeCount", toSafeArray(new Array()),
"The Employee Count Link was unailable");
    throw "The Employee Count Link was unailable";
  }

  if (innerText == "") {
    _util.Report(micDone, "GetEmployeeCount", toSafeArray(new Array()),
"Company does not have the Employee Count label.");
    throw "Company does not have the Employee Count label";
  }

  return innerText;
}
```

Likewise, the remaining methods GetPatentCount, GotoEmployeeList and GotoPatentList respectively are shown below:

```
//////////////////////////////////////////////////////////////
// Retrieve the patent information from the custom WebExtCompanyTable class
// Note: This function is just a sample. Its recommended to support error
```

```
// handling and unexpected behavior as shown in GetEmployeeCount()
// Returns: Variant
//////////////////////////////////////////////////////////
function GetPatentCount(){
  var innerText = _elem.getElementsByTagName('a')[1].innerText;

  _util.Report(micDone, "GetPatentCount", toSafeArray(new Array()),
innerText);

  return innerText;
}


//////////////////////////////////////////////////////////
// Navigates to the list of employees for the selected Company
// Note: This function is just a sample. Its recommended to support error
// handling and unexpected behavior as shown in GetEmployeeCount()
// Returns: None
//////////////////////////////////////////////////////////
function GotoEmployeeList(){
  _util.Report(micDone, "GotoEmployeeList", toSafeArray(new
Array()),"Navigating to Employee List");

  _elem.getElementsByTagName('a')[1].click();
}


//////////////////////////////////////////////////////////
// Navigates to the list of patents for the selected Company
// Note: This function is just a sample. Its recommended to support error
// handling and unexpected behavior as shown in GetEmployeeCount()
// Returns: None
//////////////////////////////////////////////////////////
function GotoPatentList(){
  _util.Report(micDone, "GotoPatentList", toSafeArray(new
Array()),"Navigating to Patent List");

  _elem.getElementsByTagName('a')[1].click();
}
```

NOTE: _util.Report(status, method, parameters, details) is responsible for sending a report step to the results viewer. If _utilReport(args) is not utilized in Extensibility, QTP will detect the name of the event but will not report what happened when the event was performed.

This section concludes the custom operations for our WebExtCompanyTable control. In the next section, let's see how to define properties that the custom control will use for identification. *For simpler and shorter identification for _elem, jQuery can be used as well.*

E.   Defining Properties of the Custom Control

To define properties, click the Properties button in the left pane. The following view will be displayed:

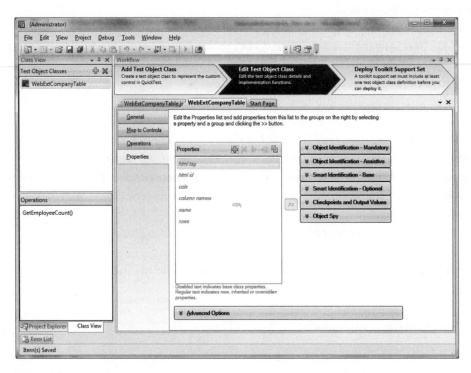

Figure 17.25 – Extensibility Accelerator - Properties view

QuickTest uses runtime values of identification properties in different standard test object methods such as GetROProperty. These runtime values are also required for different basic operations such as creating CheckPoints and outputting values. By default, to identify a control, QTP adds the control's property-values using its proprietary algorithm. The predefined properties will be added using its algorithms but any user-defined property will be added using our custom JavaScript code.

To support retrieving the runtime values of identification properties, you need to implement a JavaScript function that accepts a PropertyName parameter and returns the value of any property. You must implement this method to return a value for each identification property defined in the test object configuration file.

1. For our custom control, the following properties will be inherited from the Base Class (WebTable) by clicking the button:

   a. html tag

   b. cols

   c. name

   d. rows

   e. column names

2. In addition to the above properties, we will also add a custom property – Company Name. We would like to use this new property as the logical name when adding the company table to the Object Repository. To do so, both logical_name and company name would use the same value: the name of the company (CompanyOne, CompanyTwo etc.). Click the button to add the new property and to define the code.

The properties 'company name', 'html tag' and 'name properties' have been selected as mandatory properties for identification (see the properties under "Object Identification - Mandatory"). However, when you spy on the object to view it properties, all properties under the "Properties" pane will be displayed.

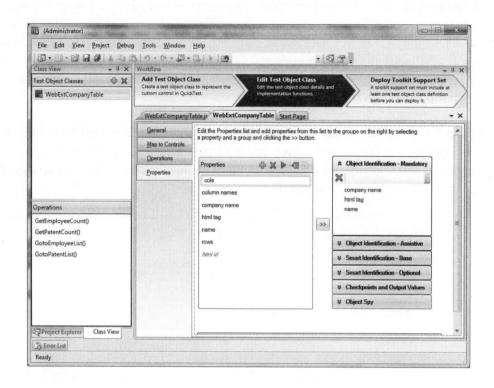

In the code view, the following code is added to define return values for identification properties:

```
////////////////////////////////////////////////////////////////
// Retrieves the run time values for the control's identification properties
// (defined in the test objects XML file).
// Parameters: property - The name of the property to retrieve.
// Returns:  Integer, String, Boolean, or Array.
//        The value of the requested property.
//        No value is returned if an error occurs or the specified
//        property is not supported by this method.
////////////////////////////////////////////////////////////////
function get_property_value(property)
{
  if (property == "cols")
  {
    return _elem.getElementsByTagName('tr')[1].getElementsByTagName('td').
```

```
length;
  }
  if (property == "column names" || property == "html tag")
  {
    // keep blank to use base class
  }
  if (property == "logical_name" || property == "company name")
  {
    return _elem.getElementsByTagName('th')[0].innerText;
  }
  if (property == "name")
  {
    return _elem.getElementsByTagName('th')[0].innerText;
  }
  if (property == "rows")
  {
      // keep blank to use base class
  }
}
```

NOTE: See the use of "property = logical_name" above. This will instruct QTP to use the company name as the logical name when adding objects to the Repository. When the Company_Table is added to the Object Repository, it will be added by the name of the company and not by the generic name (WebExtCompanyTable).

NOTE: The properties 'cols', 'column names', 'html tag', 'name' and 'rows' have no code specified because we would like these properties to inherit from the BaseClass and use the in-built methods instead.

We have now outlined all the required steps to define the identification properties. Our project can now be saved and is ready to be deployed to QTP.

F. Deploying the Solution to QuickTest

This section describes deploying the solution to QTP.

3. To deploy the solution, navigate to the Project menu and select Deploy > Deploy to QuickTest Professional as shown below.

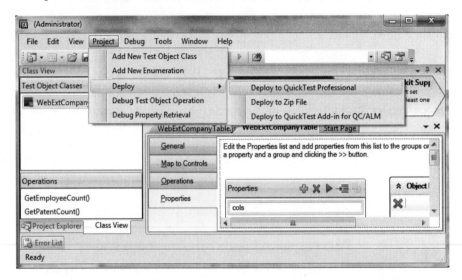

Figure 17.26 – Deploy Project to QTP

A confirmation message will appear to check that the solution was deployed correctly:

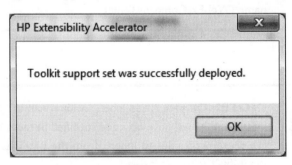

Figure 17.27 – Deployment Confirmation

Since our solution has been created and deployed to QTP, we can now start using the custom test object class.

G.   Using the Custom Test Object Class with QTP

To test whether all steps were performed successfully, start QTP and check that the solution name (WebExtCompanyApplication) appears under the Web add-in list.

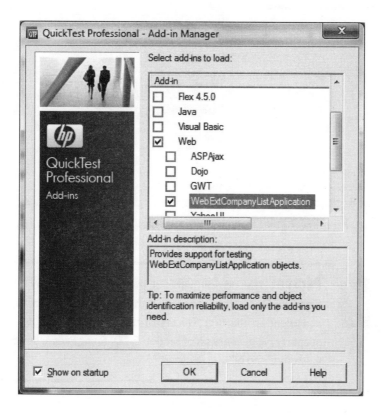

Figure 17.28 – Add-in Manager - Extensibility support displayed for WebExtCompanyListApplication

Launch the application under test and add the company table to the Local Object Repository. After adding the custom control in the Object Repository, we can see that the object was indeed added as the custom class we defined in the Extensibility Accelerator. Also notice the "Description Properties" which are the same as selected as the Mandatory properties for this object in Figure 17.26.

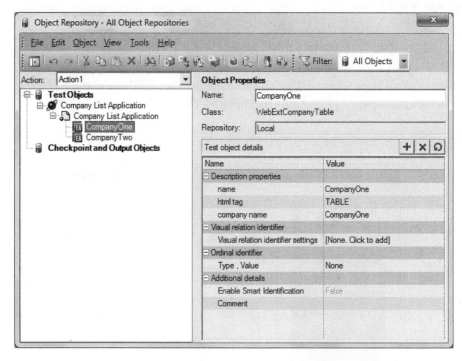

Figure 17.29 – Dialog showing WebExtCompanyTable's (CompanyOne) properties

NOTE: The logical name of the WebExtCompanyTable is CompanyOne because the logical_name property will always be equivalent to the first TH tag of the table (see step #2, get_property_value function of section E. "Defining Properties of the Custom Control").

When spying the company table, the following will be shown with all the properties (cols, colum names, company name, html tag, name and rows) defined for the custom test object:

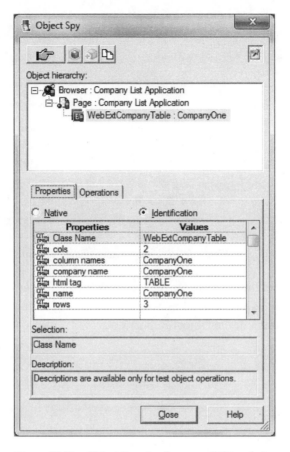

Figure 17.30 – Object Spy view for extensibility solution

When you write code for WebExtCompanyTable in the Expert View, complete IntelliSense with all methods available for WebTable (BaseClass) as well as the four methods we defined in section D. "Defining Operations" of this chapter.

The following figure shows IntelliSense for the Page object containing the custom control as a list of possible choices:

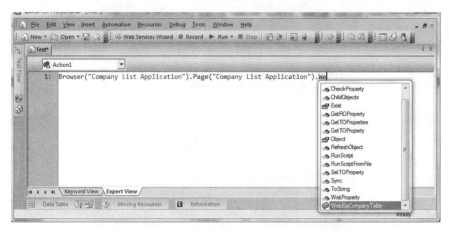

Figure 17.31 – IntelliSense for extensibility solution

The figure below shows IntelliSense for the added WebExtCompanyTable's companies. If there are more companies available, they will also be displayed as part of the IntelliSense as long as they are present in the Object Repository.

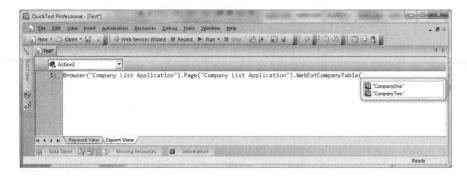

Figure 17.32 – IntelliSense for extensibility solution

Finally, when writing code for WebExtCompanyTable, notice that all the methods are available from the base WebTable class and all the custom operations are defined.

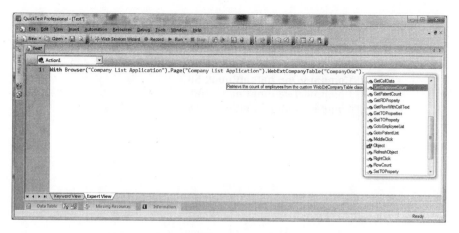

Figure 17.33 – IntelliSense for extensibility solution

Let's now test to see whether or not our code is able to retrieve the correct values from the AUT using the code below:

```
Print "CompanyOne empCount: " & _
  Browser("Company List Application") _
  .Page("Company List Application") _
  .WebExtCompanyTable("CompanyOne").GetEmployeeCount()

Print "CompanyOne patentCount: " & _
  Browser("Company List Application") _
  .Page("Company List Application") _
  .WebExtCompanyTable("CompanyOne").GetPatentCount()

Print "CompanyTwo empCount: " & _
  Browser("Company List Application") _
  .Page("Company List Application") _
  .WebExtCompanyTable("CompanyTwo").GetEmployeeCount()

Print "CompanyTwo patentCount: " & _
  Browser("Company List Application") _
  .Page("Company List Application") _
  .WebExtCompanyTable("CompanyTwo").GetPatentCount()
```

Output:

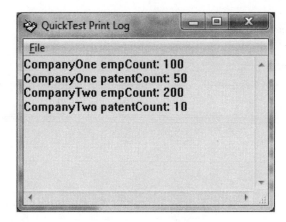

Figure 17.34 – Output log

After running the code, the results file can be viewed.. It should have the correct values retrieved for each entity:

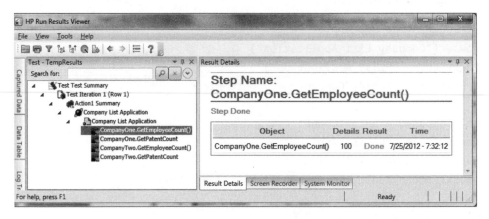

Figure 17.35 – Run Results window showing WebExtCompanyTable events

QTP was able to retrieve and report values for each of the custom operations because we had explicitly specified this in our operations code.

```
_util.Report(micDone, "GetEmployeeCount", toSafeArray(new Array()),
innerText);
```

Error handling is important here and can help us report errors if there are any changes in the UI. For example, if the name of the Employee Count column changes to 'Number of Employees', our GetEmployeeCount() function will throw an error:

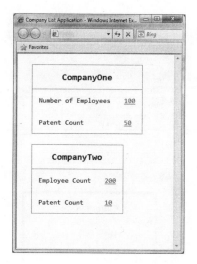

Figure 17.36 – Modified demo web page

Figure 17.37 – Run Error dialog

The same will be reported in the results viewer as shown in Figure 17.38.

This concludes our testing custom object class in QTP. A final step still remains: how to deploy the support set on other machines that will utilize the custom control.

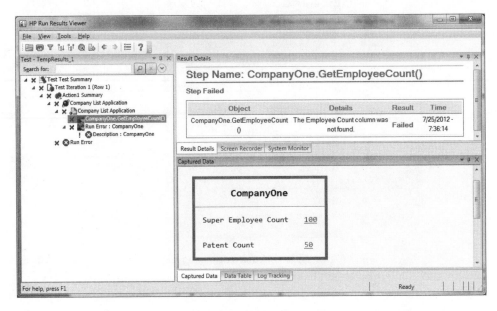

Figure 17.38 – Run Results Viewer

H.   Deploying Toolkit Support Set on Other Machines

The final stage of extending support for a custom toolkit is deploying the toolkit support set. On the main development machine, deployment can be done simply by using the Extensibility Accelerator. On other machines, to deploy support, you must place all files in the correct location. Once the files are deployed, the custom toolkit will appear as an option under the web add-in from the Add-in Manager window.

To deploy the Toolkit Support Set, follow these steps:

1. Move the Test Object Configuration file <CustomToolkitName>TestObjects.xml

to <QuickTest Installation folder>\dat\Extensibility\Web.

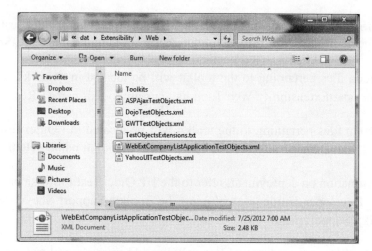

Figure 17.39 – Test Object Configuration file location

2. Create a folder with the name of your custom toolkit in the <QuickTest Installation folder>\dat\Extensibility\Web\Toolkits folder.

3. Move the custom toolkit folder on the development machine (in <QuickTest Installation folder>\dat\Extensibility\Web\Toolkits\<custom toolkit>) to <QuickTest Installation folder>\dat\Extensibility\Web\Toolkits.

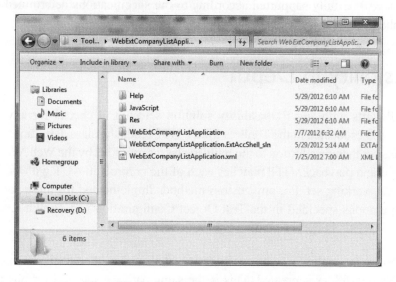

Figure 17.40 – Toolkit Configuration file location

Once the move is complete:

- All JS files pertaining to the toolkit will be located in <QuickTest Installation folder>\dat\Extensibility\Web\Toolkits\<custom toolkit name>\JavaScript.

- All icon files pertaining to the toolkit will be located in <QuickTest Installation folder>\dat\Extensibility\Web\Toolkits\<custom toolkit name>\Res.

- All Help files pertaining to the toolkit will be located in <QuickTest Installation folder>\dat\Extensibility\Web\Toolkits\<custom toolkit name>\Help.

For more information on deployment, refer to the HP QuickTest Professional Web Add-in Extensibility Developer Guide > Deploying the Toolkit Support Set > Deploying the Custom Toolkit Support menu.

In the example above, we see how the Extensibility add-in can be utilized to create custom test object classes that can hold static methods used directly in our test code. In the last step above, the custom object can store objects directly pertaining to the company name and use specific methods defined for the test object class.

This can be a very user-friendly and extremely useful approach in building robust tests. Teams can even utilize toolkit developers to write custom code and build extensibility and Test Engineers can directly employ custom operations against the UI. Each custom test object class will be fully supported according to the specifications determined during the planning phase.

Extensibility in Depth

When QTP starts with any Extensibility solution selected, it checks for any test object configuration files located in the Toolkits folder. QTP reads the class definitions and creates working sets for them in addition to the built-in classes provided by the Web Add-in. During learn, record and playback, QTP matches each of the controls in AUT with the test object classes in the working set. For any custom methods implemented for these controls, QTP uses the operations specified in the Test Object Configuration and Toolkit Configuration files.

After creating the solution, you will notice that under the Toolkits directory, the <SolutionName> folder is created. This is the same path we selected for our Solution in Step 3 above.

```
%User%\HP\QuickTest Professional\dat\Extensibility\Web\
Toolkits\<SolutionName>
```

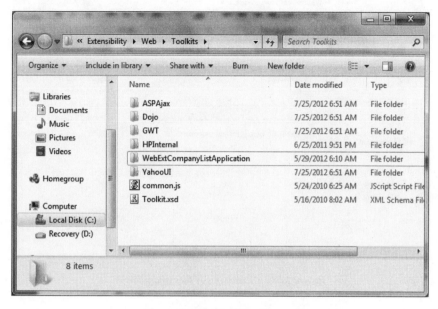

Figure 17.41 – Toolkits directory

The <SolutionName> (WebExtCompanyApplication in our case) folder contains the following files and folders:

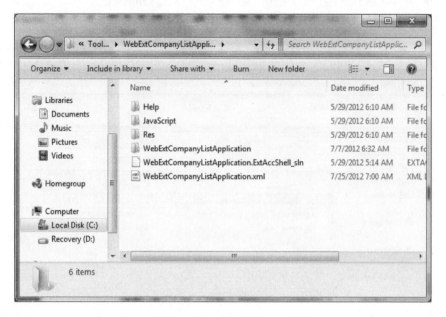

Figure 17.42 – Extensibility files and folders

Let's cover the components of the custom Web Extensibility folder.

Amongst other files in the folder, there is a set of files called the Toolkit Support Set. The Toolkit Support Set is a group of files used to instruct QTP on how to create test objects for the custom controls, how to record events against those controls and how to execute events on those controls during a Test-run. The Toolkit Support Set for the custom web control comprises of a Test Object Configuration file and a Toolkit Configuration file.

Test Object Configuration File

The Test Object Configuration file contains the name of the toolkit, the name of the QTP add-in and the definitions of the test object classes. The file can be found in the following location:

```
Toolkits\<SolutionName<\<SolutionName>\<SolutionName>TestObjects.xml
```

So, in our case:

```
Toolkits\WebExtCompanyListApplication\WebExtCompanyListApplication\
WebExtCompanyListApplicationTestObjects.xml
```

The contents of the Test Object Configuration file are shown below:

```xml
<?xml version="1.0" encoding="utf-8"?>
<TypeInformation xsi:noNamespaceSchemaLocation="file:///C:/Program Files
(x86)/HP/Extensibility Accelerator/bin/PackagesToLoad/ClassesDefintions.xsd"
xmlns:xsi="http://www.w3.org/2001/XMLSchema-instance" xmlns:xsd="http://
www.w3.org/2001/XMLSchema" PackageName="WebExtCompanyListApplication"
AddinName="Web">
  <ClassInfo GenericTypeID="Table" Name="WebExtCompanyTable"
BaseClassInfoName="WebTable">
  <Description>Custom Company List Table for the Company List Application
website. This object was created using Web Add-in Extensibility for QTP</
Description>
  <HelpInfo />
  <IconInfo IconFile="INSTALLDIR\Dat\Extensibility\Web\Toolkits\
WebExtCompanyListApplication\Res\ExtAccShell.ico" IconIndex="0" />
  <TypeInfo>
    <Operation Name="GetEmployeeCount" PropertyType="Method">
    <Description>Retrieve the count of employees from the custom
WebExtCompanyTable class</Description>
    <ReturnValueType>
      <Type VariantType="Variant" />
    </ReturnValueType>
    </Operation>
    <Operation Name="GetPatentCount" PropertyType="Method">
    <Description>Retrieve the patent information from the custom
WebExtCompanyTable class</Description>
    <ReturnValueType>
      <Type VariantType="Variant" />
    </ReturnValueType>
    </Operation>
    <Operation Name="GotoEmployeeList" PropertyType="Method">
    <Description>Navigates to the list of employees for the selected
Company</Description>
    <ReturnValueType>
      <Type VariantType="None" />
    </ReturnValueType>
    </Operation>
    <Operation Name="GotoPatentList" PropertyType="Method">
```

```
      <Description>Navigates to the list of patents for the selected
Company</Description>
    </Operation>
  </TypeInfo>
  <IdentificationProperties>
    <IdentificationProperty Name="cols" ForVerification="true"
ForDefaultVerification="true" />
    <IdentificationProperty Name="column names" ForVerification="true"
ForDefaultVerification="true" />
    <IdentificationProperty Name="company name" />
    <IdentificationProperty Name="html tag" ForVerification="true"
ForDefaultVerification="true" ForDescription="true" />
    <IdentificationProperty Name="name" ForVerification="true"
ForDefaultVerification="true" ForDescription="true" />
    <IdentificationProperty Name="rows" ForVerification="true"
ForDefaultVerification="true" />
  </IdentificationProperties>
  </ClassInfo>
</TypeInformation>
```

TypeInformation element

The TypeInformation element is the topmost element of the Test Object Configuration file. This element contains all of the test object classes which are defined by ClassInfo elements.

- AddinName [required]: The name of the add-in to which this file applies. The test object created in the example belongs to standard web and must be specified or the file will not be loaded. The AddinName_Type can take the following possible values:

```
<xs:simpleType xmlns:xs="http://www.w3.org/2001/XMLSchema" name="AddinName_
Type">
  <xs:union memberTypes="xs:string">
    <xs:simpleType>
      <xs:restriction base="xs:string">
        <xs:enumeration value="ActiveX" />
        <xs:enumeration value="Delphi" />
        <xs:enumeration value="Java" />
        <xs:enumeration value=".NET" />
```

```
        <xs:enumeration value="Oracle" />
        <xs:enumeration value="PeopleSoft" />
        <xs:enumeration value="PowerBuilder" />
        <xs:enumeration value="SAP" />
        <xs:enumeration value="SapGui" />
        <xs:enumeration value="Siebel" />
        <xs:enumeration value="Silverlight" />
        <xs:enumeration value="Standard" />
        <xs:enumeration value="Stingray" />
        <xs:enumeration value="TEA" />
        <xs:enumeration value="Terminal Emulators" />
        <xs:enumeration value="Visual Basic" />
        <xs:enumeration value="VisualAge Smalltalk" />
        <xs:enumeration value="Web" />
        <xs:enumeration value="Web Services" />
        <xs:enumeration value="Windows Applications" />
        <xs:enumeration value="WPF" />
      </xs:restriction>
    </xs:simpleType>
  </xs:union>
</xs:simpleType>
```

- PackageName [required]: The name of the toolkit set to which this file applies. This name is determined by the name of the solution created in HP Extensibility Accelerator IDE. This value also appears in the list of available add-ins in the Add-in Manager dialog box.

ClassInfo element

The ClassInfo element defines the name of the custom control and to what GenericClass and BaseClass it is mapped to. The ClassInfo element supports the following arguments:

- Name [required]: Name of the (custom) test object class.

- BaseClassInfoName [optional]: Name of the base test object class. In the XML above, WebTable is the base class which belongs to the standard set of objects provided by the web add-in. The BaseClass can be one of the standard classes or one of the classes created from Extensibility.

- DefaultOperationName [optional]: The default operation of the (custom) test object class. A custom control may or may not have a default operation associated with it. If this is not defined but the BaseClassInfoName is, the default operation of BaseClassInfoName will be used. For example, if the BaseClassInfoName is WebEdit but the DefaultOperationName is not defined, "Set" will be used by default.

- GenericTypeID [optional]: This attribute points to the generic test object class. For example, the generic class for WebTable, SwfTable and JavaTable is Table. In cases where this attribute is not defined but BaseClassInfoName is, the generic type is built from the BaseClassInfoName.

Description element

The Description element is simply a string description for the elements ClassInfo or Operation. In the XML above, the Description element is created for the ClassInfo (test object class). The following XML shows the Description element created for an Operation:

```
<Operation Name="GetEmployeeCount" PropertyType="Method">
  <Description>Retrieve the count of employees from the custom
WebExtCompanyTable class</Description>
  <ReturnValueType>
     <Type VariantType="Variant" />
  </ReturnValueType>
</Operation>
```

IdentificationProperty element

The IdentificationProperty defines the identification property for the test object class. For the custom WebExtCompanyTable, the following identification properties have been selected:

- cols

- column names

- company name

- html tag

- name

- rows

```
<IdentificationProperties>
    <IdentificationProperty Name="cols" ForVerification="true"
ForDefaultVerification="true" />
    <IdentificationProperty Name="column names" ForVerification="true"
ForDefaultVerification="true" />
    <IdentificationProperty Name="company name" ForDescription="true" />
    <IdentificationProperty Name="html tag" ForVerification="true"
ForDefaultVerification="true" ForDescription="true" />
    <IdentificationProperty Name="name" ForVerification="true"
ForDefaultVerification="true" ForDescription="true" />
    <IdentificationProperty Name="rows" ForVerification="true"
ForDefaultVerification="true" />
</IdentificationProperties>
```

The properties 'column names', 'html tag' and 'name' were selected as mandatory properties, which is why they have the 'ForDescription' attribute equaling 'TRUE'.

IconInfo element

The IconInfo element provides icon information for the ClassInfo or Operation elements. For operations, the IconInfo is only displayed in the run results. If IconInfo is not defined, a default icon is used. IconInfo supports the following two attributes:

- IconFile [required]: Path to the file that contains the icon. This file can be a .dll, .exe or .ico file.

- IconIndex [optional]: Index of the icon's location in the file. It is only required when specifying a .dll or .exe file.

ReturnValueType element

This element defines the type of value returned by the operation performed.

Load element

Load [optional]: The Load attribute can be used to specify whether the toolkit file is to be loaded by QTP or not. Instead of removing the file from the folder to prevent QTP from reading it, the Load attribute can be set to False. Possible values are:

- True: file will be loaded and instructions available will be used.

- False: file will not be loaded and instructions available will not be used.

The Toolkit Configuration file

The Toolkit Configuration file provides details for Object Identification, recording, filters applied, Run-time operations and settings for custom events supported by the control. The location of this file is:

```
Toolkits\<SolutionName> \<SolutionName>.xml
```

So, in our case:

```
Toolkits\WebExtCompanyListApplication\WebExtCompanyListApplication.xml
```

The contents of the Toolkit Configuration file are shown below:

```
<?xml version="1.0" encoding="utf-8"?>
<Controls xsi:noNamespaceSchemaLocation="file:///C:/Program Files
(x86)/HP/Extensibility Accelerator/bin/PackagesToLoad/Toolkit.xsd"
xmlns:xsi="http://www.w3.org/2001/XMLSchema-instance" xmlns:xsd="http://
www.w3.org/2001/XMLSchema">
  <Control TestObjectClass="WebExtCompanyTable">
  <Settings>
    <Variable name="default_imp_file" value="JavaScript\WebExtCompanyTable.
js" />
  </Settings>
  <Identification>
    <Browser name="*">
    <Conditions type="IdentifyIfPropMatch">
      <Condition prop_name="className" expected_value="company" />
      <Condition prop_name="tagName" expected_value="TABLE" />
    </Conditions>
    </Browser>
  </Identification>
  <Filter>
```

```
     <Learn learn_children="No" />
   </Filter>
   </Control>
</Controls>
```

In order to support the custom control, HP Extensibility Accelerator created a Toolkit Configuration file, which contains the test object class to represent the given control. The following elements make up the Toolkit Configuration file:

Control element

The Control element of this file points to the test object classes created in the solution. In the example, there is a single test object class created: WebExtCompanyTable. If there are additional classes, the number of Control elements would increment to equal the number of custom classes defined.

Identification element

The Identification element (the most basic element of the web add-in Extensibility) defines which controls should be represented by the test object class. For QuickTest to record or replay against a control against the application under test, it checks the Identification element defined for each of the test object classes in scope.

Conditions element

The Conditions element of the Identification element contains the Condition elements which must be met for the target object to be recognized as the custom Test Object class.

- In the above XML file, an object with className=company and tagName=TABLE will be identified as a WebExtCompanyTable test object.

- Each Condition (child) element can contain a single definition only.

- The value of the specified prop_name must match the expected specified value. QuickTest uses case-insensitive comparisons to execute the match.

- The above Identification element hierarchy can be modified to the below format for better performance as it instructs QTP to perform identification against test objects only on TABLE html tags.

For each of the Conditions elements, it is possible to use the TYPE attribute to instruct QTP to treat the control if its properties match the conditions. There are three TYPE attributes possible for Conditions:

- IdentifyIfPropMatch: If conditions are met, use the current test object class.

- CallIDFuncIfPropMatch: If conditions are met, call the Identification function to check this control or do not use the current test object class.

- SkipIfPropMatch: If conditions are met, do not use the current test object class.

```
<Identification>
  <Browser name="*">
  <HTMLTags>
    <Tag name="TABLE">
  </HTMLTags>
  <Conditions type="IdentifyIfPropMatch">
    <Condition prop_name="className" expected_value="company" />
  </Conditions>
  </Browser>
</Identification>
```

Settings element

In the XML file, the Settings element contains the required path to the JavaScript file necessary to execute custom-built methods (events) against the WebExtCompanyTable test object class.

- This instructs QTP to search for JavaScript files in <QuickTest installation folder>\dat\Extensibility\Web\Toolkits\<SolutionName>\JavaScript folder.

- If this file is not found or is corrupt, a Run-time error will occur.

- The example in the previous section demonstrates <Method1>, <Method2> and <Method3> created for the test object class.

Filter element

The Filter element of the Control element helps determine which dependants of the Test Object class are to be learned when adding them to the Object Repository.

- In the above file, the learn_children attribute of the Filter element is marked "No" – this will prevent QTP from learning child objects of the WebExtCompanyTable class.

- Simply mark this property as "Yes" or change it from the "Filter Options" of the Extensibility Accelerator as shown in <Step 10> in the previous section.

Using Functions to Define Filters

In the example above it was specified in the Extensibility Accelerator to not learn any of the custom control's children when recording. In the Toolkit Configuration file, an entry was added after making this selection:

```
<Filter>
  <Learn learn_children="No" />
</Filter>
```

So what if you would like to add some objects? What if in the example above, you simply wanted to add LINK objects and nothing else? This can be done by defining a Filter function. To add only the link objects for the custom test object class WebExtCompanyTable, a new filter function 'CallFilter()' can be used.

```
function ChildrenToLearn() {
  return toSafeArray(_elem.getElementsByTagName('a'));
}
```

The function can be set from General > Advanced > Filter Options.

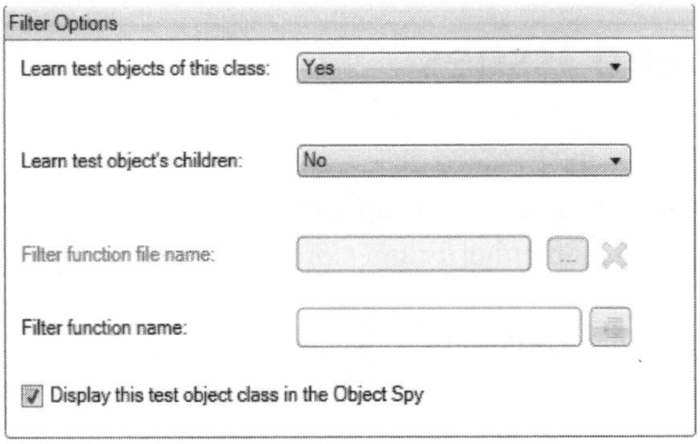

Figure 17.43 – Filter Options

Making the above change will also change the Filter element of the Toolkit Configuration file as shown below:

```
<Filter>
  <Learn function="ChildrenToLearn"
    file_name="JavaScript\WebExtCompanyTable.js"
    learn_children="CallFilterFunc" />
</Filter>
```

Using Functions to Define Operations

As covered in this chapter's section 'Defining operations to be supported by the custom control', custom operations can be defined for the test object class. A new function can be added using the Operations button from the left pane of the Extensibility Accelerator.

Using Functions to Get Property Values

Functions can be used to get property values, in cases where a custom property is defined, the return value of the base property is to be customized or in the way in which QTP defines the logical name of an object. The function below shows how get_property_value can be used to instruct QTP to add the content from the TH tag as the logical name of the object.

```
function get_property_value(property) {
  if (property == "loglcal_name")
    return _elem.getElementsByTagName('th')[0].innerText;
}
```

Limitations and Issues

Web add-in Extensibility can be used to create support for objects within a Page or a Frame, although it is not possible to add support for Pages or Frames themselves. In other words, it is not possible to map either Frames or a Page as a test object class.

If testing a web application in Mozilla Firefox, it is not possible to use Click or FireEvent to click a link. A workaround is given in the QTP documentation (shown below):

```
function clickOnLink() {
  if (_util.GetBrowserType() == QtpConstants.IE) {
```

```
      link.click();
  }
  else {
    var evObj = window.document.createEvent("MouseEvents");
    evObj.initEvent("click", true, true);
    _util.FireEvent(link, "click", evObj);
  }
}
```

If the custom control is a hidden HTML element in an area of the application that is accessed via scrolling to its location, QTP may fail to scroll to its location. A workaround as per the documentation is available, but only for Internet Explorer. In the Toolkit Support Set, implement the following properties for the test object class:

- x – control's x-coordinate relative to the frame in pixels.

- y - control's y-coordinate relative to the frame in pixels.

- width – control's width in pixels.

- height – control's height in pixels.

You must also make sure that your code is perfectly valid before deploying and testing your toolkit. If there is any error which you have missed, the toolkit may fail to work and any function with an error will not execute. A downside to this is not just us retrieving an incorrect value, but that the error in the function will not be shown either.

Creating Reserved Objects

Introduction

A reserved object allows you to add a specialized keyword to QuickTest which unlike custom classes provides you with IntelliSense. For example, the Environment object is a reserved object with the ProgId of "Mercury.MicEnvironment". Similarly, a Description object (Description.Create) is another reserved object with ProgId of "Mercury.DescObjCreator". Just like with these reserved objects, it is also possible to create custom reserved objects.

At runtime, QuickTest creates a single instance of the reserved object as required by the test code. Unlike instances of other objects, such as references to custom classes or classic COM objects (Scripting.Dictionary or FileSystemObject objects created explicitly during Test-run, for example), a reserved object is created on demand when referenced during Test-run. Usage and creation of Reserved Objects was first shown in the documentation made available with QTP Plus (QTP 8.2).

How to Create Reserved Objects

A reserved object must be an COM object registered (using RegAsm for .NET DLL or RegSvr32 for Windows DLL) on the system before it can be used. To demonstrate, a reserved object for the below math operations class will be created. It is assumed that the object has been registered to the system and its relevant keys are present in the Registry Editor.

```csharp
namespace RelevantCodes.MathOperations
{
  using System;
  using System.Runtime.InteropServices;

  [ComVisible(true)]
  [InterfaceType(ComInterfaceType.InterfaceIsIDispatch)]
  [Guid("51C85580-1190-4348-AE21-1B52965AC45D")]
  public interface IMath
  {
    int Add(int lhs, int rhs);
    int Substract(int lhs, int rhs);
    int Multiply(int lhs, int rhs);
    int Divide(int numerator, int denominator);
  }
  [ComVisible(true)]
  [Guid("FE477873-0966-4c80-915F-77B333316C98")]
  [ProgId("RelevantCodes:MathOperations")]
  [ClassInterface(ClassInterfaceType.None)]
  [ComDefaultInterface(typeof(Math))]
  public class MathClass : IMath
  {
    public int Add(int lhs, int rhs)
    {
      return (lhs + rhs);
    }
    public int Substract(int lhs, int rhs)
    {
      return (lhs - rhs);
    }
```

```
    public int Multiply(int lhs, int rhs)
    {
      return (lhs * rhs);
    }
    public int Divide(int numerator, int denominator)
    {
      return (numerator / denominator);
    }
  }
}
```

NOTE: To register the above class with ProgId "RelevantCodes.MathOperations" to the system, create a new class library project in Visual Studio, mark it for COM Interop and build it. This should create the required keys in the Registry. The ProgId will later be used as the reference to calling the reserved object in QuickTest.

After building the above project, it can now be registered as a reserved object in QuickTest using the ProgId marked for the class. The following 4 steps demonstrate this:

1. Run the Registry Editor (regedit.exe)

2. Create a logical name (key) for the reserved object under:

    HKEY_CURRENT_USER\SOFTWARE\Mercury Interactive\QuickTest Professional\MicTest\ReservedObjects

    In this case, a key named 'Math' is created as shown in Figure 18.1

3. Add 'String Value' under the key to point to the object class ProgId. This should be the same ProgId that you defined when you created it. In this case, the value to be used is RelevantCodes.MathOperations as shown in Figure 18.2

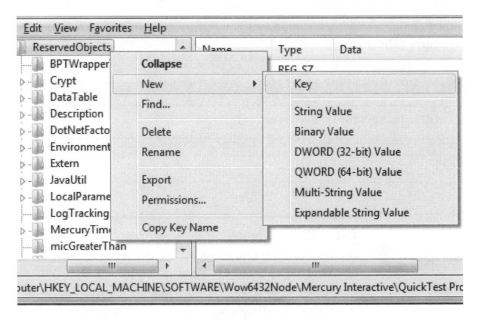

Figure 18.1 – Registry Editor - Creating New Key

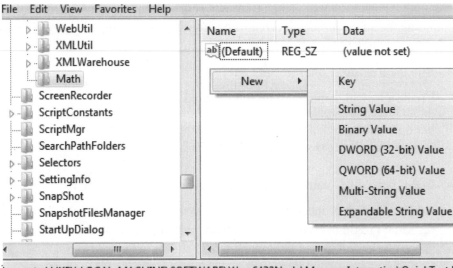

Figure 18.2 – Registry Editor - Creating New String Value

4. Now start QuickTest and enter 'Math' followed by a dot. The four methods of the interface (IMath) should now be displayed.

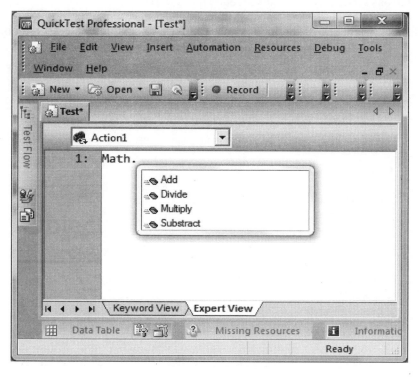

Figure 18.3 – IntelliSense in QTP

Creating an Icon for the Reserved Object

It is also possible to create icons to associate with your custom reserved object. Even though this is not required for Expert view, any operation against this object in the Keyword view will show a custom icon. The icons should be added to the resource file of your COM application.

1. To add an icon to your reserved object, navigate to the following path in Registry Editor (regedit.exe):

    ```
    HKEY_CURRENT_USER\SOFTWARE\Mercury Interactive\QuickTest
    Professional\MicTest\ReservedObjects\<Custom Reserved Object>
    ```

    In our example, since the name of the reserved object is Math, the resulting path becomes:

    ```
    HKEY_CURRENT_USER\SOFTWARE\Mercury Interactive\QuickTest
    ```

```
Professional\MicTest\ReservedObjects\Math
```

2. Create a new key called Icons under the above Registry key (reserved object).

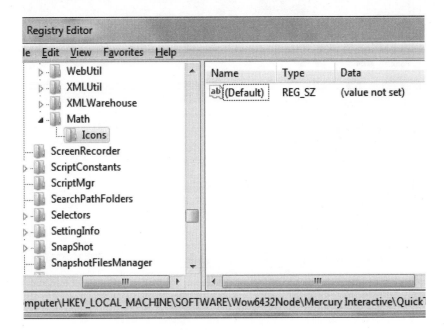

Figure 18.4 – Icons Key

3. Add the following entries to the Icons key to enable QuickTest to use the relevant icons for your custom methods. The format is:

```
<Resource DLL>, <Regular-Icon ID>, <Focused-Icon ID>
```

 NOTE: You can use the same icon for regular and focused states (as we will be using in this example).

In this sample case, the path for the default value is:

```
C:\RelevantCodesMathOperations.dll, 101, 101
```

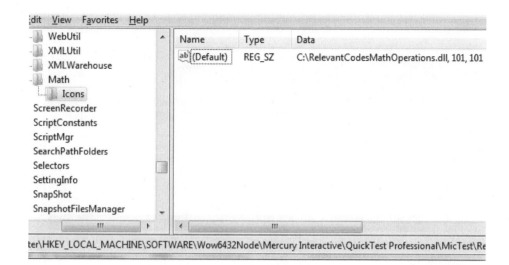

Figure 18.5 – Icon Reference Path

 NOTE: A direct path to the .ico file can also be used. Example: C:\icon.ico.

The icon used for the math class is shown below:

RC

Figure 18.6 – Logo

4. Open QTP and type the following statement in the Expert View (or using Step Generator in Keyword view):

```
MsgBox Math.Add(5, 5)
```

5. Switch over to the Keyword view and the new icon will be displayed.

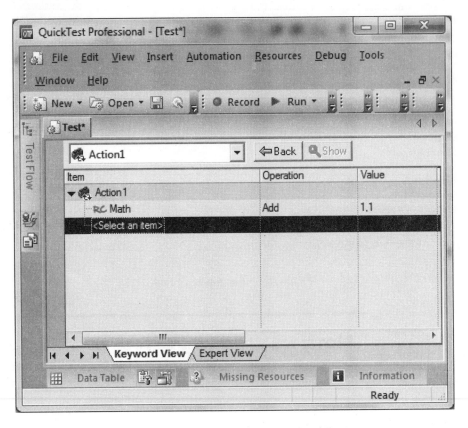

Figure 18.7 – Logo Displayed in Keyword View

NOTE: The techniques in this chapter show creation of Reserved Objects using .NET (Visual Studio, C#). It is also possible to create them using Windows Script Host (WSC) as demonstrated at AdvancedQTP.com in the following 2 articles:

1. http://www.advancedqtp.com/intellisense-and-com/
2. http://www.advancedqtp.com/reserved-objects-as-an-env-objectreplacement/

Appendix A - Approaches for Issue Resolution

Problem 1 – Application crashes when launched with QTP already open

Some applications have problems with QTP's ActiveX add-in. In such cases the application crashes when QTP is open, but works fine when QTP is closed. We can unload the ActiveX add-in if it is not required which usually fixes the problem. If the ActiveX add-in needs to be loaded, there are a few possible Registry fixes that we can try:

1. **If IE crashes with a Non-Silverlight application**

Open regedit.exe. Browse to below mentioned key:

```
HKEY_CURRENT_USER\Software\Mercury Interactive\QuickTest
Professional\MicTest\ActiveX Add-in
```

Create a new value with the name 'UseBBHook' and set the value as 1.

2. If IE crashes with a Silverlight application

Open regedit.exe. Browse to below mentioned key:

```
HKEY_CURRENT_USER\Software\Mercury Interactive\QuickTest
Professional\MicTest\ActiveX Add-in\ProgID\AgControl.AgControl.4.1
```

Create a new value with the name 'Category' and set the value as 'MultiMedia'.

Create a new value with the name 'Trapping' and set the value as 0.

Problem 2 – Java application crashes when launched after installing QTP's Java add-in

Some Java applications crash when the Java add-in hooks interfere with the JVM. There are a few possible ways to fix this issue:

1. QTP installation with spaces in the path

Sometimes blank spaces in QTP's installation path causes problems with the Java add-in. Installing QTP on a direct path like C:\QTP will help in fixing the issue.

2. Disabling the Java add-in on the machine

The Java add-in can be disabled by renaming or disabling the following Windows environment variables:

- IBM_JAVA_OPTIONS
- _JAVA_OPTIONS
- JAVA_TOOL_OPTIONS

This will disable the Java add-in on the machine and QTP will not recognize any JAVA application even if the Java add-in is loaded.

3. Disabling Java add-in for a specific application

If the Java application runs as an exe then by using Registry entry, we can disable the Java add-in.

Open regedit.exe. Browse to the below mentioned key:

```
HKEY_LOCAL_MACHINE\SOFTWARE\Mercury Interactive\JavaAgent\Modules
```

Create a new data value named 'ApplicationName.exe' with value set as 0.

 NOTE: If the application runs as a JAR file or directly using JAVA.exe or JAVAW.exe then this solution will not help.

4. **Running the application using custom batch file**

If we need to disable the Java add-in just for a specific application, we can create a batch file as below:

```
C:\LaunchApp.bat
set _JAVA_OPTIONS=
set IBM_JAVA_OPTIONS=
set JAVA_TOOL_OPTIONS=
java -jar MyApplicationName.jar
```

Problem 3 – QTP identifies IE Browser as window object

There are many possible reasons if your IE Browser is recognized as a Window object:

1. If IE is launched before QTP then QTP will not be able to identify the Browser correctly.

2. If the Web Add-in is not loaded, QTP will not identify the Browser object correctly.

3. If Record and Run settings are not set to record and run on any Browser. To fix this, browse to menu Automation->Record and Run Settings, browse to the Web tab and make sure the radio button for 'Record and run test on any open browser' is selected.

4. If you are using a version of QTP that doesn't support the version of IE, QTP may not identify the browser properly and therefore crash.

   o QTP 10 – Supports IE7 by default, and IE8 using patch QTPWEB_00035 or QTP_00626 o   QTP 11 – Supports IE8 by default, and IE9 using patch QTPWEB_00078

Make sure the correct patches are installed based on the version you have.

5. Protected mode in IE settings is ON. QTP 11 with QTPWEB_00073 patch supports record and replay on browser with Protected Mode ON. Without this setup the Protected Mode should be kept off at all times.

6. User Access Control (In case of Windows Vista and Windows 7) can also cause issues with QTP identifying objects correctly. Run the UserAccountControlSettings. exe to disable UAC control.

7. BHOManager is disabled in IE. QTP uses an add-on named BHOManager to communicate with IE. If this add-on is disabled, the identification may not work correctly. To check the status of the add-in, go to Tools->Manage Add-ons and make sure BHOManager Class add-on is enabled.

8. User profile is corrupt. At times the windows user profile gets corrupted. In such cases, the issue only persists for the affected user(s) on a system. To check if this is the case, create a new user on the machine and login with this new user. If QTP works fine with IE, this indicates a corrupted profile. The fix is to have your old user profile deleted from windows and logon again to create a new profile

9. Corrupt QTP installation. A corrupt installation can also cause identification issues. Run the setup again in Repair mode to fix it.

Problem 4 – QTP fails to identify the parent of the target object

This is one of the most common errors encountered by QTP engineers. When targeting a field in the AUT, QTP throws the error: "Cannot find the [Child] object's parent [Parent]." Here, even though we expect the error to arise from the field, the error instead is thrown because of a recognition issue caused by the [Parent]. Below is a snapshot of such an error:

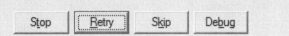

Cannot find the "[WebElement]" object's parent "[Browser]" (class Browser). Verify that parent properties match an object currently displayed in your application.

Line (1): "Browser("title:=KnowledgeInbox").Page("micclass:=Page").WebElement("innertext:=Tarun").Click".

Tip: If the objects in your application have changed, the Maintenance Run Mode can help you identify and update your steps and/or the objects in your repository.

| Stop | Retry | Skip | Debug |

Figure A.1 – Run Error - Object's Parent not found

The error itself is self-explanatory, but there may be several reasons why this error occurs:

1. The [Parent] object's properties have changed from design/record time. Make sure your code is accounting for dynamic properties used to identify the [Parent] object.

2. The loaded add-ins are not sufficient to recognize the AUT. For example, you may be testing a web application without the web add-in loaded at startup.

3. The [Parent] object is not available for testing. This error may also arise in cases where, even though all properties in the context are valid, the Parent itself is not launched or available for testing. Always make sure to launch the Parent and verify if it is available before proceeding with the rest of your code.

4. You may be working with a version of the application which is not supported by QTP. Assume that your tests were created on IE7 but you have now upgraded to a latest version of IE as per your enterprise policies. Unfortunately, the latest version of IE may not be supported by QTP. The lack of support will also can cause this error.

5. QTP was launched after the application, preventing it from injecting the required hooks.

Problem 5 – QTP is unable to find the target object

This error is quite similar to the previous Problem #4. In this case, the [Parent] object is locatable but the [Child] is not. Since the [Parent] is locatable, even though chances of an incorrect add-in become relatively low, they are not completely eliminated. Also, point #3 from the previous problem no longer applies here.

Cannot identify the object "[WebElement]" (of class WebElement). Verify that this object's properties match an object curren displayed in your application.

Line (1): "Browser("title:=KnowledgeInbox").Page("micclass:=Page").WebElement("innertext:=Tarun").Click".

Tip: If the objects in your application have changed, the Maintenance Run Mode can help you identify and update your steps and/or the objects in your repository.

Stop   Retry   Skip   Debug

Figure A.2 – Run Error - Cannot Identify the Object

1. The [Child] object's properties have changed from design/record time. Make sure your code is accounting for dynamic properties used to identify the [Child] object.

2. The required add-ins are not loaded. It may be possible that the required add-in for the [Child] object is different from the one for its [Parent]. This is especially true for Flash/Flex applications. Flash and Flex controls are embedded in a browser, so with the web add-in, QTP may be able to identify the [Parent] but fail to identify any of the [Child] controls. Example of Flex hierarchy in QTP is shown below:

```
Browser("Browser").FlexApplication("App").FlexForm("Form").
FlexRadioButton("Radio")
```

Problem 6 – QTP finds multiple objects of the supplied description

This error is very similar to the previous Problem #5, but point #2 from the same will never apply because QTP is able to find more than a single match.

The "[WebElement]" object's description matches more than one of the objects currently displayed in your application. Add additional properties to the object description in order to uniquely identify the object.

Line (1): "Browser("title:=KnowledgeInbox").Page("micclass:=Page").WebElement("innertext:=Tarun Lalwani").Click".

Tip: If the objects in your application have changed, the Maintenance Run Mode can help you identify and update your steps and/or the objects in your repository.

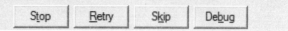

Figure A.3 – Run Error - Multiple matches

1. Identification properties are not sufficient for QTP to uniquely identify the object. This is a common reason for failure in Automation scripts.

      a.   To fix this error, ensure that the properties are unique enough. You may have to make use of Ordinal Identifiers (index, location) here.

      b.   Creating an object collection (ChildObjects) may also be considered.

      c.   Provide additional properties to make the description unique.

Problem 7 – 'General Run Error' occurs while performing an operation

QTP uses different threads for execution of associated library files and Actions. When we call a method from one thread to another and an error is raised, then at times the error text is not communicated between the two threads. These errors with missing text are thrown as a general run error by QTP. The resolution of these errors is dependent upon the root cause. In some cases it is possible to get the exception text by viewing the DescribeResult(Err. Number) in QTP's Debug window.

Some situations in which a general run error can occur are as follows:

- ⊙ Performing an operation on an object when the object or its parent doesn't exist.

- ⊙ Passing less or more than required arguments to a function.

- ⊙ Performing operations on an object derived from ChildObjects when the application has changed after using ChildObjects.

- Saving a test to HP QC/ALM when you don't have appropriate rights or there is no space left on the server.

- Saving a test to HP QC/ALM when the connection to the server has already disconnected.

Note that the above is not an exhaustive list and that the error can occur in other cases as well.

Problem 8 – ChildObjects returns 0 objects even when the objects exist

The ChildObjects method can return an empty collection in the following cases:

- When you are trying to get objects from a web application which are of type WebElement and the description's micclass has not been set to WebElement (case-sensitive).

- When you have create a description which actually doesn't match the desired set of properties in the application.

- When you have used a Regular Expression in a property which doesn't support Regular Expression. oDesc("x").value = "2|30|50", properties like x, y, abs_x, abs_y don't support Regular Expression.

- When you have used the wrong data type for the property. For some properties which take numeric values, the value should be given as below:

```
oDesc("prop").value = 1
instead of
oDesc("prop").value = "1"
```

Problem 9 – QTP only recognizes Browser and Page object after opening or closing of a popup opened by application

In rare instances we have noticed that QTP loses its object recognition capabilities for a WebBrowser and only identifies the Browser and the Page object. This is an unusual situation and HP support should be contacted. There does, however, exist a hidden and undocumented method named RefreshWebSupport that you can try as a workaround. Just call the method on the Browser object and it will try to restore the Object Identification mechanism with the Browser.

```
Browser("Browser").RefreshWebSupport
```

 NOTE: Refreshing the web page using Browser("Browser").Refresh or by sending the F5 keys to the browser can also help fix the issue.

Problem 10 – I get different errors when using Mercury.ObjectRepositoryUtil. How can I fix these errors?

ObjectRepositoryUtil is one of the most unstable and problematic APIs in QTP and the cause of many of its errors remains unknown. Here are few solutions to help fix some of the know issues:

- ◉ If the API throws a Pure Virtual Function Call error with QTP 10 then make sure you have installed the QTP_00598 Hotfix patch.

- ◉ If you get a general error when using the Load method, then it possible that the file path specified doesn't exists. This error will also be thrown if the file has the ReadOnly flag set in the filesystem.

- ◉ If you don't destroy the created object, QTP will throw an error on the next run when calling the load method. The only way to fix this issue is to restart QTP or, failing that, restart the machine. One way to avoid the issue is to create the object using the below class, rather than directly:

```
Class MicORUtil
  Public API

  Sub Class_Initialize()
    Set API = CreateObject("Mercury.ObjectRepositoryUtil")
  End Sub
```

```
      Sub Class_Terminate()
        Set API = Nothing
      End Sub
   End Class

   Dim ORUtil, clsORUtil
   'Create the object repository automation API
   Set clsORUtil = New MicORUtil
   Set ORUtil = clsORUtil.API

   'Load the object repository
   ORUtil.Load "C:\temp\SharedOR.tsr"
```

◉ If you try and perform any operation on an object derived from ORUtil, QTP will throw an error:

```
   Set Obj = ORUtil.GetObject("Browser(""KnowledgeInbox"")")
   Obj.Navigate "http://KnowledgeInbox.com"
```

ObjectRepositoryUtil is an API tool for reading and modifying objects in external Shared OR files. It is not an API that can be used to generate objects at runtime and then use them, hence the above code will not work.

Problem 11 – How can I keep a Browser or Window always on Top?

At times, there is a requirement to keep a specific window on top of other windows during a run session. The function below can be used to set a window of any type (Browsers included) to be the uppermost one:

```
Public Const SWP_NOMOVE = 2
Public Const SWP_NOSIZE = 1
Public Const HWND_TOPMOST = -1
Public Const HWND_NOTOPMOST = -2
'Declare Function SetWindowPos Lib "user32" Alias "SetWindowPos"  _
' ( _
'    ByVal hwnd As Long, _
'    ByVal hWndInsertAfter As Long, _
```

```
'    ByVal x As Long, _
'    ByVal y As Long, _
'    ByVal cx As Long, _
'    ByVal cy As Long, _
'    ByVal wFlags As Long _
' ) As Long
Extern.Declare micLong, "SetWindowPos", "user32", "SetWindowPos", _
micLong, micLong, micLong, micLong, micLong, micLong, micLong
Public Function SetTopMostWindow(object, bTopMost)
  Dim hwnd
  hwnd = GetWindowFromBrowser(object).GetROProperty("hwnd")
  If bTopMost = True Then 'Make the window topmost
    SetTopMostWindow = Extern.SetWindowPos(hwnd, HWND_TOPMOST, _
      0, 0, 0, 0, (SWP_NOMOVE or SWP_NOSIZE))
  Else
    SetTopMostWindow = Extern.SetWindowPos(hwnd, HWND_NOTOPMOST, _
      0, 0, 0, 0,(SWP_NOMOVE or SWP_NOSIZE))
    SetTopMostWindow = False
  End If
End Function
RegisterUserFunc "Window", "SetTopMostWindow", "SetTopMostWindow"
RegisterUserFunc "Browser", "SetTopMostWindow", "SetTopMostWindow"
```

The following function, which is called by SetTopMostWindow, retrieves the handle if the target is a Browser:

```
Function GetWindowFromBrowser(oBrw)
  Dim hwndBrw, hwndWindow
  hwndBrw = oBrw.GetROProperty("hwnd")
  Const GA_ROOT = 2
  'Declare Function GetAncestor Lib "user32.dll" (ByVal hwnd As Long, ByVal
gaFlags As Long) As Long
  Extern.Declare micLong, "GetMainWindow", "user32" ,"GetAncestor",micLong,
micLong
  'Get the main IE window handle
  hwndWindow = Extern.GetMainWindow(hwndBrw, GA_ROOT)
  Set GetWindowFromBrowser = Window("hwnd:=" & hwndWindow)
End Function
```

411

To use this concept and keep the window on top, it is necessary to simply call the function in the following manner:

```
Window("Calculator").SetTopMostWIndow True
Browser("KnowledgeInbox").SetTopMostWindow True
```

Likewise, if the window no longer needs to stay on top of other windows, the parameter bTopMost can be set to False:

```
Window("Calculator").SetTopMostWIndow False
Browser("KnowledgeInbox").SetTopMostWindow False
```

AppendixB-PerformanceBenchmarks

Introduction

You have decided what test cases need to be automated. You have selected the right automated tool for your environment. You have even created automated tests that are robust and tend to be resistant to changes in the UI. However, how do your tests perform? Are there unnecessary Wait statements in your code? Are you using techniques that place more than the required stress on the Automation tool?

Until now, we have described in depth how to work with Object Identification in different scenarios and with different technologies. In this section, we will describe which techniques result in code that performs faster. Please note that we are not comparing the advantages and disadvantage of one approach over another. Each approach detailed up until now has its own pros and cons. This chapter merely compares the performance difference between techniques we routinely use in Object Identification.

To run our tests and compare difference between different techniques, we are going to use the sample HTML source below:

```html
<html>
  <head><title>Performance</title></head>
  <body>
    <table border='1'>
      <tr>
        <td>TextBox</td>
        <td><input type='text' name='txtDemo' /></td>
      </tr>
      <tr>
        <td>Button</td>
        <td><input type='button' value='Button' name='btnDemo' /></td>
      </tr>
      <tr>
        <td>Link</td>
        <td><a href='#'>Link</a></td>
      </tr>
      <tr>
        <td>List</td>
        <td>
          <select name='lstDemo'>
            <option value='item1'>Item1</option>
            <option value='item2'>Item2</option>
            <option value='item3'>Item3</option>
            <option value='item4'>Item4</option>
          </select>
        </td>
      </tr>
    </table>
  </body>
</html>
```

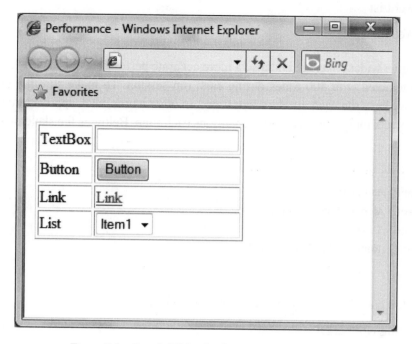

Figure B.1 – Sample UI for Conducting Performance Tests

The machine specifications are as follows:

- QTP Version: 11.0

- QTP Run Mode: Fast

- OS: Windows 7 x64 SP1

- Processor: Intel Core i3-2310M @ 2.10GHz

- RAM: 4.00GB

Performance Comparison between OR and DP

To compare performance between different techniques, we will perform Actions on five different types of objects:

- WebEdit

- WebButton

- Link

- ⊙ WebList

- ⊙ WebTable

This will give wider coverage and also a more accurate performance measure. Each object will be interacted with 500 times during each run session. To make sure the results are accurate, we have run each measure four times. In other words, each approach runs against the four objects four times, with 500 repetitions each time. Below is the skeleton code that will be used:

```
For i = 0 TO 499
  Browser().WebEdit().Set i
  Browser().WebButton().Click
  Browser().Link().Click
  Browser().WebList().Select Value
Next
```

The skeleton code is divided into the following eight sets:

1. Using Normal DP

2. Using Normal OR

3. Using DP Object Reference

4. Using OR Object Reference

5. Using DP with .Object

6. Using OR with .Object

7. Using DP Object Reference with .Object

8. Using OR Object Reference with .Object

Set 1: Using Normal DP

```
StartTime = Timer
For i = 0 To 499
  Browser("name:=Performance").WebEdit("html id:=txtDemo").Set "testing"
  Browser("name:=Performance").WebButton("html id:=btnDemo").Click
  Browser("name:=Performance").Link("innertext:=Link").Click
  Browser("name:=Performance").WebList("html id:=lstDemo").Select "Item" &
RandomNumber.Value(1, 4)
```

```
Next
Print Timer - StartTime
```

Total time: 116.98 sec

Average time: 116.98 sec / 500 iterations = 0.23 sec/iteration

Set 2: Using Normal OR

```
StartTime = Timer
For i = 0 To 499
  Browser("Performance").WebEdit("WebEdit").Set "test"
  Browser("Performance").WebButton("Button").Click
  Browser("Performance").Link("Link").Click
  Browser("Performance").WebList("lstDemo").Select "Item2"
Next
Print Timer - StartTime
```

Total time: 98.73 sec

Average time: 98.73 sec / 500 iterations = 0.20 sec/iteration

Set 3: Using DP Object Reference

```
Set oWebEdit = Browser("name:=Performance").WebEdit("html id:=txtDemo")
Set oWebButton = Browser("name:=Performance").WebButton("html id:=btnDemo")
Set oLink = Browser("name:=Performance").Link("innertext:=Link")
Set oList = Browser("name:=Performance").WebList("html id:=lstDemo")
StartTime = Timer
For i = 0 To 499
  oWebEdit.Set "testing"
  oWebButton.Click
  oLink.Click
  oList.Select "Item" & RandomNumber.Value(1, 4)
Next
Print Timer - StartTime
```

Total time: 70.51 sec

Average time: 70.51 sec / 500 iterations = 0.14 sec/iteration

Set 4: Using OR Object Reference

```
Set oWebEdit = Browser("Performance").WebEdit("html id:=txtDemo")
Set oWebButton = Browser("Performance").WebButton("html id:=btnDemo")
Set oLink = Browser("Performance").Link("innertext:=Link")
Set oList = Browser("Performance").WebList("html id:=lstDemo")
StartTime = Timer
For i = 0 To 499
  oWebEdit.Set "testing"
  oWebButton.Click
  oLink.Click
  oList.Select "Item" & RandomNumber.Value(1, 4)
Next
Print Timer - StartTime
```

Total time: 69.50 sec

Average time: 69.50 sec / 500 iterations = 0.14 sec/iteration

Set 5: Using Normal DP with .Object

```
StartTime = Timer
For i = 0 To 499
  Browser("name:=Performance").WebEdit("html id:=txtDemo").Object.Value =
"testing"
  Browser("name:=Performance").WebButton("html id:=btnDemo").Object.Click
  Browser("name:=Performance").Link("innertext:=Link").Object.Click
  Browser("name:=Performance").WebList("html id:=lstDemo").Object.
options(RandomNumber.Value(0, 3)).selected = True
Next
Print Timer - StartTime
```

Total time: 70.68 sec

Average time: 70.68 sec / 500 iterations = 0.14 sec/iteration

Set 6. Using Normal OR with .Object

```
StartTime = Timer
For i = 0 To 499
  Browser("Performance").WebEdit("html id:=txtDemo").Object.Value =
"testing"
  Browser("Performance").WebButton("html id:=btnDemo").Object.Click

  Browser("Performance").Link("innertext:=Link").Object.Click
  Browser("Performance").WebList("html id:=lstDemo").Object.
options(RandomNumber.Value(0, 3)).selected = True
Next
Print Timer - StartTime
```

Total time: 51.64 sec

Average time: 51.64 sec / 500 iterations = 0.10 sec/iteration

Set 7. Using DP Object Reference with .Object

```
Set oWebEdit = Browser("name:=Performance").WebEdit("html id:=txtDemo").
Object
Set oWebButton = Browser("name:=Performance").WebButton("html
id:=btnDemo").Object
Set oLink = Browser("name:=Performance").Link("innertext:=Link").Object
Set oList = Browser("name:=Performance").WebList("html id:=lstDemo").Object
StartTime = Timer
For i = 0 To 499
  oWebEdit.Value = "testing"
  oWebButton.Click
  oLink.Click
  oList.options(RandomNumber.Value(0, 3)).selected = True
Next
Print Timer - StartTime
```

Total time: 9.78 sec

Average time: 9.78 sec / 500 iterations = 0.02 sec/iteration

Set 8. Using OR Object Reference with .Object

```
Set oWebEdit = Browser("Performance").WebEdit("html id:=txtDemo").Object
Set oWebButton = Browser("Performance").WebButton("html id:=btnDemo").
Object
Set oLink = Browser("Performance").Link("innertext:=Link").Object
Set oList = Browser("Performance").WebList("html id:=lstDemo").Object
StartTime = Timer
For i = 0 To 499
  oWebEdit.Value = "testing"
  oWebButton.Click
  oLink.Click
  oList.options(RandomNumber.Value(0, 3)).selected = True
Next
Print Timer - StartTime
```

Total time: 9.63 sec

Average time: 9.63 sec / 500 iterations = 0.02 sec/iteration

Summary

In order of performance, the execution sets are organized below:

Technique	Overall Time (sec)	Sec per Iteration
Normal DP	116.98	0.23
Normal OR	98.73	0.20
DP Object Reference	70.51	0.14
OR Object Reference	69.50	0.14
Normal DP with .Object	70.68	0.14
Normal OR with .Object	51.64	0.10
DP Object Reference with .Object	*9.78*	*0.02*
OR Object Reference with .Object	*9.63*	*0.02*

The majority of the above results were as expected. However, the combination of Object Reference with the .Object extension was surprising to say the least: the time difference is just immense. Using both DP, OR and .Object, the completion time per iteration was less than 20 millisec.

WARNING: This chapter only compares performance of various techniques used to automate applications. We are in no way suggesting that the high-performing techniques are the best ones to use in all scenarios. Generally, a technique that is robust enough should be treated with greater importance. Techniques that utilize .Object (native methods) should be used as a last resort or when performance is of utmost importance. For more information on .Object, please refer to "Chapter 6 - HTML DOM

C

Appendix C - XPath vs CSS

XPath vs. CSS: A Comparison

This table summarizes both XPath and CSS Selectors. Both Selectors have been discussed in detail in Chapters 11 and 12. This appendix compares both side-by-side.

Select By	XPath	CSS
Element	`//p`	`P`
ID	`//span[@id='user']`	`span#user`
Class	`//span[@class='user']`	`span.user`
Attribute	`//span[@name='user']`	`span[name='user']`

Select By	XPath	CSS

Attribute (non-exact match)	`//span[contains(@name,'er')]`
	
	`//span[starts-with(@name,'us')]`
	
	`//span[ends-with(@name,'er')]`
		`span[name*=er]`
		
		`span[name~=er]`
		
		`span[name^=us]`
		
		`span[name$=er]`

Child	`//table/tr`
	
	`//table[@id='t']/tr`
	
	`//table/tr[2]`
	
	`//tr/child::td`
		`table > tr`

Descendant	`//table//tr`
	
	`//table[@id='t']//tr[1]`
	
	`//tr/descendant::td[1]`
		`table tr`
		
		`table#t tr`

Index	`//li[2]`
	
	`//table[1]`
		`li:nth-child(2)`

Content	`//p[contains(text(),'Hello')]`	`p:contains('Hello')`

Sibling	`(//tr[3])/preceding-sibling::tr`
	
	`(//tr[3])/following-sibling::tr`
		`tr + tr`
		
		`#id + td`

Parent	`//tr/ancestor::table`	`tr + table`

The biggest difference between XPath and CSS is that unlike XPath, CSS was not created for locating elements in an unique fashion. Instead, it was created for styling elements in an HTML document where a style can be applied to multiple elements. A few notable differences between the two locators are summarized below:

⊙ XPath is bidirectional. It can locate previous and following nodes from the target. CSS locates only the following nodes; it cannot even identify a target's parent (although this will change with CSS 4.0).

- XPath is slower than CSS.

- In certain situations, it is not possible to locate elements uniquely by using CSS without the use of additional properties or Ordinal Identifiers. With XPath, this is never the case. A single XPath statement can be used to select any element in the document. This also makes XPath very powerful as it could totally eliminate the need for multiple locators.

- CSS does not support arithmetic functions and certain logical operators (>=, <=, mod etc).

- Unlike XPath, CSS is only equipped to perform case-sensitive comparison.

Appendix D - Nesting of RegisterUserFunc Methods

We have already seen how RegisterUserFunc works in QTP. Now let's see what happens when RegisterUserFunc is used in a nested fashion. Consider the following code:

```
'User default timeout method
Private DEFAULT_TIMEOUT
DEFAULT_TIMEOUT = 10
'The new exist method
Function NewExist(ByVal Obj, ByVal timeout)
  If timeout = -1 Then timeout = DEFAULT_TIMEOUT
  If Obj.Exist(timeout) Then
    Print("Object does exist")
    NewExist = True
  Else
    Print("Object doesn't exist")
    Reporter.ReportEvent micFail, "New Exist", "The object doesn't exist"
    NewExist = False
  End If
```

```
End Function

'Register the NewExist method to Browser as "Exist"
RegisterUserFunc "Browser", "Exist", "NewExist"

'Print the return value of exist method
Print "Browser with hwnd 0 existence check = " & Browser("hwnd:=0").
Exist(-1)
```

In the above code, when the Exist method gets called at the last line, QTP has a call registered to NewExist method because of the RegisterUserFunc. Below is the output of the Print statement:

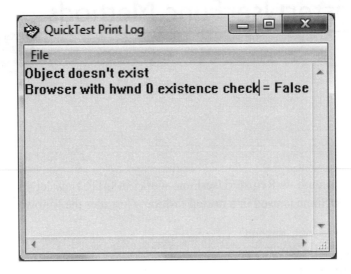

Figure D.1 – Print Log

Now instead of calling the Exist methods, we will create another method that in turn calls the Exist method. Below is the updated code:

```
'User default timeout method
Private DEFAULT_TIMEOUT
DEFAULT_TIMEOUT = 10

'The new exist method
Function NewExist(ByVal Obj, ByVal timeout)
   If timeout = -1 Then timeout = DEFAULT_TIMEOUT
```

```
  If Obj.Exist(timeout) Then
    Print("Object does exist")
    NewExist = True
  Else
    Print("Object doesn't exist")
    Reporter.ReportEvent micFail, "New Exist", "The object doesn't exist"
    NewExist = False
  End If
End Function

'The new exist method
Function NewNavigate(ByVal Obj, ByVal URL)
  If obj.Exist(5) Then
    obj.Navigate(URL)
  End If
End Function

'Register the NewExist method to be used when we call Exist on Browser
object
RegisterUserFunc "Browser", "Exist", "NewExist"
RegisterUserFunc "Browser", "Navigate", "NewNavigate"

'Print the return value of exist method
Print "Browser Navigating"
Browser("hwnd:=0").Navigate "http://relevantcodes.com/"
```

Notice the Print window after script completion:

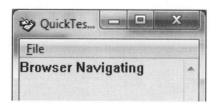

Figure D.2 – Print Log

There is no message for 'The object doesn't exist' from the Print statement. This happens because once the code is inside the method called by RegisterUserFunc, QTP will no longer allow any other registered method. To make things clearer, we will update the existing code and change the Exist method into NewExist, as shown below:

```
'User default timeout method
Private DEFAULT_TIMEOUT
DEFAULT_TIMEOUT = 10

'The new exist method
Function NewExist(ByVal Obj, ByVal timeout)
  If timeout = -1 Then timeout = DEFAULT_TIMEOUT

  If Obj.Exist(timeout) Then
    Print("Object does exist")
    NewExist = True
  Else
    Print("Object doesn't exist")
    Reporter.ReportEvent(micFail, "New Exist", "The object doesn't exist")
    NewExist = False
  End If
End Function

'The new exist method
Function NewNavigate(ByVal Obj, ByVal URL)
  If obj.NewExist(5) Then
    obj.Navigate(URL)
  End If
End Function

'Register the NewExist method to be used when we call Exist on Browser
object
RegisterUserFunc "Browser", "NewExist", "NewExist"
RegisterUserFunc "Browser", "NewNavigate", "NewNavigate"

'Print the return value of exist method
Print "Browser Navigating"
Browser("hwnd:=0").NewNavigate "http://relevantcodes.com/"
```

Running the above code will produce the following error:

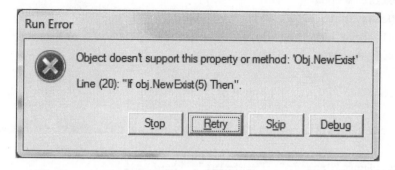

Figure D.3 – Run Error "Object doesn't support this property or method"

This error occurs because QTP doesn't honor any registered method inside another registered method, which is an understandable limitation for the existing object method, as that will cause infinite recursion. Assume we override the Navigate method and inside this method call the actual Navigate method again. QTP will not call the registered method again, but will instead call the default Navigate method on the object. There is a simple solution to this problem – we can call the overridden method directly inside the function. The updated code and output are shown below:

```
'User default timeout method
Private DEFAULT_TIMEOUT
DEFAULT_TIMEOUT = 10

'The new exist method
Function NewExist(ByVal Obj, ByVal timeout)
  If timeout = -1 Then timeout = DEFAULT_TIMEOUT

  If Obj.Exist(timeout) Then
    Print("Object does exist")
    NewExist = True
  Else
    Print("Object doesn't exist")
    Reporter.ReportEvent(micFail, "New Exist", "The object doesn't exist")
    NewExist = False
  End If
End Function
```

```
'The new exist method
Function NewNavigate(ByVal Obj, ByVal URL)
  If NewExist(obj, 5) Then
    obj.Navigate(URL)
  End If
End Function


'Register the NewExist method to be used when we call Exist on Browser
object
RegisterUserFunc "Browser", "NewExist", "NewExist"
RegisterUserFunc "Browser", "NewNavigate", "NewNavigate"
'Print the return value of exist method
Print "Browser Navigating"
Browser("hwnd:=0").NewNavigate "http://relevantcodes.com/"
```

Figure D.4 – Print Log

Appendix E - Eval and Execute

Eval and Execute

The Eval function and Execute statement provide the ability to evaluate and execute dynamic code at runtime. Eval's purpose is to evaluate a string and return the evaluation result. Execute simply interprets a string expression and executes it. An example of Eval and Execute is shown below:

```
Execute "Dim x, y : x = 2 : y = 4"
MsgBox Eval("x = y")
```

NOTE: Unlike the Execute statement, Eval is a function and it can return a value.

As stated earlier, Eval returns the result of the string evaluation whereas Execute will execute a string statement but will not return a result. The following example demonstrates this:

```
Dim x, y
x = 2
y = 4

MsgBox Eval("x = y") 'False
Execute "x = y" 'Assign y to x
```

The result of the Eval function is False whereas the Execute statement will simply set the value of y to x. To return a value using Execute, either of the two can be used:

```
Execute "MsgBox Eval(x = y)"
Execute "MsgBox(x = y)"
```

NOTE: In the statements above, Execute is not returning the value but just executing the string expression that throws a MessageBox with the string evaluation.

Option Explicit applicability

With Option Explicit, if a variable is not declared but used, QTP will complain. This is not the case with Execute. Consider the code below:

```
Option Explicit

'x is not declared using Dim
x = 2
MsgBox x
```

When the statement "x = 2" is executed, the following error will be thrown:

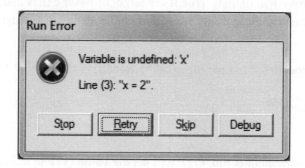

Figure E.1 – Run Error "Variable is undefined"

When QTP runs the Execute statement, no error will be thrown. Instead, x will be dynamically assigned the new value.

```
Option Explicit

'x is not declared using Dim
Execute "x = 2"
MsgBox x
```

Using Eval and Execute with Test Code

This is where Eval and Execute are used most often." The concept here and the concepts covered by previous examples will remain the same: we create action strings and execute them. This section will also demonstrate how to implement events on supplied test objects (as strings).

A quick example below shows how to check whether a browser exists using both Eval and Execute:

```
strBrowser = "Browser(""title:=Relevant Codes"").Exist(0)"
Execute "MsgBox " & strBrowser
MsgBox Eval(strBrowser)
```

NOTE: The entire statement passed to Eval and Execute is in string form.

Both statements above will display True if the target browser exists and False if it doesn't. Now, let's consider an example where some dynamic code is run against a WebEdit control to set a value:

```
strBrowser = "Browser(""title:=Google"").WebEdit(""name:=q"").Set ""QTP"""

Execute strBrowser
Eval strBrowser
```

When the Execute statement is run, QTP will set the value QTP in the Google Search box. When the statement with Eval executes, QTP will complain:

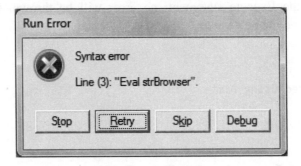

Figure E.2 – Syntax Error

This is because Eval is a function and when it executes the Set method (which is a subroutine and hence does not return a value), no evaluation is performed so an error is thrown. If the same statement was run to check for an object's existence, the code would work fine.

```
strBrowser = "Browser(""title:=Google"").WebEdit(""name:=q"").Exist(0)"

MsgBox Eval(strBrowser)
```

It is not always possible to know what is to be executed at Run-time, which is why most dynamic code is executed using Execute instead of Eval.

Appendix F - Cross-Browser Tests

DOM Differences between Browsers

DOM methods used in Firefox are case-sensitive as opposed to IE and Chrome, which are case-insensitive.

When using DOM to access HTML nodes, give consideration to the method's case. For example, in Firefox 'getElementsByTagName' will work but 'getelementsbytagname' will fail. With IE, case is not an issue so either will work. Consider the statement below:

```
MsgBox Browser("Google").Page("Google").Object.
getelementsbytagname("input").length
```

If you run the above statement in Firefox, QTP will complain:

Figure F.1 – Run Error "obj[FuncName] is Undefined"

Running the same code in IE or Chrome will give the following output:

Figure F.2 – Output

To ensure that your scripts work well in all Browsers, always make sure the case DOM methods are in the correct case.

When it comes to native properties, there are some differences as well. For example, the 'class' property is valid for both Firefox and Chrome. For IE, 'className' should be used.

```
'For Firefox and Chrome
Browser("B").Page("P").Link("URL").GetROProperty("attribute/class")

'For IE
Browser("B").Page("P").Link("URL").GetROProperty("attribute/className")
```

Another example is the Float property. To retrieve the relevant value for it in IE, styleFloat must be used. For Firefox, it is cssFloat.

Object Hierarchy

Statements with partial hierarchy are valid for both IE and Firefox. The statement below with the Page object missing will work in both IE and Firefox.

```
Browser("B").Link("L").Click
```

The above will not work for Google Chrome. The complete hierarchy must be used as shown below.

```
Browser("B").Page("P").WebElement("W").Click
```

CreationTime

The CreationTime ordinal identifier works for IE and Firefox, but does not work for Chrome. It is advisable to use other properties such as "application version", "title", "openTitle" etc. as a replacement.

CurrentStyle

The currentStyle property has been widely used by QTP practitioners until now. But, it is valid only for IE. For Firefox and Chrome, getComputedStyle must be used instead. Engineers developing cross-browser tests must keep this in mind as their current tests would break if they were to be run against browsers other than IE.

Dialog-Box Differences

For this section, let's consider the following HTML source:

```html
<html>
  <head>
    <title>Dialogs</title>
    <script type="text/javascript">
      function doConfirm() {
        if (confirm("Sample JavaScript Dialog box")) {}
      }
```

```
      </script>
  </head>
  <body>
    <form>
      <input type="button" value="Clicky" style="width:100px; height:50px;"
onclick="doConfirm()" />
    </form>
  </body>
</html>
```

The HTML is displayed as the following in IE and Firefox respectively:

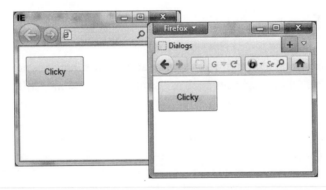

Figure F.3 – Dialog Box in IE (left) and Firefox (right)

Clicking the button throws the following pop-up:

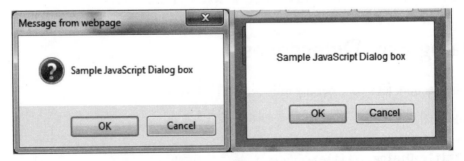

Figure F.4 – Pop-ups in IE (left) and Firefox (right)

Let's first see the differences in properties (left: IE, right: Firefox) using the Object Spy:

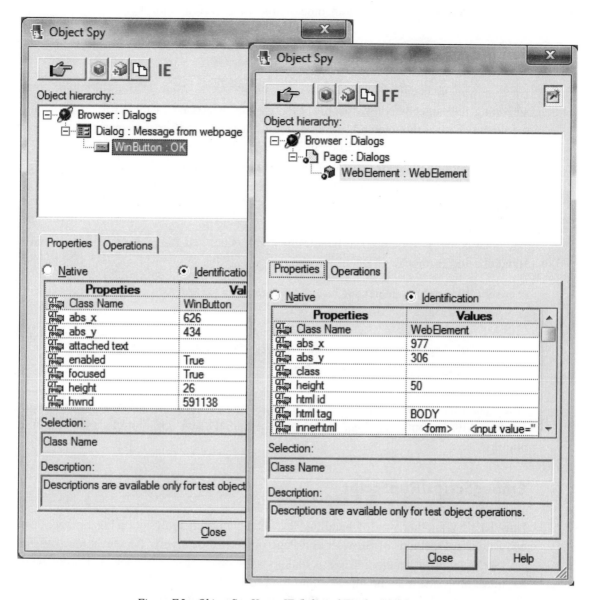

Figure F.5 – Object Spy View - IE (left) and Firefox (right)

Notice the differences between the two snapshots. IE throws a dialog box whereas Firefox's mechanics differ – it offers an embedded look. In IE, you must click the WinButton to handle the dialog whereas in Firefox, you must interact with a WebElement (because it's embedded within the page).

Let's now examine a few ways to handle dialogs in both IE and Firefox.

SendKeys

Another way to handle dialog is using the SendKeys method of WScript.Shell. After activating the target window, the ENTER key can be passed to the Browser to handle the dialog. To use this method, different logic must be used for different browsers. For example, dialog boxes for IE (different versions), Chrome and Firefox all differ - thus, it would be required to create separate mechanism to handle each.

HandleDialog

The code below will be used to handle the Click event and the pop-ups with Browser's HandleDialog method:

```
Browser("Dialog").WebButton("value:=Clicky").Click
Browser("Dialog").HandleDialog micOK

Browser("Dialog").WebButton("value:=Clicky").Click
Browser("Dialog").HandleDialog micOK
```

After running the above code, the Click event and both pop-ups get handled correctly with Firefox. With IE, only the Click event works; HandleDialog does not close the resulting pop-ups.

EmbedScript/RunScript

Now let's try another way of handling this dialog in both browsers using EmbedScript and RunScript methods of Browser and Page objects respectively. This technique utilizes JavaScript code to handle and close dialogs as soon as they are opened. Unlike other methods, this code must be injected into the browser before the dialog box appears. The following code shows how to accept the dialog box parameters (return true).

```
js = "window.confirm = function() {return true;}"

Browser("Dialog").EmbedScript js
Browser("Dialog").WebButton("value:=Clicky").Click
```

```
Browser("Dialog").EmbedScript js
Browser("Dialog").WebButton("value:=Clicky").Click
```

We notice that this dialog was handled correctly in both Firefox and IE. The above code can also be used with RunScript with the same result:

```
js = "window.confirm = function() {return true;}"
```

```
Browser("Dialog").Page("micclass:=Page").RunScript js
Browser("Dialog").WebButton("value:=Clicky").Click
```

```
Browser("Dialog").Page("micclass:=Page").RunScript js
Browser("Dialog").WebButton("value:=Clicky").Click
```

 NOTE: This technique works only with JavaScript dialogs.

Index

Symbols

A

B

C

D

E

G

H

I

J

L

O

T

U

V

W

X

And I thought I knew QTP!

How many times have you wished that there was somebody who could clear some niggling doubts about a particular aspect of QTP? Or explain some difficult-to-grasp concepts and smart workarounds? Or maybe show you some of QTP's lesser-known features?

Written by the author of the best-selling 'QuickTest Professional Unplugged', this book does just that in the form of a gripping story which will keep you turning every page in anticipation. 'And I Thought I Knew QTP! – QTP Concepts Unplugged' is unique in the way it seeks to explain the various concepts through its interesting, easy-to-follow and innovative story-telling style (rarely used for technical books). Instead of following a textbook format, this book is more like a technical novel.

The story follows the journey of Nurat, who encounters a series of challenging interviews in a search for his dream job. The question-and-answer style of the book addresses many of the questions frequently asked by QuickTest practitioners and aims to correct common mistakes and misunderstandings surrounding QTP by providing clear and concise explanation of the topics at hand.

Whether it is to brush up your QTP knowledge and skills or simply to satiate your curiosity about how a seasoned IT veteran fared in a no-holds-barred 'intellectual duel' on QTP, this book is sure to leave you astonished with its pace of narration, expertise, and sheer breadth of topics covered.

ISBN: 978-0-9836759-0-7

For more details, please visit www.KnowledgeInbox.com/books/

QuickTest Professional Unplugged

'QuickTest Professional Unplugged', the first book released by Tarun Lalwani, has received much recognition for being the most detailed and creative book on QTP. It was awarded the Best Automation Book in the 2nd ATI Automation Honors.

Even though this book contains a plethora of information to help QTP starters come up to speed, there are also many never-seen-before topics and techniques that will give advanced users an edge. This mix makes it the recommended option for those aspiring to be not only advanced users, but experts. Containing previously untouched and undocumented features which are not offered in standard QuickTest documentation, 'QuickTest Professional Unplugged' has served as the key desktop reference for QuickTest issues for over three years and continues to set an unrivaled example.

'QuickTest Professional 2nd Edition' includes all features of QTP 11 as well as additional updates that have been introduced over the years. With a brand new, in-depth chapter on Object Repository, this book delivers a clear message: QuickTest is an immensely powerful automated testing tool. 'QuickTest Professional 2nd Edition' brings to light a plethora of hidden and highly innovative features and is a must-have volume for any QTP user's bookshelf.

ISBN: 978-0-9836759-1-4

For more details, please visit www.KnowledgeInbox.com/books/